**An Altitude
SuperGuide**

Alberta

D0981723

An Altitude SuperGuide

Alberta

Bruce Patterson

Altitude Publishing
Banff Alberta Canada

Photo, front cover: Spirit Island is the scenic destination for boat tours on Maligne Lake in Jasper National Park.

Photo, inset: John George "Kootenai" Brown, lawman, whisky trader, pony express rider, and buffalo hunter was a driving force behind the establishment of Waterton Lakes National Park.

Photo, overleaf: Farm near Cowley in southwest Alberta lies on the edge of the foothills. The front ranges of the Canadian Rockies are on the horizon.

Photo, back cover: The Calgary skyline sparkles under a full moon.

Copyright © 1992
Altitude Publishing Ltd.
Post Office Box 490
Banff, Alberta
Canada T0L 0C0

Extreme care has been taken to ensure that all information in this book is accurate and up to date, but neither the author nor the publisher can be held legally responsible for any errors that may appear.

Canadian Cataloguing in Publication Data

Patterson, Bruce
Alberta

Includesindex.
ISBN 0-919381-94-4
1. Alberta – Guidebooks.
2. Alberta – Description and travel – 1981-
* I. Title.
FC3657.P38 1992   917.123'043
C92-091205-2   F1076.P38 1992

Supplementary copy and listings information for this book was supplied by Mary McGuire

Editor: John F. Ricker
Proofreader: Oscar Watchman

Maps: Paul Beck

Design: Robert MacDonald, MediaClones Inc., Vancouver, Banff, and Toronto, Canada

Printed and bound in Canada
by Friesen Printers

The publisher gratefully acknowledges the assistance of Alberta Culture and the Alberta Foundation for the Arts in the production of this book.

Contents

How to Use the Alberta SuperGuide

The *Alberta SuperGuide* is your comprehensive guide to the diverse attractions of the province. It will help you discover and appreciate all that the province has to offer from the hot springs, ski slopes, and golf courses of the Canadian Rockies to the rodeos and guest ranches of the foothills and wide open prairies.

There are descriptions of the province's fascinating human and natural history. Wherever possible, there are tips on the best ways to explore that history – to see the remnants of the Ice Age, follow the path of the early explorers, or sense the hardships of the fur-trading voyageurs.

SuperGuide takes you to Edmonton and Calgary with world-renowned attractions such as the West Edmonton Mall and Calgary Stampede. There are also tips on smaller centres such as Lethbridge in southern Alberta with its thriving arts community, and Fort McMurray in the north where tours are offered of the massive oil sands projects.

If you are interested in the Wild West, there are opportunities to watch cowboys in action not only at the Calgary Stampede, but at small town rodeos where it is often easier to get close to the steer-wrestlers and calf-ropers.

There are also several excellent ways to experience the rich culture of western Natives. Pow-wows and Native rodeos are held throughout the summer. An innovative interpretive centre at Head-Smashed-In Buffalo Jump near Fort Macleod provides a vivid look at the traditions of the plains Natives in Western Canada.

SuperGuide caters to specific interests as well. The chapter on recreation and adventure provides details on activities for summer and winter including cycling, fishing, swimming, canoeing, camping, and skiing.

SuperGuide also offers suggestions for the best scenic drives to take in the mountains, foothills, prairies, and the southeastern badlands where dinosaurs once roamed. Dinosaurs have a chapter of their own, with the focus on the internationally known Royal Tyrrell Museum of Palaeontology.

A handy listings section provides information on accommodation, restaurants, shopping, entertainment, transportation, and other useful topics.

SuperGuide is designed for first-time and returning visitors as well as Albertans who want to explore other parts of the province. The guide also includes an extensive collection of full-color photographs and archival material to enrich your enjoyment of a magnificent part of the world.

Opposite: Stephen Avenue Mall in downtown Calgary provides relaxed strolling for pedestrians.

Introduction

A young but skilled barrel racer guides her horse at the Little Britches Rodeo in High River, south of Calgary. The event, held each May, is one of many rodeos for junior cowboys and cowgirls staged throughout the summer. Adults have their own rodeo circuit including the famed Calgary Stampede in July.

Alberta is a young province but people have been attracted for a long, long time to the soaring mountains, rolling foothills, fertile plains, and vast forests in this part of the world.

The first travellers arrived about 30,000 years ago when ancestors of North American Natives migrated across a land bridge from Siberia in pursuit of bison, mammoths, and other sources of food. Those early migrants were driven out by the last great Ice Age that ended 10,000 to 12,000 years ago. And the region has be-come much more hospitable since then.

Natives had the land to themselves for thousands of years and developed rich cultures. Some groups developed sophisticated techniques to stalk the huge herds of bison that roamed the prairies.

It was 1754 when the first white man arrived. Others followed: explorers in search of a waterway to the Pacific, traders seeking furs for the market in Europe, and finally ranchers and farmers.

It has been only in the past 100 years with the completion of the Canadian Pacific Railway that

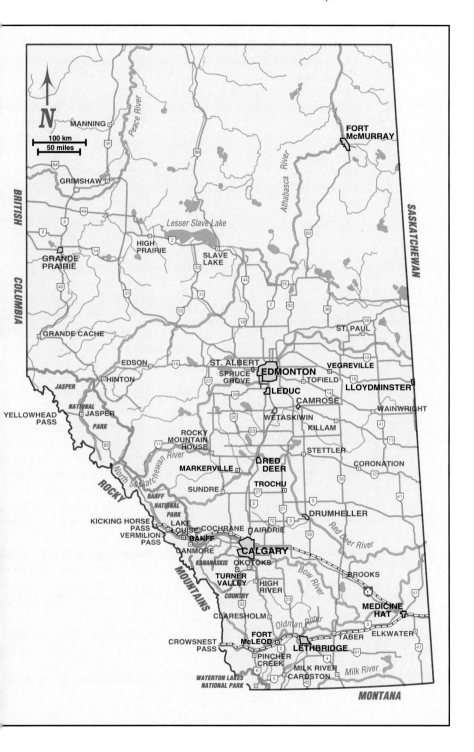

people have made the journey for pleasure. Some sought the regenerative powers of the sulphur hot springs at Banff. A few travelled from Europe or the eastern United States to scale the rugged peaks of the Rockies.

Today, visitors from around the world join Albertans and other Canadians in enjoying the diverse attractions of the province (see box p. 19).

Alberta at a Glance

Size: 661,185 square kilometres (255,303 square miles)
Population: 2,469,800 (according to 1990 census)
Name: The province was named after Princess Louise Caroline Alberta, the fourth daughter of Queen Victoria. Alberta became a province on September 1, 1905.
Capital: Edmonton
Time Zone: Mountain Standard Time (noon Greenwich Mean Time = 5 a.m. MST)
* Alberta switches to Daylight Saving Time in the spring (noon GMT = 6 a.m. Mountain Daylight Time)
Provincial Flower: Wild Rose
Provincial Bird: Great Horned Owl
Provincial Mammal: Bighorn Sheep
Provincial Tree: Lodgepole Pine
Provincial Stone: Petrified Wood
Highest point: Mount Columbia 3747 metres (12,294 feet)

The People

There is a good reason that Alberta has diverse attractions, from the giant Pysanka (Ukranian Easter egg) in Vegreville, to the historic home of Iceland's national poet, Stephan Stephansson, in Markerville west of Red Deer. The province has a long tradition of welcoming people from around the world. As early as 1921, the Canadian census recorded over 30 different languages spoken in Alberta in addition to at least 10 distinct languages of the Natives.

People came for a variety of reasons. British settlers were lured by the prospect of free farmland offered in the early years of this century. In 1913 alone, 113,000 English immigrants came to Canada with most of them headed for the west. In 1903, close to 2000 people were enticed by Reverend Isaac Barr to move from England and establish a religious community on the prairies. Reminders of the early days of the Barr Colony are still found in Lloydminster.

French fur-traders, explorers, and missionairies were among the earliest settlers in the west. French Canadians are the fourth largest ethnic group in the province after the British, Germans, and Ukrainians. Many French descendants have settled in the Edmonton area. The St. Ann Trading Co., Tea House, and Country Inn at Trochu, gives a taste of the early days of French culture on the prairies.

Chinese fortune hunters were among the prospectors who rushed to the gold fields of western Canada in the 1860s. Many stayed to take up other trades when the rush was over. In 1882 and 1883, close to 17,000 Chinese laborers were hired to help build the western section of the Canadian Pacific Railway. After the railway was built, many of the chinese took up market gardening; others established restaurants. Their descendants have continued in these traditional occupations, in cities and small towns alike.

Germans have come to Alberta for diverse reasons. Many came to settle, lured by free land in the west. Others came to escape persecution. Hutterites immigrated to North America because their religious beliefs, particularly their refusal to serve in the military, were not tolerated in central Europe. The Hutterites' pacifism created problems during times of war. However, Hutterite colonies, where German is still the predominant language, have been highly successful agricultural operations in rural Alberta. Elsewhere, German influence is readily apparent each fall with Oktoberfest celebrations.

Ukrainians have been attracted to Alberta since the 1890s when the pioneers told their friends and relatives about the agricultural potential of the lands east of Edmonton. By the time Alberta was established as a province in 1905, there were already more than 13,000 Ukrainians.

Now, Edmonton has close to 60,000 residents of Ukrainian descent. There are 25,000 in Calgary and there are thriving communities throughout Alberta. Ukrainian culture is evident in the restaurants and in the performing groups such as the renowned Shumka Dancers. The Ukranian Cultural Heritage Village 50 kilometres east of Edmonton on Highway 16 depicts the early way of life of Ukrainian settlers.

There are many other cultural influences – American cowboys, Norwegians, Italians, and more recent additions: Vietnamese,

Shumka Dancers perform spectacular leaps and other acrobatics in celebration of their Ukrainian heritage. Ukrainian traditions are particularly strong in the Edmonton area. Specialty restaurants feature perogies and other ethnic dishes. The town of Vegreville displays a giant pysanka – a Ukrainian Easter egg.

Thais and Cambodians. It is a mixture that has made Alberta a rewarding place for residents and visitors. Most cultural groups celebrate their traditions on Heritage Day, the first Monday of August.

Alberta at Work

In the early days, it was the plentiful wildlife that attracted Natives, and later, the fur-traders and buffalo hunters. That way of life has passed into history. Today agriculture, oil and gas, and tourism provide the mainstay of Alberta's economy. However, wildlife continues to play an important role. The big-game animals are not prized so much for their meat and furs any more. Today, they are much more valuable

Ten questions about agriculture

How much did a farm cost in 1901?
Ten dollars. Homesteaders were given tracts of land for $10 with the stipulation that they had to break a specific amount of sod each year, build a house, and stay on the land for at least three years. There were 40,000 homesteads granted in the territory by the time Alberta became a province in 1905.

How big is the industry now?
Total receipts for both livestock and crops amount to more than $4 billion a year. But farm incomes have been declining in recent years, primarily because of slumping grain prices. The number of farms in Alberta dropped from 62,702 in 1971 to 57,777 in 1986.

What's growing in all those fields?
It's most likely wheat or barley. One-third of the cultivated farmland in Alberta is used to produce wheat. Barley is a close second. Canola, oats, rye, and flax make up the rest of the top six major cereals and oilseeds.

Canola, formerly called rapeseed, is particularly noticeable in midsummer when the fields are a bright yellow. Flax fields appear blue when flax is in flower.

What are the crops used for?
Wheat is used for flour and occasionally livestock feed. The flour is mainly used to make bread, although Alberta durum wheat is among the best for making pasta. Barley is used for both livestock feed and for making beer. Oats and rye are used mainly for livestock feed. Some rye is used for bread and some for whisky. Alberta flax is used mainly in the production of linseed oil.

Rapeseed oil was used as a lubricant for engines during World War II. Not only the name has been changed in recent years. New varieties of canola produce an oil that is suited to human consumption, and much of it becomes salad dressing.

How big is the beef business?
There are more than 4 million head of cattle and calves in Alberta, almost double the human population. Beef cattle account for about 30 percent of farm receipts in the

alive, as links to the wilderness and an important element in Alberta's appeal to tourists.

Oil and Gas

Rich deposits of fossil fuel have been important in the development of Alberta. During boom years such as the early 1950s and the 1970s, soaring oil prices sparked intense activity in the oil patch. Fortunes were made and government royalties helped finance everything from new hospitals and medical research to the development of recreational areas and tourist attractions such as Kananaskis Country and Head-Smashed-In Buffalo Jump Interpretive Centre, west of Fort MacLeod.

The coal, oil, and natural gas reserves in Alberta have been around many millions of years. These resources have been used for at least several hundred years. Fur traders who travelled through the northern forests in the 1700s

province. Alberta has 40 percent of Canada's beef-breeding herd.

What about milk?
There are about 125,000 dairy cows in Alberta. The average cow produces about 6000 litres of milk per year.

What about vegetables?
Vegetables account for only a small fraction of Alberta's agricultural industry. The area around Taber in the southeast corner of the province is one of the most productive regions, especially for corn. There is also a thriving sugar beet industry in the south. Many communities have a farmers market throughout the summer.

Has the horse been replaced?
Modern machinery has taken over many of the tasks handled by traditional horsepower, but working cowboys still use the horse for a variety of ranch jobs.

There are close to 160,000 horses in Alberta. Most are for recreation, but there is a thriving business producing speedy thoroughbreds and standardbreds for racing.

What are those giant sprinklers?
Close to 3 million hectares (1.2 million acres) of farmland are irrigated in southern Alberta, mainly by rolling wheel or pivotal sprinkler systems. Irrigation has been heavily promoted in Alberta since the early 1900s, when the Canadian Pacific Railway constructed massive irrigation systems to attract settlers.

Why aren't there any rats in Alberta?
Alberta has operated a rat patrol since 1950 to keep Norway rats from invading across the Saskatchewan border. The Rocky Mountains keep the pests out from the west. The joint program of Alberta Agriculture and municipalities along the Saskatchewan border includes public education and provides pest control inspectors. They exterminate any rats that are sighted in the province. The program costs about $250,000 a year, but far outweighs the potential damage from rats.

Above: Grain elevators stand tall on the prairie landscape. A modern elevator stores up to 160,000 bushels (4,000 tonnes) of wheat, barley, and other crops. Alberta ships more than 5 million tonnes of field crops each year to markets around the world.

Right: Upper Waterton Lake is the deepest body of water in the Canadian Rockies with a depth of almost 150 m. The lake straddles the international border at the 49th parallel of latitude.

saw Natives patching their canoes with tar-like sand. The Athabasca oil sands in the Fort McMurray area contain enormous reserves, but only in recent years has it been economic to extract the oil.

Kootenai Brown became one of Alberta's first oilmen when he collected seeping black oil from the banks of Cameron Creek near Waterton Lakes (see box p. 131). It was an ideal lubricant for wagon wheels, and one enterprising settler started selling the oil for one dollar a gallon.

In 1901, the Rocky Mountain

John D. Snow

I'm a landman with Shell Canada Limited, a contracts negotiator for subsurface minerals. I obtain leases and orchestrate the closing of a deal. I have to interact with lawyers, geophysicists, geologists, and other technologists. From that I compose an agreement in conjunction with all the parties involved. It's really exciting being able to work with people from diverse backgrounds. You're met with a challenge or a problem, and you need to find a creative solution. Probably the most gratifying thing for me is to achieve the ultimate objective: to strike a deal to explore for oil and gas.

My family goes back centuries in this area, and is part of the important group who signed the treaty with the Crown in 1877 at Blackfoot Crossing. Kichipwot (Chief Jacob Goodstoney) signed on behalf of what, today, we call the Goodstoney Band. And from that treaty emanates the bilateral relationship with the Crown. Kichipwot was a heriditary leader. Today leaders are elected. Even so, my father, Chief John Snow, is of the bloodline of Chief Goodstoney and has been chief since 1969.

So there's a long history of leadership in our family in the development of Indian rights and aboriginal concerns. On behalf of Shell Canada, I sit on the Calgary Chamber of Commerce. And I'm the Shell representative to the Aboriginal Opportunities Committee. We're one of the leading committees in the country dealing with aboriginal issues. We've organized Native Awareness Weeks and brought in aboriginal leaders for discussions.

The Indians see themselves as stewards. They have to maintain harmony throughout the land and nature. For example, when an Indian would take a deer, he would give a prayer for it. He would burn sweet grass or tobacco and make an offering to the Creator, so there is a spiritual relationship that binds the act of creating and the act of tying oneself to the land.

I think that technology must be guarded by wisdom, and that Indian people can provide a linkage, a philosophy, and an understanding for the use of that technology. I think that's where we have yet to see the contribution of Indian people in this country, and it will come.

Rolling wheel (shown above) and pivotal irrigation systems bring needed water to 485,000 square kilometres (1.2 million acres) of Alberta farmland. Four percent of the province's farmland is irrigated but that land accounts for 12 percent of the crop production.

Development Company drilled for oil on the site and the discovery set off the first of many oil booms in Alberta. Like many of the booms, however, it was short-lived and Oil City was abandoned when other wells came up dry. A historic marker has been erected near Waterton Park townsite to commemorate the event.

Natural gas had already proven itself as an inexpensive energy source by the turn of the century. A railway crew was drilling for water near Medicine Hat in 1883 when they discovered gas instead.

By 1900, the community was using natural gas to light its streets. The first significant oil discovery was in Turner Valley in 1914 when A.W. Dingman, a veteran of the Pennsylvania oil fields, tapped into a major oil reserve (see box p. 17). Speculators and stock promoters quickly got into the act, and though there was plenty of oil and gas, the field did not live up to overblown expectations. The region became a steady producer, however, and the focus of Canada's oil and gas industry until February 13, 1947 when Imperial Oil's Leduc No. 1 came in.

Leduc is the 200-million barrel oil field southeast of Edmonton that created fortunes for some and attracted a wave of workers. The original derrick has been preserved and is on display at the Gateway Park Oil Interpretive Display on the south edge of Edmonton.

The Oil Sands Interpretive Centre in Fort McMurray shows much more recent technology used to separate oil from sand and water in the rich northern deposits, the Athabasca Tar Sands.

Alberta continues to be the major oil and gas producing region of Canada, and the industry has a pervasive impact on the province. Many of Calgary's skyscrapers were built during the boom of the 1970s when oil prices rose dramatically.

The overheated economy led to some bold ventures. In Edmon-

A.W. Dingman

"Carry on. We want and need more crude oil."

That was the credo of A.W. Dingman, the pioneer oilman who ushered in the great Calgary oil boom of 1914.

Dingman might never have made his historic discovery of oil at Turner Valley southwest of Calgary if it hadn't been for a devastating fire that raged through Toronto in 1900.

Dingman was raised in Ontario and toiled in the oil fields of Pennsylvania in the 1880s. He tried his hand at a variety of trades in Eastern Canada including manufacturing brakes and installing electric lights. He claimed to have installed the first electric street light in Toronto. Dingman

seemed destined to find riches with a soap company in Ontario, but the manufacturing plant was destroyed by the Great Toronto Fire.

He headed west in 1902 and began trying to tap into the rich oil reserves that awaited discovery.

Dingman founded the Calgary Gas Company that gradually developed a market, providing fuel for the Calgary Brewing and Malting Company and street lighting for the young city.

He branched out to establish the Calgary Petroleum Products Company in 1912 and two years later, the Dingman Well came in, and Turner Valley was at the centre of the rush for "black gold".

Tourism

Tourism was well established in the Canadian Rockies even before Alberta became a province in 1905. Since then, it has grown to become one of the most important sectors in the economy.

Tourism is worth an estimated $2.7 billion per year in Alberta employing about 100,000 people.

Private operators and Alberta Tourism department have been working to make the industry more competitive internationally through training programs.

The Alberta government has invested millions in new interpretive centres throughout the province and offered incentives for improvement to private tourist facilities.

Two new interpretive centres have been built to house extensive collections of antique vehicles and farm equipment. the Reynolds-Alberta Museum in Wetaskiwin traces the history of transportation and faming technology since the days of early settlement. Pioneer farm equipment, antique cars, vintage aircraft, and restored farm machinery are on display.

The Remington-Alberta Carriage Centre in Cardston was constructed to display a wide variety of horse-drawn vehicles. The meticulously restored wagons and carriages from the late 1800s include an elegant British "Cinderella" coach and a stagecoach that once carried passengers on bumpy rides across the Canadian West.

The Rocky Mountain Development Company drilled the first oil well in what is now Alberta near Waterton Lakes in 1901. About 17,000 producing wells are found throughout the province. Alberta is the major oil and natural gas producing region of Canada. Pumpjacks resemble nodding horses with their up and down action.

ton, a family of Iranian immigrants parlayed a family carpet business and a thriving real estate business into a consumer wonderland, the West Edmonton Mall. The Ghermezian brothers created this mall, the world's largest shopping complex, with everything from working submarines and an indoor roller coaster to a fantasy hotel with Roman, Polynesian, and other theme rooms.

There are still some difficulties. Many jobs in the tourist industry are filled by inexperienced students during their summer holidays. Service can be very erratic in late summer when the workers leave to go back to school.

Standards have improved in recent years as operators recognized the need to compete for a share of the international travel market.

Top 10 foreign visitors

1.	United States	1,002,900
2.	United Kingdom	99,800
3.	Japan	91,200
4.	West Germany	47,700
5.	Australia	29,900
6.	Hong Kong	15,000
7.	The Netherlands	14,800
8.	Switzerland	13,700
9.	France	13,100
10.	New Zealand	10,800

Source Statistics Canada 1989

Native dance demonstrations are held each summer at the $10 million Head-Smashed-In Buffalo Jump Interpretive Centre near Fort Macleod. The ancient hunting grounds have been declared a World Heritage Site by United Nations Educational Scientific and Cultural Organization.

Lay of the Land

Chinook winds bring warm air across the Rocky Mountains from the Pacific Coast each winter. The winds often bring clouds and shape them into distinctive chinook arches over the western horizon (see page 40).

The Alberta landscape has been shaped and sculpted for millions of years by some of the most powerful and subtle forces of nature.

The result is a province of diversity from jagged mountain peaks and sprawling icefields to rolling hills and vast tracts of forest and grasslands.

It was not always like this. For 1.5 billion years, the land that now forms Alberta was under the Bearpaw Sea. Over that period sediments and the remnants of marine life formed layers on the ancient sea bed. The deposits reached up to six kilometres thick in places and the enormous pressure turned the material into limestone and other forms of sedimentary rock.

The Rocky Mountains were born 120 million years ago when a plate in the earth's crust that lay beneath the North American continent collided with rigid land masses to the west. The gradual compression of the sedimentary layers caused the rock formation to fold and buckle. At weak points, the layers fractured and turned upward. The contortions brought some of the oldest rocks on earth

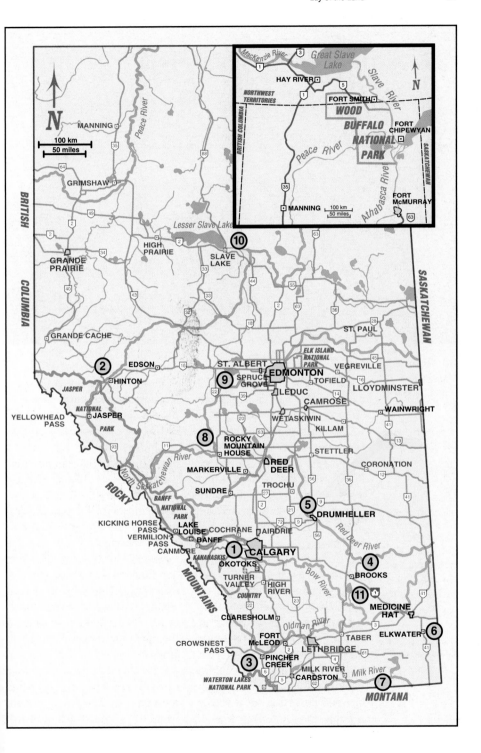

Badlands along the Red Deer River in Dinosaur Provincial Park show the powerful force of erosion. Flooding meltwater at the end of the Ice Age carved deep into the layers of the Earth revealing sediments deposited millions of years ago. Rain and wind continue to erode the lands and reveal dinosaur fossils and other remnants of ancient times.

to the surface. In Waterton Lakes National Park, Precambrian rock dating back 1.6 billion years can be seen in the exposed layers.

The shifts in the earth's crust continued until about 45 million years ago. At one point, the Rockies may have soared as high as the 8000 metre peaks in the Himalayas. They have been steadily eroded down to less than half that size.

The Ice Ages

Over the past 500,000 years, climatic changes have initiated a series of ice ages with glaciers advancing from the cold regions in the north and from the higher elevations of the mountains. Remnants of the ice age are still found in the glaciers of the Rockies, most notably the Columbia Icefield

between Banff and Jasper.

During the ice age a layer of ice, up to one kilometre thick in places, gouged and scraped across the mountains, foothills, and plains. The glaciers carved out valleys and smoothed over the lower peaks. Changes in temperatures caused the ice to advance and melt back several times before the last major retreat about 10,000 years ago.

Even in retreat, the glaciers continued to shape the land and waterways. Floods in lowlands such as the lower Red Deer River valley, cut deep into the layers of the earth and created the badlands.

The slowly moving ice flow carried massive boulders from the mountains far into the plains and when the glaciers melted away,

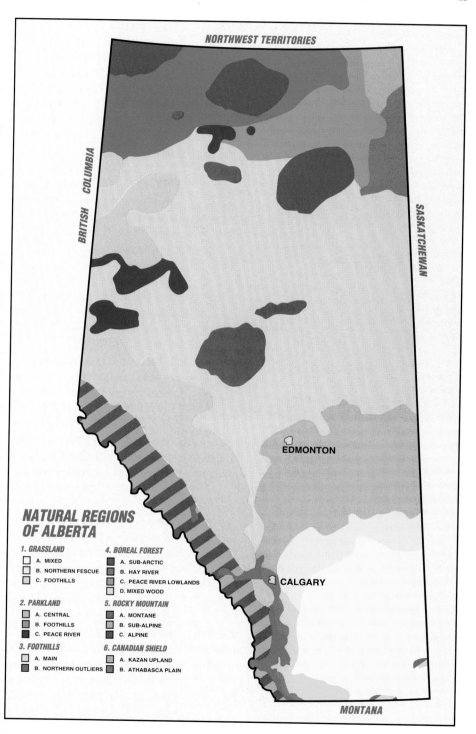

NATURAL REGIONS OF ALBERTA

1. GRASSLAND
- A. MIXED
- B. NORTHERN FESCUE
- C. FOOTHILLS

2. PARKLAND
- A. CENTRAL
- B. FOOTHILLS
- C. PEACE RIVER

3. FOOTHILLS
- A. MAIN
- B. NORTHERN OUTLIERS

4. BOREAL FOREST
- A. SUB-ARCTIC
- B. HAY RIVER
- C. PEACE RIVER LOWLANDS
- D. MIXED WOOD

5. ROCKY MOUNTAIN
- A. MONTANE
- B. SUB-ALPINE
- C. ALPINE

6. CANADIAN SHIELD
- A. KAZAN UPLAND
- B. ATHABASCA PLAIN

Mt. Louis, near the town of Banff, is a typical dogtooth mountain and shows sedimentary layers tilted skyward in an almost vertical formation.

The Mountains

The Canadian Rockies stretch for 760 kilometres along the western edge of Alberta. The southern part of the boundary between Alberta and British Columbia was delineated by the Continental Divide, the high ground in the Rockies. Rivers to the west flow to the Pacific Ocean. Rivers to the east flow into the Arctic or Atlantic oceans.

While the mountains form one natural region, they vary in shape and appearance and in the kinds of plants and animals found at different elevations.

There are five types of mountains found in the Canadian Rockies.

Overthrust mountains such as Mt. Rundle in Banff are distinguished by their gradual slopes to one side (southwest) and steep faces on the other (northeast).

Dogtooth mountains such as Mt. Louis near Banff were formed when sedminentary layers were broken and pushed into a vertical formation. The exposed rock has turned into a series of jagged peaks.

Sawtooth mountains such as Mt. Ishbel have sharper teeth than dogtooth peaks due to the nature of the rock, and erosion. The ridges in the sawtooth formations are perpendicular to prevailing winds from the southwest.

Castellated mountains are prevalent in the Rockies. Castle Mountain and Mt. Temple are two prime examples of peaks in which the layers of rock have remained horizontal as they have been

rocks, known as glacial erratics, were left sitting out on the flats. The "Big Rock" near Okotoks is the largest and best known erratic in the province.

With the retreat of the ice, Alberta slowly developed into six distinct natural regions: mountains (the Rocky Mountains), foothills, grassland, parkland, boreal (northern) forest and the Canadian Shield.

Both the climate and the unique features of the different landscapes have played major roles in determining the types of vegetation and wildlife that can be found in each.

forced up. The result is an appearance that looks like a cross between a layer cake and a medieval fortress.

Horn mountains (or horns) such as Mt. Athabasca have sharply defined features because of severe erosion by glaciers on different faces.

Mountain Ecoregions

Much of the fascination with mountains comes from the variety of plants and animals found there. Elevation is critical in determining where life is found in the mountains. Other factors that shape the complex ecosystems include the prevailing westerly winds, the higher rainfall and snowfall on the western slopes, and fire.

Fire

Fire, most often caused by lightning, clears out tracts of land and enables new growth to replace the old. In the national parks, conservationists have seen that years of forest-fire fighting have upset the balance of nature. The heat from fires helps trees such as the lodgepole pine to flourish by popping open their insulated cones and freeing the seeds inside. Fire suppression is still critical for the safety of wildlife and visitors, but park wardens have experimented with controlled burns in recent years to help restore the balance of nature.

Top: Castle Mountain, between Banff and Lake Louise, is a prime example of a castellated mountain with horizontal layers turned into a fortress shape by erosion.

Middle: Mt. Temple, overlooking Lake Louise, is also castellated. It is named after Sir Richard Temple, patron of an 1884 expedition to the Canadian Rockies.

Bottom: Sawtooth Range, along the Bow Valley Parkway, shows sawtooth formation where sedimentary layers have also been thrust upward. Points are sharper than in dogtooth mountains.

Top: Treeline marks the upper limit of forests on mountain slopes. Stunted evergreens are known as krummholz, translated as "crooked or elfin wood".

Bottom: Indian paintbrush can be found anywhere from valley bottoms to alpine meadows.

Elevation

Elevation is most important in determining where plants and animals are found. The growing season is very short at high altitudes.

A typical mountain in the Rockies is covered by a thick forest at the base that thins out and ends at a distinct treeline. There may be scrubby trees at higher elevation, and in some treasured spots there are magnificent alpine meadows. Here beautiful wildflowers come out in spectacular colors during a very brief summer. At the highest altitudes, there appears to be only a landscape of rock. But even here, lichen can often be found clinging to rocks.

These different zones where plants and animals live are called ecoregions. In the mountains there are three ecoregions, according to elevation – montane, subalpine, and alpine.

The Montane Ecoregion
The montane ecoregion covers the valley bottoms and the lower sun-exposed mountain slopes from about 1200 to 1500 metres elevation (4000 to 5000 ft). Deciduous trees such as trembling aspen are interspersed with conifers, such as lodgepole pine and white spruce. The relatively abundant vegetation provides food for many animals including elk, moose, and deer. The montane ecoregion is crucial for the survival of many species in winter since conditions here are less harsh than at higher elevations. The highways and tourist facilities in the mountains are built primarily in the montane zone. Any further development must be carefully considered since it means a loss of relatively scarce habitat.

The Subalpine Ecoregion
The subalpine ecoregion is the most extensive in the mountains, covering the terrain generally between 1500 and 2200 m (5000 to

7200 ft). The subalpine ecoregion begins where the forest changes from lodgepole pine and Engelmann spruce, to spruce and fir. Higher up, the trees thin out, and they finally stop growing altogether at treeline. Stunted trees known as krummholz struggle to survive at the upper limits of the subalpine. It is also the zone where distinctive larch trees use some colorful magic to endure the extreme cold of winter (see box). A variety of wildlife can be found in the subalpine. But some, like the elk, head down to lower elevation in winter when conditions become too harsh and food is scarce. The subalpine gets higher snowfall than the montane ecoregion. Black bears and grizzlies have their own solution to the harsh winters. They hibernate until spring.

The Alpine Ecoregion

The alpine ecoregion extends from treeline to the mountain peaks. Wildlife such as bighorn sheep and mountain goats will find enough food to remain on the upper slopes during the brief summer growing season, but they have to move to lower elevations for most of the year. Flowers have to be extremely hardy to cling to life and grow at an extremely slow rate. Alpine meadows are among the most beautiful sights in the mountains, but extreme care must be taken not to disturb them since the plants take decades to grow even a centimetre or two.

A Golden Treasure

When the first taste of winter arrives in the mountains in late September or early October, a remarkable transition takes place near treeline in a few special spots.

There are magnificent forested areas made up of Lyall's larch scattered throughout the Rockies. The larch is an oddity since it is coniferous with delicate bright green needles. But unlike its evergreen relatives, those needles turn color and drop off each autumn.

By stripping its branches bare, the slow-growing tree manages to retain scarce nutrients and moisture during the extreme winter conditions. Before the needles are scattered by the wind, they turn a brilliant gold and attract photographers and sightseers from far and wide.

Larch Valley near Moraine Lake and Lake Louise is a prime destination and national park officials have become concerned about overuse of the 2.4-kilometre trail up to the valley.

There are some beautiful displays of larch atop "The Beehives" overlooking Lake Louise and Lake Agnes. There are also several scenic spots for motorists on Kananaskis Trail west of Calgary.

Mountain Scenery

Banff, Jasper, and Waterton Lakes national parks are the obvious choices for exploring the mountains in Alberta. Kananaskis Country is an excellent place to see the jagged eastern slopes of the Rockies. Waterton Lakes National Park is the place to see the oldest exposed rock formations in the mountains.

Foothills

The foothills lie along the eastern edge of the Rockies in a belt 24 to 65 kilometres wide. The hills were formed in a way similar to the mountains, but the greater amount of softer sandstone (rather than limestone) has left them prone to erosion.

At low elevations, there are stands of trembling aspen, balsam poplar, and willow among the lodgepole pine and white spruce forest.

The Peigan Natives named the rolling foothills west of Claresholm the Porcupine Hills because of the quill-like appearance of the Douglas Fir and lodgepole pine that blanket the slopes.

A large portion of the foothills is dry and grass covered. Deer, elk, black bear, and the occasional grizzly are found in the foothills, but much of the land has been turned over for cattle grazing.

Deer

There are two species of deer in Alberta. Mule deer are prevalent in the mountains and foothills, whereas white-tailed deer are more common in the eastern parklands.

To tell them apart, look for distinctive markings on their tails. The tail of the mule deer is narrow and white with a black tip. The tail of the white-tailed deer is wider and is dark on top with an all-white underside. When a white-tailed deer is alarmed or running, its tail is erect.

Mule deer also have larger ears.

Both species are much smaller than elk. Mule deer bucks weigh from 90 to 115 kilograms and white-tailed males range from

70 to 140 kilograms. In each species, does are much smaller than bulls. The coloring of both species change seasonally. Mule deer are brownish-grey with a tendency toward more grey in late fall and winter. White-tailed deer are reddish brown in summer, tending toward grey in winter.

Deer browse on brush, twigs, and new growth on trees as well as grasses and wildflowers. Deer tend to lose their wariness of humans in the national parks, especially Waterton Lakes National Park where they stroll across lawns and sidewalks. Do not feed deer or approach them too closely. They can cause injury with their hooves if alarmed.

Foothills Scenery

There are several picturesque provincial parks in the foothills including Bragg Creek, southwest of Calgary, William A. Switzer, near Hinton, and Beauvais Lake, southwest of Pincher Creek. The provincial government's Bow-Crow Forest includes the eastern slopes of the Rockies and a vast portion of the foothills in southern Alberta.

Grassland

The southeast corner of Alberta is made up of shortgrass and mixed-grass prairie. Rainfall is low, particularly in the shortgrass region around Medicine Hat. The area receives less than 40 centimetres of annual moisture.

Captain John Palliser saw little potential in the parched prairie in 1857:

There is a region, desert or semi-desert in character, which can never become occupied by settlers. It can never be much advantage to us as a possession.

However, time has proven Palliser wrong. Vast irrigation systems and advances in agriculture, especially the development of hardy grain varieties, have allowed most of the land to be cultivated. However, there are still patches of native grass, including blue grama and rough fescue.

Trees are scarce out on the prairies, except along river valleys where dwarf aspen and willows grow. The rivers cut deeply into the flatlands during floods and bursts of heavy rain, carving

out steep ravines known as coulees along the sides of the river.

Deer find a ready source of food and shelter in the greenery along the rivers. Great blue heron frequently take up residence on the shores and gracefully patrol the river for fish.

Bison once roamed the prairies in vast numbers but they are now found only in domesticated herds or on wildlife reserves such as Wood Buffalo and Elk Island national parks. Still, there is other wildlife along the roadside. Richardson's ground squirrels, more commonly but incorrectly

Canada Geese are common in Alberta. During spring and fall migration, they fly in V-formation and often make a considerable amount of noise with their loud honking. Adults are 56 - 92 cm in length with greyish brown bodies and long black necks. Heads are black with white cheek patches.

Cypress Hills Provincial Park

The 200 square kilometres park is a misnamed but intriguing landmark in southeastern Alberta. The hills, which rise more than 450 metres above the surrounding plains, were only partially covered by the last ice age. The forested slopes receive about 8 centimetres more rainfall than the surrounding plains and the vegetation resembles the foothills country along the edge of the Rockies. There are delicate orchids, tall prairie grasses, and evergreens, along with the poplar and trembling aspen. But don't expect to find cypress trees. The region was named "Montagnes de Cypres" by French-Canadian fur-traders who mistook the lodgepole pine for jack pine (*cypres* in French). The error was compounded through a loose translation into English.

The park is a wonderful oasis in summer. There are 548 sites in 14 campgrounds offering everything from walk-in tent spots to full-service hookups for recreation vehicles. There is swimming, fishing, and power boating at Elkwater Lake. There are several hiking trails including a path up to the Horseshoe Canyon viewpoint (4 km one way) with a panorama of the surrounding plains.

called gophers, are easy to spot. Motorists tend to find them difficult to avoid since they dart across the highways throughout the summer.

Pronghorns can also be seen, especially in the Medicine Hat-Cypress Hills area.

Grassland Scenery
It is easy to think of the grasslands as flat and uninteresting, but there are fossil beds and badlands in Dinosaur Provincial Park near Brooks and in Midland Provincial Park near Drumheller. At Cypress Hills Provincial Park, southeast of Medicine Hat, you can see a unique grassland as well as foothills vegetation. And there are hoodoos and Native petroglyphs at Writing-On-Stone Provincial Park southeast of Lethbridge.

Aspen Parkland

The Aspen Parkland covers 60,000 square kilometres of east central Alberta and marks the change from the southern grasslands to the boreal or northern forests.

Not surprisingly, there is a mixture of forested areas of aspen, willow, poplar, and spruce and clearings containing fescue grass. The parkland also has more lakes than the grasslands to the south.

Wildflowers can be found throughout the region. The lovely prairie crocus is one of the first to bloom, in bright purple clusters. The Alberta rose or wild rose is also readily found along riverbanks and shorelines.

Much of the land has been

cleared for farming, but wildlife can still be observed, especially in wooded areas. White-tailed deer, beaver, muskrat, and waterfowl are common.

Parkland Scenery

Some of the finest examples of aspen parkland can be found within the city limits of Edmonton and Red Deer. Waskasoo Park in Red Deer and Capital City Recreation Park in Edmonton both provide lovely riverbank green spots. Elk Island National Park east of Edmonton is a magnificent sanctuary for plains and wood bison, moose, and deer.

Boreal Forest and Canadian Shield

The largest ecoregion in Alberta is the boreal or northern forest. This ecological zone covers more than half the province.

Parts of the vast forested area extend down in a narrow band to Rocky Mountain House and Sundre northwest of Calgary but most of the region lies north of Edmonton.

Due to the harsh climate, hardy trees such as spruce, pine, and poplar dominate the landscape, but birch, fir, larch, willows, and aspen can also be found. There are also bogs, muskeg marshes, and lakes to support a varied wildlife population. The northern lakes are among the world's finest fishing spots.

The remote forests are home to moose, black bears, beaver, and to a lesser extent, elk and

woodland caribou. Caribou have become more scarce in northern Alberta because of extensive logging. However, conservation efforts have been increased to protect caribou habitat.

The remote northeastern corner of Alberta encompasses a

Pronghorn

The pronghorn has achieved a remarkable comeback after being hunted to near-extinction early this century. Wildlife sanctuaries were established in Alberta and Saskatchewan after the pronghorn population dipped to less than 2000 in 1906. Now, there are approximately 20,000 pronghorn on the prairies, even after several harsh winters when many starved. Conservationists in the Medicine Hat area help out in severe conditions by supplying food.

The deer-like pronghorn are easy to identify. They are tan with white patches on their cheeks and rumps. They have a dark muzzle. Both bucks and does have pronged horns. Adults weigh about 50 kilograms (110 lb). Pronghorn have extremely good eyesight, an important protective trait in the wide open prairies. They can run faster than 80 kilometres per hour (50 mph).

small part of the Canadian Shield where the landscape consists mainly of exposed 600-million-year-old Precambrian rock.

Boreal Forest Scenery
Crimson Lake Provincial Park west of Rocky Mountain House is one of the most accessible examples of boreal forest as is Wabamun Lake Provincial Park just 65 kilometres west of Edmonton. Lesser Slave Lake Provincial Park, between Edmonton and Peace River, is not only in the heart of the boreal forest but is also on one of the largest lakes in the province, with excellent swimming and fishing. Wood Buffalo National Park, which lies both in Alberta and the Northwest Territories, covers a wilderness area the size of Switzerland (see p. 35).

Conservation

The conservation ethic has grown steadily over the past 100 years, to protect not only the wild animals, but also their native habitat – the natural ecological regions.

Canada's first national park was established around the Banff hot springs in 1885 to prevent commerical interests from spoiling the landscape. Many of Alberta's other parks and wilderness reserves have been established to protect natural treasures.

The process has been a long one, with awareness and sophistication evolving slowly. Hunting was allowed in the early days of Rocky Mountains Park, the forerunner of Banff National Park. Sportsmen hired local guides to lead them to prized grizzlies and bighorn sheep. The impact on the wildlife was devastating, since the best breeding specimens were also prized as the greatest trophies.

Even after conservationists gained new laws against hunting, there was still a misconception that some animals (such as cougars and wolves) were "bad" and should be killed to protect "good" animals (such as deer and elk). From 1924 to 1941, park wardens killed 80 cougars in Banff and Jas-

Moving Mountains

During the Ice Age, glaciers not only carved their way through the mountains, they also carried chunks of debris far out onto the plains. When the ice melted away 10,000 years ago, huge boulders were left strewn across the countryside from Edson to Cardston. They are known as glacial erratics, and the largest one known sits on the edge of a farmer's field west of Okotoks on Highway 7. The Big Rock may have once been part of Mt. Edith Cavell near Jasper.

per national parks. The practice was stopped decades ago but the population of big cats has never recovered, and they are rarely seen.

With the number of predators drastically reduced over the years, other species flourished. And they suffered from overpopulation. From 1941 to 1970, park wardens had to kill high numbers of elk to keep them from destoying their own habitat.

Wildlife management has become much more sophisticated in recent years. Specialists look for ways to ensure that natural balances are maintained. For example, some roads, such as the southern stretch of Kananaskis Trail are closed in winter to keep traffic away from sensitive elk habitat. Also, hunting limits in the province are set to protect big game animals.

Alberta has also joined the international conservation efforts

Weather

Thanks to the Rocky Mountains and the other interior ranges of British Columbia, Alberta is the sunniest province in Canada. The prevailing westerly winds lose most of their moisture as they rise to cross the mountains. There are some rainy spells, particularly in June, but you can expect plenty of days with brilliant blue skies.

What to expect:

Summer: Average high temperatures are a comfortable 20–23°C (about 70–75°F) in Calgary and Edmonton, and a few degrees lower in Banff and Jasper. Even on extremely hot days, it cools off at night to about 10°C (50°F) in Calgary and Edmonton and a little cooler in the mountains. There are occasional mid-summer snowfalls in the mountains, providing a beautiful frosting on the mountaintops. There is rarely any snow in the mountain valleys.

Fall: September and October are excellent months to tour the province. Temperatures

are pleasant with highs of about 16°C (60°F) in September and 10–12 °C (50–54°F) in October. November is much cooler and usually marks the arrival of the first winter storms.

Winter: January is the coldest month of the year with average highs of -6°C (21°F) in Calgary, -11°C (12°F) in Edmonton, -7°C (19°F) in Banff, and -8°C (18°F) in Jasper. Temperatures tend to be a little more moderate in December and February, but each winter there seem to be cold spells when temperatures dip to -30°C (-22°F) and special care is needed to prevent frostbite and hypothermia.(See Winter Safety, p. 218.)

Spring: Winter officially ends on March 21, but snow usually lingers into April out on the prairies and much longer in the mountains. Some ski resorts stay open until late May. Visitors to Banff may have a choice of playing tennis in town or spring skiing in the mountains. Average highs are 14–16°C (57–61°F) in May and rise a few degrees in mid-June. June tends to be the wettest month of the year.

Whooping cranes nest in Wood Buffalo National Park, a World Heritage Site that is in Alberta and the Northwest Territories.

of the United Nations Educational Scientific and Cultural Organization. It is fitting that some of the most magnificent spots in Alberta have been singled out for international recognition.

Several national parks, including, Banff, Jasper, and Wood Buffalo have been named World Heritage Sites along with Dinosaur Provincial Park and the Head-Smashed-In Buffalo Jump.

Saving the Whooping Crane

Wood Buffalo National Park is the site of one of the greatest international efforts in history. Forestry officer G.M. Wilson and pilot J.D. Landells were on a routine helicopter patrol over park wetlands in 1954 when they solved a crucial ecological mystery. They spotted a group of majestic snow

white birds with long graceful necks and brilliant red crowns fringed with black. More importantly, there was a young bird with them, still not able to fly.

A ground search by the Canadian Wildlife Service confirmed the discovery of the spring nesting grounds of the rare and endangered whooping crane. It also marked a significant advance in the painstaking joint effort by Canada and the United States to save the magnificent species.

Whooping cranes were once common sights on the western plains of North America. With a wingspan of 2 metres or more and a height of 1.5 metres, they are the largest bird on the continent. Unfortunately, they were once prime targets for hunters and they became prized even more as their numbers declined dramatically 100 years ago. Collectors placed even more value on the rare species and hastened their demise.

Conservationists began to take action and in 1937, the Aransas National Wildlife Refuge was established in Texas to protect the winter habitat of the cranes.

That sanctuary on the Gulf of Mexico helped the cause, but it still seemed that the species was headed for extinction. In the early 1950s, there were only 21 whooping cranes left.

The discovery of the nesting

Wood Buffalo National Park

The wholesale slaughter of buffalo across North America sparked laws to protect the endangered animals as early as 1877 in the Northwest Territories, which included Alberta at the time.

The laws were difficult to enforce however, and in 1922 one of the world's largest national parks was established to protect the most significant remaining wild herd of bison.

Wood Buffalo National Park encompasses 45,000 square kilometres (17,300 sq mi) in both Alberta and the Northwest Territories. Administrative headquarters for the park are in Fort Smith, NWT, which also has commercial services including accommodation, groceries, restaurants and air transportation There are also park offices and services in Fort Chipewyan, on the Alberta side of the border.

The park can be reached by road by driving to the northern limit of the MacKenzie Highway in Alberta and continuing on to Fort Smith.

Although the herd of 3500 bison has been protected on park lands, the animals have been stricken with disease in recent years.Researchers are trying to find a way of fighting the latest threat to the animals. Aside from the bison herd, the park contains the nesting area for the endangered whooping crane.

For more information contact:
The Superintendent
Wood Buffalo National Park
Box 750, Fort Smith
Northwest Territories
X0E 0P0

site at Wood Buffalo National Park enabled conservationists to step in and help mother nature. Researchers found that whooping cranes tend to hatch two chicks each spring. But there is fierce competition for food and only one chick survives to migrate south in the fall.

By carefully removing one egg from nests each spring, wildlife workers have established foster homes for whoopers among sandhill cranes in Idaho. A captive flock has also been established in Maryland.

The population of the whooping cranes has climbed steadily

Martha Kostuch
Veterinarian/
Environmentalist

What brought me to Alberta and Rocky Mountain House? The mountains, the rivers, the streams, the forests, and the wildlife. Rocky Mountain House also provided a good business opportunity; I'm a veterinarian and environmentalist. Both are very important.

My life is never boring. Yesterday, for example, after getting breakfast and the kids off to school, I went out and performed fertility exams on a herd of cattle. Then I was called out on an emergency to examine two sick cows. I came back to answer phone calls from the media regarding environmental issues, and then I spent most of the afternoon preparing and printing my brief on the Old Man Dam hearings. The Old Man River and the Kootenay Plains have become very, very special to me, partly as a result of my battles to try to save them.

Then while making supper, I was called out on an emergency to sew up a cow, and I came back to more printing. So that's the sort of day I have, very eventful.

Rocky Mountain House is the last town before entering the foothills and has a population of about 5800. Although it isn't in the Rockies, you certainly have a beautiful view of them. We depend on agriculture, tourism, and the oil and gas industry. Many people live here because of the environment. Some would like to develop it; others see it as something to be protected. We are a diverse community with a large Native population; we have primarily Cree, as well as Stoney at the Big Horn Reserve farther west.

The Stoney also have a special interest in the Kootenay Plains – about 158 kilometres west of here on the David Thompson Highway (Highway 11). It is a sacred place for them; they hold Sun Dances there every year. There is a dry, desert-like environment with diverse landforms – alkali flats, hoodoos, and the Siffleur Falls. There are rare plants and orchids, and it is all fragile and easily disturbed by man. The only other two places like it are in Banff and Jasper, and they have been largely destroyed by the development of the townsites.

and is now above 200. There are still serious threats to the species. Researchers do not know if the whooping cranes raised by sandhills will have the mating capabilities to establish a self-sustaining flock.

There are also serious hazards on the 3500 kilometre migration route between Wood Buffalo National Park and the Aransas refuge. Though the cranes occasionally cross northern Alberta, they are most likely to be seen in central Saskatchewan, when the birds stop to feed in stubble fields as they head south.

Enjoying the Environment

Alberta's diversity: mountains, badlands, river valleys, prairies, foothills, and forests are enhanced by the wonderful variety of plants and wildlife.

Here are some suggestions on the best ways to enjoy the environment without disturbing the wildlife and plants.

1. Do not feed the animals. It's against the law in the national parks and other protected areas. It can also be quite dangerous. Deer may look very friendly, but they can become aggressive in pursuit of handouts. The practice also spoils the animals.

Campers should also be careful to store food safely. A bear that finds easy access to food around campgrounds will pose a danger.

It's okay to sniff and photograph the wildflowers but do not pick them. Fragile flowers can take decades to mature in the harsh mountain environment. Park regulations prohibit disturbing the flowers. It's best to enjoy them without touching and hikers should keep to established trails to avoid trampling vegetation.

Moose

The moose is the largest animal with antlers in the world and is found in forests throughout Alberta. A mature bull stands 1.8 m at the shoulder and weighs 450 kg or more. Cows are slightly smaller. Moose are dark brown with humped shoulders and large prominent noses. Both bulls and cows have a piece of loose skin under the chin known as a bell. Bull moose have palmated antlers that begin to grow each spring and reach full size by the fall mating season. Palmated antlers resemble the shape of a hand and are wide and flat with tines along the edge.

The name "moose" comes from a native word for twig-eater. Moose eat new growth on bushes and trees as well as aquatic vegetation in marshes and wetlands. In winter, they venture onto avalanche slopes and browse on willow, aspen, and poplar. They are also frequently found along river valleys.

Unlike elk, moose are solitary animals. Whereas it is common to see 20 or 30 elk grazing together in a clearing, it is rare to see more than one moose in an area unless it is a cow and calf. Do not approach a cow and calf or adults of either sex during the autumn mating season. Moose can be quite aggressive and people have been killed in attacks.

Park staff try to relocate problem bears to the remote backcountry, but some bears become reliant on food left out by careless humans. And the bears have to be destroyed.

2. Do not disturb the animals. It is tempting to get close to wildlife for a better look or close-up photograph. It can be a very serious mistake. If you spot a bear at a distance, leave the area. Bears, especially females with cubs, are very protective and it is important not to get between a mother and her young. (For more on bear safety, see page 208)

Use a telephoto lens for photography and carry binoculars or a spotting scope to best observe the wildlife.

3. Check with staff in the national and provincial parks about wildlife in the area. Some interpretive programs are offered with hikes to prime viewing areas.

4. Watch for wildlife in the early morning and in the evening. Many species are most active at those times. As well, the lighting is often best then.

5. Do not pick wildflowers. It is against the law in the parks and it can take decades for some alpine plants to recover. Stay on designated trails wherever possible to keep from walking on fragile vegetation.

6. Watch for wildlife on the road. Park officials had to build fences on either side of the Trans-Canada Highway through much of Banff National Park because of the number of elk, deer, and bears that were hit by traffic. Most of the highways do not have that safeguard and extreme care is needed, especially at night. If you spot wildlife by the highway and want to stop for a look, pull over safely and avoid blocking traffic.

7. Keep your pets under control. Dogs must be on a leash in national and provincial parks.

8. Report suspicious activities. Poaching is a serious threat to wildlife in Alberta. Hunting is carefully regulated in the province and is not allowed in the national parks. Contact park wardens or the Royal Canadian Mounted Police if you suspect someone is illegally hunting on park land. Elsewhere in Alberta, dial 1-800-642-3800.

Wildlife

Bear Family

Grizzlies are the largest carnivores (meat-eaters) in Alberta. Grizzlies are often spotted along the Icefields Parkway (Highway 93) between Banff and Jasper. They can also be seen from a distance on the south end of Cameron Lake in Waterton Lakes National Park. Grizzlies are found mainly in the mountains and foothills. (See page 209.)

Black bears share much of the mountain and foothills terrain, but can also be found out on the prairies and throughout the boreal forests. (See page 209.)

Deer Family

The deer family includes those with cloven hooves and branched antlers that are shed each year. (See page 28.)

Mule deer are found throughout almost all of Alberta except the extreme north.

White-tailed deer are found throughout most of the province as well but they are less common in the mountains than mule deer.

Elk are found mainly in the mountains and foothills. They are seen around the townsites of Banff and Jasper, especially in winter when they search for food in valley bottoms. (See page 51.)

Moose are the largest members of the deer family in the province and can be found in the foothills and mountains as well as the northern forest. (See page 38.)

Pronghorn are found in southeastern Alberta around Medicine Hat and Cypress Hills Provincial Park. (See page 31.)

Caribou are found in the Rockies and northern forest.

Bovid Family

Members of the bovid family are also ungulates (hooved) but unlike members of the deer family, they have horns that are not shed.

Bighorn sheep are found throughout the Rockies. (See page 111.)

Mountain goats are also found throughout the Rockies. (See page 206.)

Wild Cats

Cougars are the largest of the wild cats in Alberta and can be found mainly in the mountains and foothills. (See page 117.)

Wild Dogs

Coyotes are the most prevalent member of the wild dog family in Alberta and can be found in all types of terrain. (See page 214.)

Wolves are the largest members of the wild dog family but are less common than coyotes and are found mainly in the northern parts of the Rockies and the boreal forest.

Rodent Family

Beaver are found in wetlands throughout the province. (See page 134.)

Columbian ground squirrels and Richardson's ground squirrels are commonly called gophers. Columbian ground squirrels live in the high country. The Richardson's ground squirrels are found out on the prairies as well.

Birds

The Alberta checklist has topped 340 birds including 250 that nest in the province and another 90 birds that pass through on migration routes.

The province is well known for the variety of ducks, geese, and other waterfowl that thrive in the wetlands. There are also majestic raptors such as the bald eagle (page 41). Species range from the tiny calliope hummingbird to the tallest and rarest bird in North America, the whooping crane (page 34).

There are excellent birdwatching areas in Alberta. *SuperGuide* recommends:

1. Beaverhill Lake, 65 km east of Edmonton (Scenic Drive 3). Over 250 species have been recorded including a fine assortment of waterfowl, shorebirds (almost all of the 43 species in Alberta), raptors and songbirds. Look for pelicans at the north end of the lake.

2. Capital City Recreation Park, Edmonton. An extensive park system has been established along the banks of the North Saskatchewan River (Scenic Drive 10). Over 120 species can be spotted in the river valley. Bald and golden eagles migrate through the city. Bohemian waxwings are

---

Chinooks

In the depths of winter, Alberta is treated to warm westerly winds that sweep across the southern half of the province. Usually a dramatic arch of clouds appears over the western horizon as mild Pacific air blows in from British Columbia. (The winds are named after a band of Oregon Natives.) As the wind dips down from the mountains, it gains heat from increased pressure and can cause a sudden rise in temperature that lasts from a few hours to several days. There have been rare cases where the temperature jumped more than 20° C (over 40° F) in just 10 minutes but generally the shift is less extreme. Still, there are tales like that of a skier in 1930 who began climbing a snowpacked hill just as a chinook arrived. As the story goes, by the time he got to the top the slope was bare.

common and have attracted a high density of merlins.

3. Inglewood Bird Sanctuary, Calgary. Close to 220 species have been spotted in this lovely patch of greenery along the Bow River just east of downtown (Scenic Drive 11). Bald eagles are occasionally seen farther downstream.

4. Frank Lake, near High River, 48 km southeast of Calgery, is an excellent place to see water birds (Scenic Drive 6).

5. Waskasoo Park and the Gaetz Lake Sanctuary, Red Deer. Close to 130 species have been recorded in the mixed habitat which includes riverbank, lake, grassland, and forest. Look for osprey, great blue heron, merlin and songbirds.

6. Elk Island National Park, 35 km east of Edmonton (Scenic Drive 3). Close to 230 species have been recorded in the park which includes boreal forest and aspen parkland. Look for the great blue and crowned night herons, as well as loons and a wide variety of ducks.

7. Waterton Lakes National Park. Diverse habitat in the mountains of southern Alberta supports a variety of species. The national park is also on major migration routes and nearly 230 species have been observed. Look for an osprey nest atop the pole near the park gates.

8. Cypress Hills Provincial Park, 66 km southeast of Medicine Hat. Look for songbirds and waterfowl. More than 200 species have been recorded, including wild turkeys.

9. Banff National Park (Scenic Drive 7). Close to 250 species have been recorded including bald eagles, osprey, and ptarmigan. Magpies and whiskey jacks (gray jays), are very common around campgrounds and picnic spots. The Fenland hiking trail and Vermilion Lakes Drive near Banff townsite are recommended.

10. Jasper National Park. Over 250 bird species have been observed in Jasper National Park (Scenic Drive 8). Look for golden

Bald Eagle

The bald eagle is one of most easily identified birds, with its all-white head and tail and brown wings and body. This majestic predator is also one of the largest birds in Alberta with a wingspan that can exceed two metres.

Bald eagles are generally summer residents in the Rockies. They are usually found near water since they rely mainly on fish for food. Bald eagles can also be seen soaring along ridge tops in search of prey or carrion.

Large nests are built high in trees and are used year after year. Most bald eagles migrate to the Pacific Coast or southern United States for the winter. But some stay year-round in Alberta if they have access to open water. Bald eagles are frequently seen along stretches of the Bow River in Calgary.

Prairie crocus, also known as pasque flower or lion's beard, is found not only on the prairies, but also on the foothills and mountain slopes. The bright purple flower is one of the earliest to bloom in spring. The crocus, with fine hairs on both stem and flower, grows low on the ground.

eagles nesting near Amethyst Lake and northern pygmy owls in Jasper townsite.

11. Kinbrook Island Provincial Park, 13 km south of Brooks. Lake Newell provides ideal habitat for Canada geese, double-crested cormorants, white pelicans and about100 other species (Scenic Drive 2). Several small islands in the lake are off limits to protect water birds.

Wildflowers

There are many places to see wildflowers in summer. Naturally, the terrain, climate, and elevation are critical.

Out on the grasslands, the prairie crocus provides a burst of purple in early spring. The prickly pear cactus can survive under the dry conditions of the southeast.

In the mountains, growing conditions change dramatically with elevation. Wildflowers in the montane zone include tall bear grass, cow parsnip, and yarrow.

The plants adapt to harsher growing conditions in the subalpine zone. Some, like fireweed, take on different characteristics depending on elevation. Common fireweed, which thrives in burned out forests, grows two metres high. Mountain fireweed is less than half a metre high and has smaller leaves and fewer flowers.

Higher in the subalpine zone there are a variety of delicate twinflowers and more hardy bunchberry and huckleberry.

In the alpine zone, plants survive by adapting to a very short growing season that can be interrupted by snowfall at almost any time. Low-lying plants, often with hairy coverings and tough leaves, are well-suited to avoid heat and moisture loss. White mountain avens and a variety of heathers can survive at high altitude. Colour is supplied by pale blue alpine forget-me-nots, pink moss campion, and many other species.

SuperGuide recommends:

1. Parker Ridge, on the Icefields Parkway (Scenic Drive 8). The 2.4 kilometre trail rises steeply above the roadway to one of the most accessible alpine meadows in the Rockies. Look for white mountain avens, yellow heather, western anemone with its furry head, and moss campion with its delicate pink flowers against a deep green background.

2. **Sunshine Meadows**, at Sunshine Village off the Trans-Canada Highway in Banff National Park (Scenic Drive 7). The ski area is free of snow briefly each summer, just long enough for a wonderful display of alpine flowers. Gondola service is available.

3. **Cavell Meadows**, off Mt. Edith Cavell Road in Jasper National Park (Scenic Drive 8). The 8 km trail rises through subalpine forest to an alpine meadow and provides great views of the Angel Glacier.

4. **Blakiston Falls**, off Red Rock Canyon Road in Waterton Lakes National Park. The short walk to the falls viewpoint winds through

Andy Russell
Conservationist/Writer/ Naturalist

My family members were agriculturalists. We had a small ranch down south, west of Lethbridge. It was my grandfathers and it's still in the family. Dad moved out to Pincher Creek area in 1919, and Mother and us kids went out in 1920.

When I left home to work, I went into the mountains as a professional guide. At age 19, I was a licensed Grade A Guide and I guided hunters, fishermen, and sightseers. While guiding, I travelled between Waterton Lakes and Banff, and west to the Flathead River in BC. I have good memories; it was gorgeous country in those days.

The fires of 1935 and 1936 burned off a lot of the forest in the Waterton area. It opened up the country that was heavily timbered. There were some big changes following those fires; the moose and elk started to move on trails that the forestry cut through the mountains. And during World War II the wildlife became a lot more abundant, since there was also very little

hunting being done. We saw moose down in Waterton country in the late 1940s. In 1946 there were 2000 elk in Waterton Park. Today the elk are not numerous because, first of all, the animals overextended themselves. About 500 of them starved and quite a few were slaughtered. Also a big stretch of country that had been a game preserve was opened up for oil exploration. In the old days the only way you could hunt something bigger than a deer was with a horse, because the animals were too heavy to pack out alone.

When people come to the wilderness, they could try to learn to see. Most who come can look, but they can't see. For example, a person who can really see can trail an elk for days. You can get good at it after a while. It's detailed understanding – that's what it boils down to; and you can't learn that in a day. Still, if you're really going to enjoy the country, you've got to understand something of what you're looking at. And one can learn: it's education, it's observation; and it takes time.

Alpine wildflowers bloom in the short summer above treeline at Sunshine Meadows. The Sunshine Village ski resort near Banff has built interpretive walkways to attract visitors in July and August.

subalpine forest. Shooting stars, sticky purle geraniums, Indian paintbrush, and many other species line the trail.

5. Ptarmigan Cirque, at Highwood Pass in Kananaskis Country (Scenic Drive 9). The 2.5 kilometre hike provides ready access to an alpine meadow. A gentle mountain stream provides moisture for moss campion and a colorful array of other species.

Scenic Drive 1: Calgary to Bragg Creek and Elbow Falls

The 82 kilometre drive from Calgary to the end of Elbow Falls Trail (Highway 66) provides a look at the transition from prairies to foothills to the Front Ranges of the Rockies. Along the way, there is an opportunity to stop at day-use areas, hike a short interpretive trail, fish for trout in a stocked pond, and explore the arts and craft shops in the hamlet of Bragg Creek.

To follow the Elbow River into the foothills, take Highway 8 from the end of Richmond Road in southwest Calgary. The grassland west of the city is used primarily for cattle grazing. Deer and coyo-

tes are seen in the area, and occasionally, cougar and black bear.

Head south on Highway 22 into the hamlet of Bragg Creek. Much of the land is part of the Sarcee Indian Reserve. The Redwood Meadows Golf Course and neigbouring housing subdivision have been developed by the Natives.

Bragg Creek has a variety of galleries along with a few casual restaurants. **Bragg Creek Provincial Park (1)** is a day-use area along the edge of the Elbow River. It's a popular fishing and picnic spot. The vegetation is mainly forest, a mixture of white spruce, lodgepole pine, poplar, and some Douglas fir.

Bragg Creek Provincial Park is at the eastern edge of the Ka-nanaskis Country recreation area. It is also at the edge of the Bow-Crow Forest, one of 10 vast forest management areas in the province. The Bow-Crow Forest encompasses the eastern slopes of the Rockies and foothills from the Clearwater River west of Red Deer to Waterton Lakes National Park in the southeast corner of the province.

Detailed information on local campgrounds, hiking trails, and other attractions is available at the **Elbow Valley Visitor Information Centre (2)**, nine kilometres southwest of Bragg Creek on Elbow Falls Trail (Highway 66).

Allen Bill Pond (3), 4.5 kilometres west of the information centre, is a popular fishing spot in summer (permit required) and

Landscape quickly changes from prairie to foothills to mountains west of Calgary. And the vegetation shifts from grassland to forest.

Land is less suitable for growing crops in the foothills but can sustain cattle grazing.

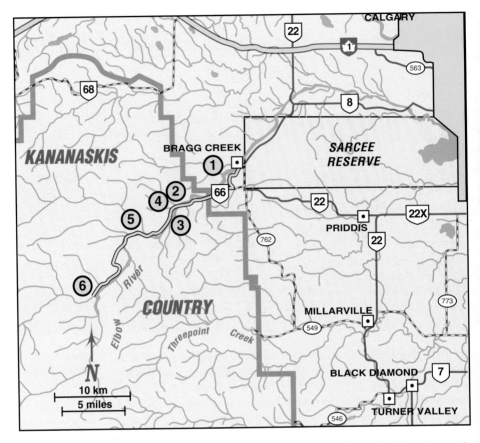

skating rink in winter. The parking lot marks the trailhead for the **Fullerton Loop (4)**, a 5 kilometre hike that offers a panorama of the foothills from the top of Ranger Ridge.

Follow the highway up the Elbow River to **Elbow Falls (5)**. A picnic area, viewpoint, and short hiking trails have been developed here.

There are rewards for those who drive on to the end of Elbow Falls Trail. The foothills terrain gets steeper and the eastern Rockies loom on the western ho-

rizon. Peaks such as Romulus and Remus, Glasgow, Fullerton, and Howard begin to dominate the skyline.

The **Little Elbow Campground (6)** marks the end of the roadway. A short interpretive trail follows the bank of the Little Elbow River.

The road (Elbow Falls Trail) is closed west of Elbow Falls from December 1 to May 15. Cyclists take advantage of the closure in spring when the road is bare enough to ride on for several weeks, before the opening for motor vehicles.

Scenic Drive 2: Badlands to Wetlands

Dinosaur Provincial Park to Kinbrook Island Provincial Park

Out on the shortgrass prairie, water is crucial in shaping the landscape and sustaining wildlife. It has been a precious commodity since the turn of the century when the Canadian Pacific Railway began promoting irrigation to turn the parched soil into productive farmland.

The 86 kilometre drive from Dinosaur Provincial Park to Kinbrook Island Provincial Park near Brooks provides a close look at the diverse influences of water.

Dinosaur Provincial Park (1), 48 kilometres northeast of Brooks, encompasses the largest and most spectacular badlands region in Canada. Reddish brown hills spread out on either side of the Red Deer River. Layers of shale and sandstone reveal that ancient sediments were deposited millions of years ago when the area was an inland sea and later a fertile coastal region.

At the end of the Ice Age, meltwater from retreating glaciers carved out much of the badland region along the Red Deer River.

Today, rainfall is infrequent but summer storms continue to sculpt the landscape. As the layers have washed away, fossilized dinosaur bones have been exposed. The park has been designated a World Heritage Site because of the many fossils. The

Royal Tyrrell Museum of Palaeontology field station (2) operates in the park, with interpretive displays on dinosaurs and the badlands. Guided bus tours and hikes are available into an ecological reserve. Look for great blue heron along the riverbanks, and prairie falcons and hawks. Fortunately, poisonous rattlesnakes and scorpions are seen only a few times each summer.

From the field station drive southwest on Highways 511, 544, and 873. Watch for mule deer, white-tailed deer, and pronghorn. Ring-necked pheasants are quite common. The **Brooks Wildlife Centre (3)** raises over 100,000 chicks for release each year. The centre also provides verterinary care for injured birds of prey.

Badlands were originally called *mauvaise terres* by early French travellers. The deeply eroded landscape looks desolate, but waterfowl can be found along the banks of the Red Deer River. And deer and coyotes are commonly seen.

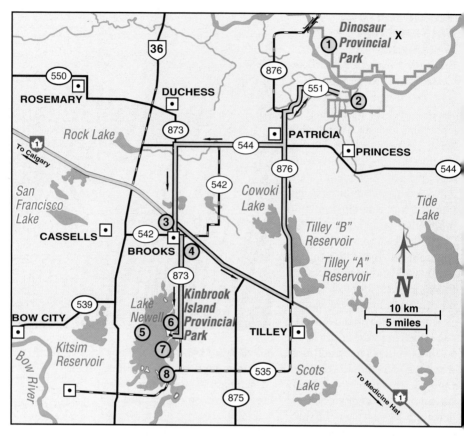

Tours are available.

The importance of water is vividly demonstrated by the 3.2 kilometre **Brooks Aqueduct (4)** south of town, patterned on the aqueducts of ancient Rome. The concrete aqueduct was built between 1909 and 1914 by the railway as part of a massive irrigation scheme to attract settlement. The aqueduct has been replaced by other systems to make the 600,000 square kilometres (1.5 million acres) of the Eastern Irrigation District extremely productive .

Lake Newell (5), 13 kilometres south of Brooks off Hwy 873, is part of the irrigation district. At 65 square kilometres, it is the largest manmade lake in the province. The reservoir is also a popular recreation area and the wetlands have become habitat for waterfowl and shorebirds.

White pelicans, double-crested cormorants, California gulls and about a hundred other species have been identified. Several small islands are off limits to visitors but camping facilities at **Kinbrook Island Provincial Park (6)**, are reached by a short causeway.

The Kinbrook Marsh (7), adjacent to the park, and **Swen Bayer Peninsula** (8) to the south are two prime spots for birdwatching.

Scenic Drive 3: Elk Island to Beaverhill Lake

Two of Alberta's best spots for wildlife viewing and birdwatching are less than 50 kilometres east of Edmonton. A drive through **Elk Island National Park (1)**, with its herds of wood and plains bison can easily be combined with a stop at the Beaverhill Lake Nature Centre and its abundance of waterfowl. Avid birders can add a short sidetrip to Miquelon Lake Provincial Park where more than 200 species have been recorded.

Elk Island National Park, 35 kilometres east of Edmonton on Hwy 16, has its origins in a conservation campaign that started in 1903. A small group of residents and farmers in the Fort Sas-

Astotin Lake provides habitat for waterfowl and mammals. About 230 species of birds have been recorded. The lake is good for canoeing and sailing and the shoreline drive provides excellent views.

Listen for elk bugling at sunset in the fall. Elk Island National Park has a high density of big game animals including elk, wood and plains bison, deer, and moose.

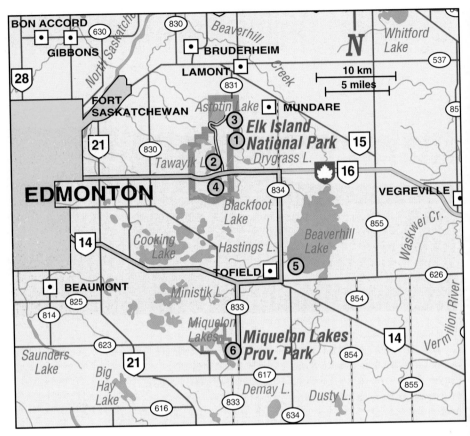

katchewan area were alarmed at the number of hunters who were stalking a herd of elk that had once flourished in the Astotin Lake area of the Beaver Hills.

A fenced reserve was created around the lake in 1906 and a hunting season that had threatened the last remnants of the herd was cancelled. In 1907, the reserve was used as a temporary home for a herd of 400 plains bison shipped north from Montana. The animals were rounded up in 1909 and transferred to a new Buffalo Park at Wainwright in eastern Alberta, but 48 animals

eluded capture and started the herd that still thrives in aspen parkland at Elk Island National Park.

The 194 square kilometre park is now home to 500 plains bison, 400 wood bison, 400 moose, 1600 elk and a variety of other species including coyotes, beaver, muskrats, and porcupines.

Approximately 230 species of birds have been seen in the park, and the wetland areas serve as nesting sites for waterfowl. Attempts have been made to reintroduce the endangered trumpeter swan. The trumpeter swan is the largest waterbird in the world and has a wingspan of over two metres.

A small herd of bison is kept in a **bison paddock (2)**, 2.6 kilometres north of Highway 16 on the main access road to **Astotin Lake (3)**. There is an interpretive centre at the lake itself. A road curves around the west edge of the lake. There are also short interpretive trails along the lakeshore.

The **Ukrainian Cultural Heritage Village (4)** is located on the east edge of Elk Island National Park with 30 historic buildings. Special events depict the early way of life of Ukrainian settlers.

It is a short drive from Elk Island south on Highway 834 to Tofield and the **Beaverhill Nature Centre (5)**. Lakeside viewing areas are 7 kilometres east of the centre. More than 250 species of birds include tundra swans, snow geese, peregrine falcons, bald eagles, and merlins. Checklists are available at the nature centre. The 129 square kilometre lake and surrounding wetland has been designated an internationally significant wetland by the International Union for Conservation of Nature.

It is a 45 kilometre drive from Tofield back to Edmonton on Highway 14. Birders can add another short sidetrip to **Miquelon Lakes Provincial Park (6)** at the south end of the Beaver Hills. The lake is another major stopping point for migratory birds, with nearly 200 species.

Elk

These majestic members of the deer family are commonly seen in the Rockies and foothills. Early Europeans called the animals "elchs," a term more correctly referring to a type of moose. Shawnee Natives named the animals "Wapiti," a more accurate term which refers to their white rumps.

Stag elk can grow to 1.5 metres at the shoulder and grow impressive antlers each year with up to six points. The antlers can be up to1.5 metres long and 1.8 metres wide.

Stags can weigh up to 450 kilograms. Females or hinds are usually in the 225 to 270 kilogram range. The coat is tan brown on the body, darker on the neck and legs, with a shaggy mane on the neck. They have cream-colored rumps.

Elk are both browsers and grazers, meaning they eat grasses and weeds along with shrubs. Aspen trees throughout the mountains and foothills are scarred by elk feeding on the bark.

Elk mate in late summer and early fall and the high-pitched bugle of the stags is intended to impress the hinds. The hinds form harems and the dominant stags make good use of their antlers to fend off other males.

In the national parks elk are accustomed to sightseers and photographers. They can be seen at close range along the roadways. But males can be very aggressive toward humans during the rutting season from late August to October. Then they are ready to use their antlers on any potential rivals, including humans.

Highlights of History

Mounted policemen established Fort Walsh on the eastern edge of the Cypress Hills (shown here), before marching west to build Fort Macleod and Fort Calgary. Formation of the North West Mounted Police in 1873 drove whisky traders out of the territory and offered security to early settlers.

9000 BC Natives migrate to western grasslands and forests after glacial ice retreats and game animals return.

3700 BC Natives develop an efficient technique to hunt bison by stampeding animals over cliffs. Communal hunting grounds known as "buffalo jumps" are used repeatedly throughout the west for more than 3500 years.

3000 BC Natives erect hilltop medicine wheels. Rocks piled in a central cairn with up to 28 spokes radiating from the centre are possibly used as astronomical instruments. Some indicate the point on the horizon where the sun rises on the first day of summer.

1730 Natives in Alberta begin to feel the influence of foreigners, with the arrival of guns and horses. Natives from eastern Canada resettle in the west.

1754 Anthony Henday travels overland 1600 kilometres (1000 miles) from York Fort on Hudson's Bay to become the first white man to set foot in what is now Alberta. He tries unsuccessfully to convince natives to travel to York Fort to trade their furs and recommends that new posts be built in the west.

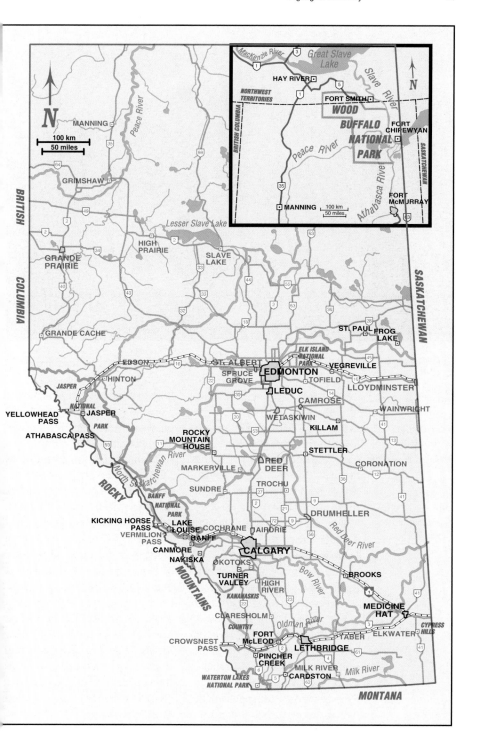

Mt. Rundle, one of the most prominent landmarks in Banff National Park, is named for Wesleyan Missionary Robert Rundle. Rundle began his missionary work in Fort Edmonton in 1840. In 1847, he became one of the first white men to journey into the Bow Valley near Banff where he preached to Stoney Natives.

1778 Peter Pond of the North West Company establishes the first fur trading post in the region on the Athabasca River.

1788 Explorer Peter Fidler signs on with the Hudson's Bay Company and begins extensive travel through the fur-trading territories. He sees potential for agriculture and mining at the frontier.

1789 Alexander Mackenzie finds a route to the Arctic Ocean from Fort Chipewyan. During his explorations he uses tar found in the ground to mend his canoes. Two centuries later, the tar sands would be used to produce oil.

1793 Mackenzie reaches the Pacific and becomes the first explorer to cross North America.

1795 Edmonton House is established as a fur-trading post on the North Saskatchewan River.

1800-1812 David Thompson uses Rocky Mountain House as a base for explorations on behalf of the North West Company throughout western Canada. He produces a detailed map that is important to opening up the frontier. In 1911, Thompson becomes the first white man to cross the Rockies when he is guided through Athabasca Pass near Jasper.

1813 Jasper House is built by the North West Company as a link in its expanding fur-trade network.

1827 Guide Pierre Bostonais, known as Yellowhead because of his fair hair, is killed in an ambush by Beaver Indians. Bostonais, who was part Iroquois, had opened up much of the west for the Hudson's Bay Company.

1840 Wesleyan Missionary Robert Terrill Rundle arrives in Fort Edmonton to begin work with the Natives. His efforts help to ensure the peaceful settlement and agricultural development in central Alberta and in the Bow Valley of the Rockies.

1857 Captain John Palliser sets out to explore the prairies for the British government and to determine the potential for settlement and development.

1858 James Hector, geologist on the Palliser expedition, is kicked in the chest by a packhorse while exploring a route through the Rockies. The incident is immor-

talized when the expedition names the Kicking Horse Pass and the Kicking Horse River after the unruly animal.

1869 Unscrupulous whisky traders head north from Fort Benton, Montana to establish an outpost at the confluence of the Oldman and St. Mary rivers near present-day Lethbridge. Blackfoot Natives bring furs and buffalo hides to Fort Whoop-Up to exchange mainly for firewater.

1870 Cree and Assiniboine Natives clash with Blackfoot, Blood, and Peigans along the banks of

Palliser and Hector

Irishman John Palliser set out from Britian in 1857 to lead a three-year exploration of the Canadian west. The Palliser expedition was important in staking out lands for development and railway routes across the vast trading region of the Hudson's Bay Company.

Palliser was well-suited to the task. The 39-year-old had travelled throughout the American west and published a popular account, *Solitary Rambles and Adventures of a Hunter in the Prairies.*

He was accompanied by James Hector, a 23-year-old doctor who was also a geologist and naturalist. Eugene Bourgeau was assigned the task of botanist and Thomas Blakiston was sent along as magnetic observer.

The expedition split into three groups and conducted scientific observations and mapping work throughout the Rockies. The young adventurers scouted mountain passes and river valleys from Waterton to Jasper.

Several places in the mountains have been named in their honor, as well as for those in the Royal Geographical Society who backed their journey.

James Hector was also responsible for one of the most memorable names for a mountain pass in the Rockies. On August 29, 1858, Hector was knocked unconscious when he was struck in the chest by the hoof of an ornery pack animal. In 1881, Kicking Horse Pass, west of Lake Louise, was chosen as part of the route for the main line of the new Canadian Pacific Railway.

Interpretrive programs at Fort Macleod Museum depict the way of life of the North West Mounted Police when they brought law and order to the west in the 1870s. A mounted patrol ride is performed daily in July and August.

the Oldman River near present-day Lethbridge. The Cree and Assiniboine succeed in launching a surprise attack but were to be massacred later. Nearly 300 warriors die in the last great battle among warring tribes in North America.

1874 North West Mounted Police trek 1600 kilometres across the prairies, arriving in October to establish Fort Macleod. They put an end to the whisky trade. There is no resistance at nearby Fort Whoop-Up. The traders learn of the approaching lawmen and abandon their trading post.

1875 Mounted Police head north to build Fort Calgary on the banks of the Bow River. Missionaries and fur traders have already established a wagon route on an old native trail between the site of the

new fort and Fort Edmonton.

1876 Chief Sitting Bull and 5000 Sioux followers seek refuge in the Cypress Hills following their victory over General George Custer.

1877 Blackfoot Natives sign Treaty No. 7, one in a series of agreements that saw the natives give up traditional lands in exchange for reserves and government payments.

1880 The dominion government promotes ranching in Alberta by offering huge tracts of leased land for an annual rent of one cent an acre.

1882 Alberta becomes one of four districts in the newly created Northwest Territories. Pioneer outfitter Tom Wilson explores the mountains near the confluence of the Bow and Pipestone rivers and comes across one of the most beautiful lakes in the Rockies. Wilson calls it Emerald Lake, but the name is changed to Lake Louise in honor of Princess Louise Caroline Alberta, the daughter of Queen Victoria and wife of Canada's Governor General, the Marquis of Lorne.

1883 Canadian Pacific Railway workers discover natural gas while drilling for water near Medicine Hat. Crews lay up to 11 kilometres of track in a day to reach Calgary. The line pushes west as part of the ambitious plan to establish a rail link to the Pacific. Railway workers discover hot springs in the mountains at Banff. Silver City west of Banff becomes a boom town of 2000, but is deserted two years later when the mine proves uneconomical.

1884 Hunters race to Cypress Hills after a small surviving herd of buffalo are spotted. The vast herds have been driven to the brink of extinction and some hunters take pride in stalking the final remnants. Geologist Joseph Burr Tyrrell makes dramatic finds of dinosaur fossils in the badlands along the Red Deer River near Drumheller.

1885 Sam Steele leads the Alberta Field Force to put down a Native uprising that was part of the widespread but unsuccessful North West Rebellion. Cree Natives on the Frog Lake Reserve, east of Edmonton had killed nine men, but fled when confronted by policemen and soldiers.

Prime Minister John A. Macdonald establishes a reserve for

Colonel James Walker

In 1874, the Dominion of Canada established a new police force to put an end to the whisky traders and ensure law and order in the west. James Walker was among the first to sign up for the North West Mounted Police and help lead them on their historic 1600 kilometre journey to the plains of Alberta.

The force had little trouble rousting the whisky traders but Superintendent Walker stayed on and played a key role in reaching peaceful treaties with the Plains Natives. In 1880, he travelled the west with $100,000 in one dollar bills to distribute treaty payments to the Indians.

Walker was not just a lawman. He was hired to establish the first major cattle operation in the province, the sprawling Cochrane Ranche. Walker hoped to have 10,000 head of cattle on a 100,000 acre (40,000 ha) spread northwest of Calgary and organized a cattle drive of 3000 from the Washington area in 1881. That herd was ravaged by harsh winters.

Undaunted, Walker got out of ranching and started a sawmill. He also began a pony express service and later a telephone system in Calgary.

His riverside home in east Calgary has now become the Inglewood Bird Sanctuary.

Short steam engine rides are offered at Calgary's Heritage Park (shown above). Longer excursions are offered by Alberta Prairie Steam Tours Ltd. They operate day trips and dinner excursion packages originating from Stettler. For more information, contact Alberta Prairie Steam Tours Ltd., Postal Bag 800, Stettler AB T0C 2L0 (1-800-282-3994). The Alberta Railroad Museum in Edmonton has rolling stock and locomotives from 1877-1950.

the hot springs at Banff and resolves a dispute over commercial development.

1886 Natives near the central Alberta town of Killam predict ill-fortune when a 175 kilogram (386 lb) spiritual Manitou Stone is taken from its creekside location. The rock was a meteorite. The predictions of misfortune proved to be true for the Natives, since they found it harder and harder to track the bison, their main food source.

Lady Agnes Macdonald, wife of the Prime Minister, decides on a unique way to tour the Rockies. She sits on the cowcatcher at the front of the locomotive for a wild ride on the new rail line.

1887 Parliament creates Rocky Mountains Park, Canada's first national park surrounding the Banff hot springs.

Charles Ora Card leads a group of Mormons from Utah to establish a settlement at Lee Creek in southern Alberta. The town of Cardston remains an important centre for members of the Church of Latter Day Saints.

1888 The Canadian Pacific Railway opens Banff Springs Hotel.

1892 Edmonton incorporates as a town and Calgary incorporates as a city.

1895 Rancher F.W. Godsal and frontiersman Kootenai Brown coax the federal government into establishing the forest reserve in southern Alberta that will become Waterton Lakes National Park.

1896 North West Mounted Police Sergeant W.B. Wilde is shot and killed by a Blood Native near Pincher Creek. The outlaw, who is suspected of murdering another Native, is captured by members of his band and turned over to police. He is convicted and executed in March, 1897.

1897 The Klondike Gold Rush turns Edmonton into a supply centre for fortune hunters heading north.

1901 The first oil well in western Canada is drilled in the Rocky Mountains near Waterton Lakes. The Rocky Mountain Development Company strikes oil at a depth of 312 metres (1024 ft). Production begins at 300 barrels a day but quickly tapers off.

1903 At 4:10 a.m. on April 29, the Crowsnest Pass coal-mining town of Frank is devastated by a huge rockslide that sweeps down from Turtle Mountain and kills 70.

The CPR finds coal deposits for its steam engines at the foot of Cascade Mountain near Banff and the mining town of Bankhead is quickly established.

The first automobile arrives in the territory.

1904 Booming Edmonton becomes a city.

1905 Alberta becomes a province with Edmonton established as the capital.

1907 Jasper Forest Park is established to create a wilderness region surrounding the new rail line being pushed through the Rockies across Yellowhead Pass.

1908 More than 500 square kilometres of wilderness in northern

The Frank Slide

The coal mining town of Frank was devastated at 4:10 a.m., April 29, 1903 when 82 million tonnes of limestone crashed down from the top of Turtle Mountain in southwestern Alberta. The rockslide killed 70 people but another 23 miraculously escaped even though their homes were in its path. Three young daughters of Alexander Leitch all managed to escape even though their house was destroyed. The slide trapped 17 coal miners underground but they managed to dig their way out to safety.

Almost 3 square kilometres of land was covered by rock up to 30 metres thick. The slide lasted less than 100 seconds.

On June 19, 1914, the nearby Hillcrest coal mine was the scene of one of Canada's worst mining disasters when an explosion killed 189 men.

The Frank Slide Interpretive Centre tells the stories of the families who settled in Crowsnest Pass region.

American trick rider Guy Weadick convinced four Calgary businessmen to back his idea for the finest rodeo and wild west show the world had ever seen. The 1912 Calgary Stampede was a success with the spectators, but was costly to produce and it took another seven years before the "Greatest Outdoor Show on Earth" was staged again and became an annual event.

Alberta is set aside as a preserve for wood buffalo. Today, Wood Buffalo National Park serves as an important refuge, not only for the endangered buffalo but also as a nesting site for the whooping crane, which also was almost driven to extinction.

1909 The CPR begins an irrigation project to improve agriculture in southeast Alberta. Over five years, an elaborate irrigation system is developed surrounding the town of Brooks. The irrigation system involves dams, 48,000 kilometres of ditches, and a 3.2 kilometre aqueduct.

1910 The ban on automobiles in Rocky Mountains Park is lifted, and drivers begin making the arduous journey from Calgary on a newly opened route in 1911.

1912 Guy Weadick stages the first

Calgary Stampede. Financial problems prevent a return engagement for a few years, but when the Stampede does return, its popularity turns it into the "Greatest Outdoor Show on Earth."

1913 Elk Island National Park is established thanks to the efforts of conservationists who lobby for a big-game sanctuary in central Alberta, to protect elk from overhunting.

1914 The Dingman Well in Turner Valley "comes in" marking the discovery of the first major oil and natural gas field in western Canada. Initial activity died down due to World War I, but development resumed in 1936. The area was to become Canada's major oil-producing region for the following 12 years.

On June 19, an explosion within Hillcrest Mine at Crowsnest Pass kills 189, Canada's worst mine disaster. The victims are buried in mass graves and their families receive $1,800 each as compensation.

1916 Alberta women earn the right to vote.

1917 Louise Crummy McKinney, a prominent member of the Women's Christian Temperance Union, becomes the first woman elected to any legislature in the British Empire.

1919 Prominent suffragettes, known as the "Group of Five" go to court and succeed in having women officially recognized as "persons" under Canadian law.

1922 Wood Buffalo National Park is created on the border of Alberta and the Northwest Territories to protect the only remaining herd of wood buffalo.

1930 The Great Depression hits the west. Calgary Member of Parliament R.B. Bennett becomes prime minister. Despite measures that include massive relief projects, the economy fails to recover. One most visible sign of the depression is the "Bennett Buggy," an automobile adapted for towing by a horse because fuel is unaffordable.

1932 Construction begins on the Banff-Jasper Highway as a relief project for the unemployed. When the highway opens in 1940, it is hailed as one of the most scenic drives in the world.

1945 During World War II, German prisoners of war are kept in remote camps including the converted Kananaskis Forest Experi-

Passengers on the stage coach between Calgary and Edmonton had plenty of unscheduled stops. The 294 km journey took days to complete on deeply rutted tracks. Now it's a three-hour drive on a four-lane highway.

ment Station. Some prisoners are so captivated by the scenery that they return to Alberta after the war.

1947 On February 13, the oil business begins to boom again with a major strike by Imperial Oil's Leduc No.1 well near Edmonton.

1964 Development begins to tap the Athabasca tar sands, near Fort McMurray.

Mormon Temple

Members of the Church of Latter Day Saints (Mormons) travelled north from Utah in 1887 and settled in the Cardston area of southern Alberta. The town is named for Charles Ora Card, leader of the 40 families that made the trek.

In 1913, construction began on the landmark Cardston temple. Granite for the temple was quarried in the Kootenay Lake area of British Columbia and shipped 500 kilometres to Cardston. Hardwoods were imported from overseas for interior finishing work.

The eight-sided building is shaped like a Maltese cross. The temple was completed and dedicated as a spiritual center in 1923.

Three years of renovation were completed in 1991. Only members of the church are allowed inside the temple, but a visitor information centre is open to the public.

1967 Canada celebrates its 100th birthday. Communities throughout Alberta commemorate the centennial with unique projects, including the development of the ornate Nikka Yuko Japanese Gardens in Lethbridge and a landing pad for UFOs in St. Paul.

1973 The economy booms, based on dramatic oil price increases fostered by Arab producers. The Alberta government uses revenue from the sale of oil and gas rights to establish the Heritage Savings and Trust Fund. Part of the fund is used to develop major tourist attractions.

1977 The Alberta government opens Kananaskis Country multiple-use recreation area along the eastern slopes of the Rockies. The boundaries are expanded in 1982 to encompass 4200 square kilometres.

1978 Edmonton hosts the Commonwealth Games. Athletes from 48 countries assemble before 60,000 spectators to hear Queen Elizabeth open the competition.

1981 The first phase of the West Edmonton Mall opens at a cost of $1.1 billion. Two more phases are completed over the next four years making it the largest shopping mall in the world, with over 800 stores and services.

1988 Calgary hosts the Winter Olympics. A variety of major sports facilities are built including ski jumps, a speed skating oval, the Nakiska downhill ski resort in Kananaskis Country, and the Canmore Nordic Centre. A worldwide television audience of 2.5

billion watch as an 11-year-old Calgary girl lights the Olympic flame.
1989 Albertans set a national precedent when they vote to elect Reform Party candidate Stan Waters as their representative in the Canadian senate. Prime Minister Brian Mulroney refuses to give up his power to make appointments to the senate, but eventually appoints Waters. Two years later, the Mulroney government endorses the concept of an elected senate.

Scenic Drive 4: Crowsnest Highway

Lethbridge to Crowsnest Pass
The Crowsnest Highway (Highway 3) extends from Medicine Hat into British Columbia, providing a scenic route to Vancouver. Scenic Drive 4 follows a historic section of the route for 161 kilometres, from Lethbridge to Crowsnest Pass.

Start this scenic drive on the peaceful riverbank at **Indian Battle Park (1)** on the west edge of Lethbridge. A violent confrontation between Indian nations occured here in 1870. The park also includes a replica of the notorious Fort Whoop-Up whisky trading post. The **High Level Bridge (2)**, which dominates the Oldman River valley, was built by the Canadian Pacific Railway in

The Nikka Yuko Japanese Gardens in Lethbridge were built in 1967 as a symbol of peace and friendship between Canada and Japan. Japanese farmers came to southern Alberta in 1907 and played an important role in sugar beet production and market gardening. Communities expanded during World War II when Canadians of Japanese ancestry were forced to leave their homes in western British Columbia.

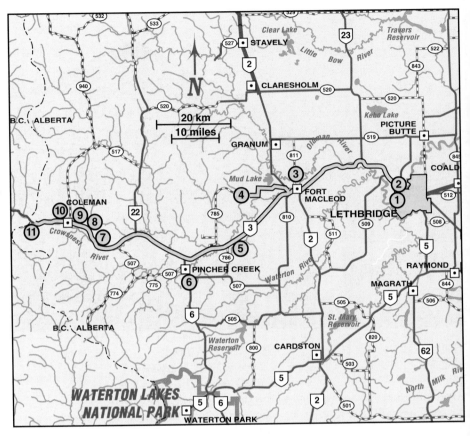

1909. It is 96 metres high and 1623 metres long.

The highway parallels the river and railway, crossing the grasslands on the north edge of the Blood Indian Reserve.

Fort Macleod (3), near the junction of Highway 2, has a replica of the 1874 fort built by the North West Mounted Police. Several historic buildings in the downtown core have been restored under the Alberta Main Street Programme.

The **Head-Smashed-In Buffalo Jump Interpretive Centre (4)** is located on Highway 785 west of Fort Macleod (see p. 70).

The Crowsnest Highway enters the Peigan Indian Reserve and the small town of **Brocket (5)** is its service centre. Local native crafts are sold in a shop on the north side of the highway.

Pincher Creek (6), 48 kilometre west of Fort Macleod, got its name in 1868 when prospectors found a pair of pinchers used to trim horse hooves by the creek. The Pincher Creek Museum is in a restored 1894 ranch house and Kootenai Brown Historical Park

contains Kootenai Brown's cabin.

Toward the mountains, the highway enters Crowsnest Pass, region of mining communities, all built in the early 1900s.

The **Leitch Collieries (7)** thrived briefly around the time of World War I. The remains are a provincial historic site with interpretive signs explaining the coal-processing operations.

In June 1914, 189 men perished in an underground explosion at the **Hillcrest Mine (8)**, the worst mining disaster in Canadian history.

Just a few kilometres west, the town of Frank was destroyed by a landslide in April 1903. Millions of tons of rock broke loose from Turtle Mountain and crashed into the valley below killing 70 people. The **Frank Slide Interpretive Centre (9)** describes the area's colorful and occasionally tragic past. (See p. 59).

The **Crowsnest Museum (10)** in Coleman also describes mining in the region. The **Crowsnest Pass (11)** may simply have gotten its name from the crows and ravens that nest in the area. However, some historians have suggested that the origin goes back to a battle when Crow Natives were killed by rival Blackfoot.

A weathered limber pine known as the "Burmis Tree" is a much-photographed landmark at the east end of the historic Crowsnest Pass corridor. Interpretive programs at the Leitch Collieries Provincial Historic Site and Frank Slide Interpretive Centre reveal the region's colourful and sometimes tragic past.

The Wild West

Chuckwagon drivers race for prize money nightly at The Calgary Stampede. Outriders accompany each wagon in the race around the oval track. Early versions of the event required cowboys to light a cookfire but rules have been changed to speed up the contest.

Welcome to the Wild West. In Alberta, western heritage is not some myth that lives only on the silver screen. It is as real as the smell of campfire coffee brewed on the open range or the sound of hoofbeats on a foothills trail.

Blackfoot, Stony, Sarcee, and other Natives continue to gather for colorful powwows and perform sacred rituals. The traditions date back thousands of years.

Cowboys still round up cattle, brand them, and drive them over the rolling grasslands in much the same way they have been doing it

since the first herds were brought up from Montana and introduced to the region in the late 1800s.

Wild horses, descendants of those imported to Mexico by the conquistadors centuries ago, still roam free in remote corners of Alberta. And, even though modern technology has helped, quarter horses, Appaloosas, and other breeds are still important to the cultures of both Natives and cowboys.

You can immerse yourself in the traditions of the Canadian west whether it is touring Banff, Jasper, or Waterton on horseback for an hour, or getting decked out in your Stetson and cowboy boots to take in the Calgary Stampede. You can even bunk in at a working ranch and see the outfits that have made Alberta beef famous.

The First Inhabitants

The history of Natives in Alberta dates back at least 11,000 years when the last Ice Age was ending and nomadic hunters began their pursuit of mammoths, great bison, and other game on the plains of North America.

Natives gradually formed diverse societies based on adaptation to their environment. In the boreal forests, woodland Natives developed hunting techniques for moose, caribou, and wood bison. They also fished and supplemented their diet with berry crops.

In the southern grasslands, plains Natives relied mainly on the bison, a close relative of the buffalo. The bison that once roamed the prairies in vast herds were a primary source of food. Although a 500 kilogram animal provided plenty of meat, it also provided material for tools, clothing, shelter, and ceremonial pieces.

Bones were turned into scrapers and needles. Horns were shaped into spoons. The stomach and other internal organs were treated and turned into containers. Hides were valuable in construction of teepees, robes, and blankets. Natives could also fabricate ropes and thread from

sinews, hair, and tails. Bison tongues were frequently used as offerings in rites held before large communal hunts.

In winter, hunters would use snowshoes to stalk prey and could easily trap the lumbering bison in deep snow. In summer, the bison hunters had to be much more ingenious. Over the centuries, an elaborate technique for conducting massive buffalo hunts was developed. The hunt required intricate planning and co-operation. One group had to sneak up on a wary herd and coax the animals into long drive lanes.

Teepees have provided shelter for natives for thousands of years. Before the arrival of the horse, teepees were quite small since they had to be hauled by humans or dogs. Designs reflect sacred symbols that are revealed in dreams. Teepee rings found throughout Alberta show where rocks have been placed to anchor walls.

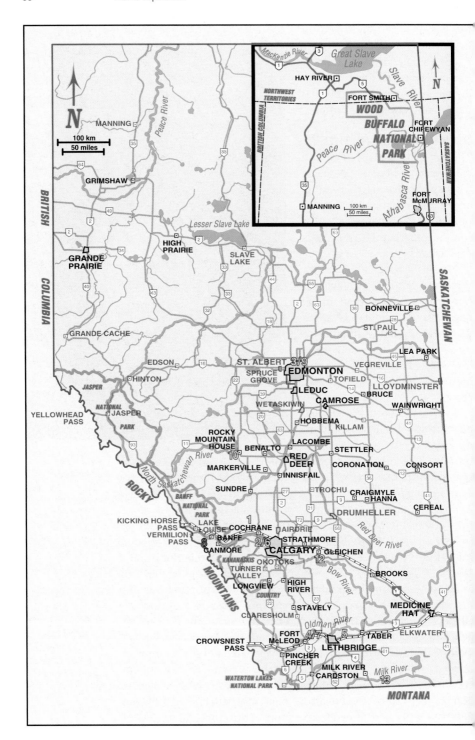

Women and children lined the route to keep the animals heading toward the brink of a high cliff. As the buffalo approached the edge, the hunters, some wearing wolf skins forced them into a stampede and they tumbled headlong over the precipice.

Down below, another group quickly moved in to kill the injured animals and process the meat. Much of it was turned into pemmican, a dried concoction made of buffalo meat, Saskatoon berries or other prairie fruits, and fat.

The practice died out in the mid-1800s when the rifle was introduced to the west and both Indians and white buffalo hunters quickly drove the bison to near-extinction.

Fortunately, early conservation efforts have succeeded and both the wood and plains bison have found sanctuary on wilderness reserves like Wood Buffalo National Park. There are also several domesticated herds and it is possible to find bison (buffalo) meat on the menus in some restaurants.

Traders and Explorers

As far back as the early 1700s, the the white man began to have an impact on the Natives in the west. Around 1730, there was an important shift in the way-of-life of the plains Natives. The first horses were introduced from the south and became prized possessions. It was an honor to be able to steal them from neighboring tribes. Horses dramatically changed the

Early Europeans described them as buffaloes but the largest land mammals of North America are correctly known as bison. Before Europeans arrived in the west, as many as 60 million bison roamed the prairies in vast herds. In less than 100 years of wasteful hunting, there were less than 1000 bison left and the species seemed doomed to extinction. Conservation efforts have brought the population back to a healthy level. There are two subspecies in Alberta, plains bison and wood bison.

Head-Smashed-In Buffalo Jump

Archeologists have counted dozens of "buffalo jumps" across the prairies. Head-Smashed-In Buffalo Jump (180 km south of Calgary on Highway 785 and 18 km west of Fort Macleod) is the largest of the sites and provides an exceptional way to examine hunting techniques of the plains Natives and the changing fortunes of Natives in the west.

According to Blackfoot legend, a young hunter wanted to see the buffalo as they were driven over a steep sandstone cliff at the southern end of the Porcupine Hills. He hid beneath the ledge and watched as the stampeding animals fell past him. The hunt that day was better than expected and the animals quickly piled up and trapped the boy against the rocks. He was found with his head crushed beneath a sprawled buffalo.

For the past 150 years, the jump has been named for the fate of that curious boy.

The Alberta government has built a $10 million interpretive centre at the edge of the 300-metre-long cliff that was used by hunters as long ago as 5700 years ago.

The interpretive centre is a multi-tiered structure built into the side of the Porcupine Hills. Architect Robert LeBlond has been honored for a unique design that complements the prairie landscape.

Displays and films provide an entertaining and informative view of the changes in a traditional way of life. Much of the story is centred on Napi, an important figure in Blackfoot legend.

Level 1, Napi's World looks at the native version of the origin of man and the evolution of hunting techniques.
Level 2, Napi's People shows the life of the Plains Indians with artifacts and reconstructions of teepees and travois.
Level 3, The Buffalo Jump focuses on hunting by stampeding herds over prairie cliffs.
Level 4, Cultures in Contact shows the influence of the whiteman in the West.
Level 5, Uncovering the Past shows the archeological methods used to piece together ancient stories from artifacts buried beneath the plains.

Archeologists have found information at the base of the cliffs and out on the rolling hills to the west where natives built their version of "scarecrows" to help steer the animals toward the jump. The area is such an important cultural relic, it has been designated a World Heritage Site by the United Nations Educational Scientific and Cultural Organization.

Short pathways along the hilltop and at the bottom of the cliff provide a view of the scene of the hunts.

The interpretive centre is staffed with Native guides who provide information about their traditions and legends. A small shop sells authentic native crafts.

Special events are held throughout the year. The most impressive is the powwow and teepee village presented the third weekend of July.

Head-Smashed-In is open seven days a week 9 a.m. to 5 p.m. in winter, and 9 a.m. to 8 p.m. in summer.

Crowfoot
Chief of Chiefs

What is life? It is the flash of a firefly in the night. It is the breath of a buffalo in the winter time. It is the little shadow that runs across the grass and loses itself in the sunset.

The words of Blackfoot Chief Crowfoot may have been embellished in translation, but there is no doubt that the philosophical Native leader played a critical role in the peaceful settlement of western Canada.

He welcomed the arrival of the North West Mounted Police as a means to control the ravages brought by unscrupulous whisky traders.

Crowfoot was a fierce warrior and stood up for his people when he felt they had been wronged. He demanded compensation before allowing the Canadian Pacific Railway across his land.

Blackfoot Chief Crowfoot urges acceptance of Treaty No. 7 at a signing ceremony with Northwest Mounted Police, Colonel J.F. Macleod in 1877. Blackfoot, Blood, Peigan, Stony, and Sarcees gave up their rights to 130,000 square kilometres (50,000 sq mi) in exchange for reservation lands and compensation rights. The original of this painting by A.B. Stapleton is at the Glenbow Museum in Calgary.

He was influential in getting other Native leaders to accept Treaty No. 7, one of the most important steps in insuring peaceful relations between Natives and white settlers.

"I will be the first to sign and I will be the last to break the treaty," he said.

Crowfoot refused to take part in the Riel Rebellion of 1885 or to join with Sitting Bull in a war against white settlers.

He was a proud leader who sought allegiance with the Great White Mother, Queen Victoria.

mobility of the Natives who had relied on dogs to haul their loads.

Using horses, they were able to travel twice as far in a day and haul four times as much load. Soon, the Natives were building much larger teepees and traveling much farther in search of food.

Another major change was the arrival of guns. Now, Natives were much more efficient in hunting and in making war. In the north, the Cree became dominant. They were active fur traders and eagerly sought the guns, axes, knives, and other marvels of the white man's world.

In the south, the Blackfoot Confederacy, linking the Blackfoot, Blood, and Peigan Natives, rose to prominence across the plains. As the tribes prospered, they were able to devote more time to crafts and the designs of ceremonial masks. Headdresses became more and more elaborate.

Sadly, the whiteman introduced great hardships and suffering to the natives. Greedy traders in the south used firewater, a vile alcohol mixture, as one of their main bargaining tools. The white men also introduced smallpox and other diseases to the tribes and epidemics took a devastating toll. The real decline in Native influence began soon after the bison, which once numbered close to 60 million, were almost completely wiped out.

In a series of treaties signed in the late 1800s, the Natives gave up much of their traditional hunting grounds to live on reserves in exchange for compensation and continuing support from the federal government.

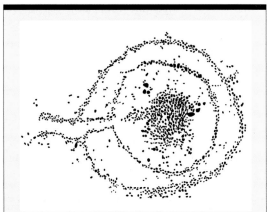

Medicine Wheel Mystery

At the time when other civilizations were creating Stonehenge or the great pyramids of Egypt, North American Natives were building their own sacred monuments.

About 50 elaborately laid out rock formations have been found on remote hilltops throughout the prairies. They are known as medicine wheels and date back 5000 years. Rocks are often found set out with a central cairn built of tons of boulders and up to 28 spokes. The spokes radiate up to eighty metres from the centre.

Some archeologists have speculated that the wheels may have been used as ancient astronomical instruments, since some spokes are closely aligned with the direction of the rising sun at the summer solstice.

The wheels are no longer used and even the elders are unsure about their origin. Unfortunately, the wheels are on private land and not available for public tours.

Opening Up the West

Rivalry between the Hudson's Bay Company and the North West Company spurred much of the early exploration of the west.

In the late 1700s, the trading companies established posts farther and farther west in search of beaver pelts and other furs that were prized by fashion-conscious Europeans.

In 1754, the Hudson's Bay Company sent Anthony Henday west to establish contact with Blackfoot trappers in the wilderness along the North Saskatchewan River, in what is now central Alberta. With Crees to guide him, he became the first white man to see the Canadian Rockies.

From 1789 to 1793, Alexander MacKenzie made extensive explorations throughout the west. In 1789, he followed the river that now bears his name to the Arctic Ocean. Three years later he travelled along the Peace River and through the Rockies continuing westward by land and river to become the first man to cross the continent.

In the early 1800s David Thompson surveyed most of the major rivers in northern Alberta as well as the Columbia and Kootenay rivers west of the Rock-

Rock Art

For centuries, natives have used sacred symbols to depict their way of life by carving and painting on rock.

Archeologists have discovered pictographs (painting on stone) and petroglyphs (carving in stone) throughout Alberta.

The finest examples are found in an archeological preserve at Writing-On-Stone Provincial Park, 43 kilometres east of Milk River on the southern border of the province.

Guides lead interpretive hikes into the restricted area throughout the summer.

ies. His map-making for the North West Company was crucial in opening up the frontier.

Rocky Mountain House National Historic Park west of Red Deer details the history of the fur trade and the rivalry between the North West and Hudson's Bay companies. Short interpretive trails along the North Saskatchewan River provide a look at remnants of the fur-trading posts along with a York boat and Red River cart that were used to travel across the prairies.

Forts

Fur-traders, explorers, the North West Mounted Police, and even the notorious whisky traders built forts as they established a presence in the Canadian West.

Many of the forts were little more than reinforced cabins built to withstand a small attack by Natives and were abandoned when no longer needed.

Others, like Fort Edmonton and Fort Calgary proved to be the starting points for major settlements. While most of the original buildings have been lost, several forts in Alberta have been restored or recreated and today house interpretive centres.

Fort Edmonton Park
(Scenic Drive 10)
A replica has been built of the original 1846 Hudson's Bay fur-trading post. Other buildings have been re-created to depict changing life in the city from 1885 to 1920. Open daily from late May to

Fort Edmonton was originally built in 1795 as a trading post for the Hudson's Bay Company. The fort was relocated several times and in 1830 was situated on the land now occupied by the Alberta Legislature Building. The fort was dismantled in 1915 and later rebuilt at Fort Edmonton Park off Whitemud Drive and Fox Drive.

early September and on Sundays and holidays the rest of the year.

**Fort Calgary
(Scenic Drive 11)**
The outline of the original 1875 North West Mounted Police fort has been restored and an interpretive centre provides information on the role of the Mounties in the settlement of the West. The fort is open daily throughout the summer and from Wednesday to Sunday the rest of the year.

**Fort Macleod Museum
(Scenic Drive 4)**
The 1874 North West Mounted Police fort has been re-created. Displays feature the history of this police force along with the natives and pioneers. A musical ride

Jerry Potts

It's ironic that the scout who helped the North West Mounted Police drive the whisky traders out of the territory was more than fond of the bottle himself.

After a few drinks, Jerry Potts was known to trim the moustache of a friend with his pistol. He helped the lawmen close down Fort Whoop-Up, the centre of the notorious whisky trade and he helped track down other outlaws. When there was whisky involved, however, the mounties had to watch that their scout didn't drink the evidence.

Potts was born in Montana in the 1840s, the son of a Scottish fur- trader and a Blood Native woman. He was a skilled frontiersman, scout, and interpreter. His life reflected the violence of the old west.

When he was very young, his father was murdered by a Peigan Native. His mother and half-brother were killed years later by Blood Natives who had drunk too much firewater.

Potts knew a variety of Native dialects and served both Natives and whites over the years. On one occcasion his knowledge of the Crow language proved to be a lifesaver. He was surrounded by seven warriors who used sign language to "invite" him to ride along to their nearby camp. The Natives were acting friendly, but did not realize that he understood them as they talked about their plans to kill him. Potts managed to draw his gun and shot four of his captors while the other three fled in panic.

is presented four times daily in July and August. The fort is open from May 1 to mid-October.

Fort Whoop-Up (Scenic Drive 4)

A replica has been built of the fortified whisky trading post of 1869. An interpretive centre features artifacts and audio-visual displays about this lawless era in the Canadian West. The centre is open daily from late May to early September.

Ranching

The 1870s and 1880s marked a turning point in the Canadian west and the start of a great ranching tradition that flourishes to this day.

In 1874, the North West Mounted Police arrived to bring law and order to the territory and put a quick end to the ruthless whisky trade. By 1880, most of the bison were gone and most Natives had signed treaties setting aside reserves.

In 1881, the federal government allowed individuals or companies to lease up to 100,000 acres of land for a rental of one cent per acre.

A Quebec senator, Matthew Cochrane quickly took the government up on its offer and staked

Cowboys pin down a calf for branding on the Mount Royal Ranch near Cochrane in 1906. Cattle are still marked for identification in much the same way, although some ranchers have started using electronic sensors to keep track of the animals.

In 1991, the Canadian Rodeo Historial Association began construction of a Western Heritage Centre at a cost of $10 million. The interpretive facility, set to open in 1992, features displays and artifacts outlining the history of rodeos and the livestock industry in the west.

The Calgary Stampede

For 10 days each July, Calgary undergoes a remarkable change. City slickers dust off their Stetsons and dig out their Levis to join genuine cowhands in an exhuberant celebration of the West: the Calgary Exhibition and Stampede.

The focus is at the Stampede grounds and its half million dollar rodeo and chuckwagon races, but the whole city gets involved. There are pancake breakfasts on streetcorners and parking lots. Hotels, bars, and restaurants bring in top name country and western acts. Square dancers perform on downtown stages and the city kicks up its heels from morning to well into the night.

It all started in 1912 when an American trick roper and vaudeville performer blew into Calgary with an idea for a frontier show that would "make Buffalo Bill's Wild West extravaganza look like a side show."

Guy Weadick convinced a group of prominent Calgarians to back his scheme. The "Big Four" – George Lane, A.E. Cross, A.J. MacLean, and Patrick Burns –

Bareback riders have to stay on for eight seconds to earn points in this popular rodeo event. Broncs are specially bred to buck cowboys. Both the rider and horse are scored.

out a vast spread along the Bow River northwest of Calgary.

The Cochrane Ranche operated out of that area for only two years before relocating to even more appealing grazing land to the south.

An small interpretive centre has been built at the site on the west edge of Cochrane, 30 kilometres northwest of Calgary on Highway 1A (Scenic Drive 5).

There are outdoor displays maintained year round with guides on hand, and a visitor centre is open from mid-May to the first weekend in September.

staked the smooth-talking promoter to $100,000 and the "Greatest Outdoor Show on Earth" was born.

With tough cowboys and Natives riding wild bulls and broncos, the Stampede was a big hit as nearly 14,000 visitors packed the exhibition grounds in southeast Calgary. However, the Stampede was expensive to stage, and the backers barely got their money back. World War I intervened and it was not until 1919 that Weadick convinced the Big Four and a group of other Calgarians to finance the second Stampede for $60,000.

In 1922, the rodeo was linked with a popular annual agricultural fair and since then the Calgary Stampede has grown into a 10-day extravaganza that attracts approximately one million visitors a year.

Cowboys and cowgirls now compete for $500,000 in the afternoon rodeo and for the top prizes of $50,000 in each of the major events on the final Sundays. Chuckwagon racers compete each evening and, aside from the prize money, top racers can earn $20,000 or more just for having a corporate logo painted on their wagon canvas.

Tickets must be purchased in advance for the afternoon rodeo, evening chuckwagon races, and evening grandstand show. They include admission to the Stampede Grounds.

There is a charge just for admission to the Stampede Grounds and there is free entertainment available on the Grounds. A vari-

Cowboys are timed as they leap from their horses and wrestle steers to the ground. Surprisingly, they manage to keep their hats on most of the time.

Ralph Thrall, Jr.
McIntyre Ranch

I was born and raised here in Lethbridge, but we never lived on the ranch. As a matter of fact, my son is the first of our family to actually live there. The ranch is roughly nine miles (15 km) north and south, by eleven miles (18 km) east and west, although it jogs a bit here and there. It would take a couple of hours to drive around it. There are 55,000 acres (22,300 ha) of land; native grassland makes up about 48,000 acres (19,000 ha). That's close to what it was like when the Natives and the buffalo were here. The remainder was farmed at one time, but we replanted it with grass over the last few years.

The ranch is in gently rolling country, part of what is called short or intermediate grass prairie – good grassland. There are maybe five or six trees in the whole place that grew there naturally; all the other trees were planted by hand. The land is much more suited to ranching than farming, although we have Hutterites near us who farm.

The ranch operation is 100 percent cattle. Today, our cow herd is a cross between Hereford and Red Angus, although we still raise some purebreds. We put bulls out with the cows in July and August, and partly September – so that calving for the main cow herd begins after the first of May. We used to start calving earlier, around the first of April, but we changed because most years we'd get a severe snowstorm in late April and we'd lose a lot of calves.

We brand the cattle in late June or late July. And today we use horses and all-terrain vehicles to round them up. We use horses for the really difficult terrain.

Our cattle graze out year around. The grasses on the plains of North America, I have been told, are unique in the world in that they cure on the stem. I'm sure that's what led to the huge buffalo herds here. But we will feed our cattle, particularly in late winter, if it's really tough.

There's been no hunting allowed on the McIntyre Ranch for about 90 years. We have around 1300 deer, 300 pronghorn, and things like that.

To a lot of people driving through southern Alberta, the prairie looks empty and desolate, but it's not. I'd suggest that people just stop for 20 minutes and walk out into a field somewhere and sit down and enjoy the life around them. They would be very surprised.

I think that to appreciate the prairies, you have to live on them for a while. I've noticed that people who live on the prairies walk with their heads up, because they're always looking at the horizon. Whereas, if you live in the city or you live in the mountains, I don't think you tend to keep your head up quite as much. And I think that has a psychological effect that I've wondered about.

I think you feel more in harmony with all of nature when you're on the prairie. It's a very peaceful kind of feeling, not as intellectually exciting, certainly, as being in the big city, but it has other qualities.

ety of theme days are held for senior citizens, teens, and children. There is an extensive midway along with agriculture displays and performances on several indoor and outdoor stages. A huge casino for blackjack players and other gamblers operates in the Big Four Building.

For tickets contact: Grandstand Ticket Office, Calgary Exhibition and Stampede, Box 2890, Calgary AB T2P 3C3, phone 1-800-661-1767

Rodeos

While the Stampede is the best known rodeo in the west it is definitely not the only one.

There are dozens of professional and amateur rodeos held throughout the province. The local rodeos are often more entertaining than the Stampede, since you can get much closer to the action.

Rodeos are far from just a summer sport. Several rodeos are held indoors including the Professional Rodeo Championships of Canada held each November in Edmonton's Northlands Coliseum.

The Calgary Stampede holds its major indoor event in March, the Rodeo Royal in the Corral Building.

You don't have to be a grown-up to compete in the rodeo arena, and kids put on some of the most entertaining shows. The Little Britches Rodeo, for junior cowboys, is a popular attraction in High River each Victoria Day holiday (the third weekend of May).

A trick rider goes through her routine at the Calgary Exhibition and Stampede rodeo. Women also take part in the barrel-racing competition at the Stampede.

Several other communities hold similar rodeos, with teenagers trying to wrestle calves and ride steers. The littlest cowboys and cowgirls also kick up the dust in the "mutton-busting" contest where they hop on a sheep and hang on for a wild, woolly ride.

How to Watch a Rodeo

There are six basic events for individual competition at a professional rodeo, although organizers frequently include team contests, such as wild cow-milking, to liven things up.

horse's back. Once again, it is an eight-second ride and cowboys are judged for their skill in spurring the horse, starting high up on its neck and sweeping toward the back. The spurs are dulled to avoid injuring the highly prized horses.

Bull Riding

There is only a loose rope around the bucking Brahma bull for the cowboy to hang onto, for eight seconds. No spurring is required since it is hard enough just to stay on. As in all the bucking events, riders can only use one arm to hang on and they will be disqualified if their free arm touches the animal.

There is luck in the bronco- and bull-riding events since cowboys draw for the animals they must ride, and the winner is chosen on the basis of the performance of both the stock animal and the rider.

Bulls like "Rambo" and "Charles Manson" or broncs like "Moonshine" and "Papa Smurf" soon earn a reputation as tough, but potentially lucrative, rides. And the bulls can go on to greater glory in the Stock Hall of Champions.

Calf Roping

Cowboys and their specially trained horses use teamwork in roping a calf. The cowboy lassos the calf. And as the horse keeps the rope tight, the cowboy dismounts, races to the calf, throws it to the ground, and ties a short "piggin' string" around three of

The fiercest bulls become almost as famous as the cowboys who try to ride them. Bull riders must stay on for eight seconds to score points. Rodeo clowns divert the attention of the stock animals to keep them from charging downed riders.

Saddle Bronc Riding

The idea is to stay on a bucking bronco for eight seconds. That is difficult in itself, but cowboys are also judged for their style, with an emphasis on good rhythm. Riders must have their spurs above the horse's shoulders when they come out of the chute. They are disqualified if they lose a stirrup or touch the animal with their hands.

Bareback Riding

Riders do not use a saddle, stirrups, or reins, just a leather pad and handhold cinched to the its legs. Fastest time wins, but cowboys are disqualified if the calf's legs don't remain tied for a minimum six seconds.

Steer Wrestling

Steer wrestling is another timed event, and once again cowboys use their own trained horses to pursue a running stock animal. This time the animal is a little bigger. And instead of using a rope, the rider reaches down and grabs the steer's right horn. He slides off his horse while still hanging onto the steer and uses a twisting motion on the animal's neck to bring it onto its side.

Ladies Barrel Racing

The only event for ladies involves riders guiding their horses around three barrels, in a cloverleaf pattern. Penalties are added on for knocking over barrels. The fastest time wins.

Professional Rodeo Events

March
Medicine Hat, Calgary, Camrose
April
Coleman, Red Deer, Lethbridge
May
Leduc, Stavely, Bonnyville, Taber
June
Stettler, Grande Prairie, Coronation, Brooks, Rocky Mountain House, Lea Park, Craigmyle, Innisfail, Sundre, Wainwright, High River, Ponoka

July
Benalto, Cerea, Calgary Stampede, Bruce
August
High Prairie, Lethbridge, Grimshaw, Strathmore, Cardston
September
Lacomb, Hanna

For exact dates, contact the Canadian Professional Rodeo Association hot line in Calgary. 291-3680.

Small town rodeos, such as the North Peace Stampede, give spectators a close view of the action in team-roping and other events. Rodeos are held year-round including indoor competitions in winter.

Native dancers are scored on their costumes and performing skills in powwow competitions. Most reserves host powwows in summer.

Klondike Days

Just as the Calgary Stampede winds down, Edmonton kicks up its heels with a 10-day celebration based on the gold rush fever that gripped the frontier city in the 1880s.

Instead of cowboy gear, the locals are decked out in prospecting costumes or dance hall finery, and they show off their attire at a Sunday Promenade.

There are parades, pancake breakfasts, gambling casinos, and an exposition and midway.

Instead of chuckwagon races, they compete in a colorful World Championship Sourdough Raft Race on the North Saskatchewan River.

Contact: Edmonton Klondike Days Association, #1660, 10020 - 101A Avenue, Edmonton AB T5J 3G2.

Pow wows

Each summer Natives have elaborate gatherings known as powwows. Everyone from tribal elders to small children celebrate a colorful tradition of dancing, singing, and displays of vibrant ceremonial clothing and intricately crafted headdresses.

The powwows, held on reserves throughout Alberta, attract up to a thousand competitors. Prizes totalling $25,000 or more are awarded to drummers and dancers based on skill, rhythm, and costume.

Outsiders are welcome and can sample traditional food such as fry-bread (a kind of bannock), and admire native craftsmanship. The gatherings offer exceptional opportunities for photographers.

The largest powwows are held by the Blood, Blackfoot, Peigan, and Sarcee Bands. Alberta Tourism keeps up-to-date information on powwow schedules throughout the summer. (See Listings).

Malcolm MacKenzie
Artist/Cowboy
Sculptor, *Men of Vision* Statue, Cochrane Ranche

Ever since I left school, I've worked in the foothills, around on the ranches. Of course, a lot of the ranches have wildlife on their land: elk, deer, moose .... And ever since I could remember, I've been drawing pictures of animals. And as soon as you begin, you run into problems of anatomy, so you pay more attention. And the more attention you give to the animals as you draw, the more ideas you get for a painting or a sculpture.

I think if you were a photographer you'd see the same thing. There are poses that are there only briefly, but you can see them. Being a sculptor or a painter, you can retain that in your memory, then put those elements together and make something that is very pleasing to look at.

I didn't model the *Men of Vision* statue on anybody in particular, because you would run into controversies. Families will say, oh no, my granddad was here first, he was here four days ahead of yours or something, so I just made it general. And, the good thing about it? When the statue was unveiled, a lot of these older people said, "god, that looks like granddad." When you come right down to it, you can't tell one cowboy from another on horseback. And as for the horse, well, many of the early ranchers had thoroughbred blood in their horses. The horses were larger than some of the ones today. So, I tried to model that larger type of horse.

When I was outfitting or working on a ranch, I was in the saddle seven days a week, five to six hours a day. I have only one secret for a person visiting Alberta and planning some horseback riding. The important thing is to ride a horse a little bit first, and get yourself in condition. Even walking will help you. If you're in good physical condition, you won't get sore horseback riding like many people do.

One time we were out with Japanese students and teachers and we'd go hiking with them since they didn't ride. We were just dismantling the camp and a black bear with three cubs comes along. We still had the washrack set up with mirrors hanging on it. So two cubs climb up on it, and one's having a drink out of the wash basin the other cub caught a glimpse of himself in the mirror, so he goes to look down behind it, and of course, there's nothing there. He did this two or three times.

I think some of the national parks are a must for visitors. If you take the old Banff Highway [Bow Valley Parkway] and then hike a bit, you'll see some fantastic things. The fall is the greatest time to be there, because of the colour of the tree leaves and the wildlife's at their peak – they're all fat and slick. In the spring, the wildlife can be thin, with their hair falling out, and they look kind of scraggly.

Trail rides range from short sightseeing outings to long pack trips in the Rocky Mountains that can last a week or more. Outfitters provide horses to match the skill levels of just about any rider. Novices can expect sore behinds until they get accustomed to their saddles.

Guest Ranches and Trail Rides

It is one thing to watch John Wayne and his counterparts in action on the late movie. It is quite another to hop on a saddle and ride over rolling grasslands or along a winding mountain trail.

There are dozens of trail-riding outfits, outfitters, and guest ranch operators throughout the Rockies and foothills. They offer a variety of tours from short sightseeing rides to extended horse pack-trips. Accommodation varies from modern cabins with whirlpool baths to backcountry teepees with outhouses and traditional wash stands. (See Listings.)

Country Music

Not surprisingly, Alberta has been home to many of Canada's top country music stars from Wilf Carter, better known as "Montana Slim" south of the border, to Ian Tyson and George Fox who both ranch near Calgary. And then there is the sensational k.d. lang of Consort, Alberta.

Songwriters have found inspiration in the prairie landscape, the Rockies, and the ranching traditions of the west.

In Edmonton and Calgary, big-name stars from Canada and the United States can fill the Northlands Coliseum and Saddledome. Country singers frequently perform in concert halls such as the Jubilee auditoriums.

Many people prefer to see the performers in a more casual set-

Town for rent. Em-Te Town, a re-created western town near Alder Flats southwest of Edmonton, has 25 buildings filled with antiques available for tours during the day. Cabins can be rented overnight. The whole town can be booked for special occasions. Write: Box 103, Alder Flats AB T0C 0A0. Phone: 388-2166.

Native Museums and Cultural Centres

Provincial Museum of Alberta
(12845 -102nd Avenue, Edmonton)
One of the major themes of the museum is native history with excellent displays, dioramas, and a collection of artifacts. There are also exhibits on fur-trading and the province's natural history. Open year-round.

Glenbow Museum
(130 - 9th Avenue SE, Calgary)
The history of Plains Natives and the development of the west are portrayed with displays and artifacts. The Glenbow, featuring a vast collection amassed by pioneer oilman Eric Harvie, ranks with the Provincial Museum in Edmonton as the province's best. Open year-round.

Sarcee People's Museum
(3700 Anderson Road S.W., Calgary):
The Sarcee Natives display artifacts and a model teepee. Crafts are available for sale. Open weekdays year-round.

Siksika Nation Museum of Human History
(1.6 kilometres south of Gleichen at Oldsun College)
Artifacts and displays reveal the traditions and changing ways of life for the Siksikas. Open weekdays year-round.

Luxton Museum
(Banff):
The mountain setting is an incongruous location for a display of Plains Native artifacts but the old stockade is packed with ceremonial costumes and dioramas showing hunting techniques and the use of the traditional travois for transportation and teepees for shelter. The museum is showing its age, but remodelling is planned.

Wilf Carter

To millions of Americans he was known as Montana Slim, and the yodelling cowboy entertained country music fans daily on the CBS radio network in the 1930s.

Back home in Alberta, he was known as Wilf Carter, a genuine cowboy who knew what it was like to work on the range and compete in the Calgary Stampede.

Carter was born in Nova Scotia but headed west to find work when he was only 12. His first break came in 1931 when he hit the airwaves in Calgary earning $5 a show.

Three years later, he was a sensation in the United States and soon earned enough to buy his own spread near Calgary.

ting. In Calgary, Ranchman's, at 9615 Macleod Trail South, bills itself as a high class honky-tonk with country-western style food and live entertainment. Also in Calgary, the Silver Dollar Bowl and Action Centre, 1010 - 42nd Avenue SE, seems like an unlikely setting, but several top-name country acts appear in a nightclub-style show.

In Calgary, most clubs and lounges feature country entertainment during the Calgary Stampede. And there are usually country bands playing at old-fashioned community dances held in conjunction with the rodeo circuit.

Poem, Poem on the Range

In mid-June, the Alberta Cowboy Poetry Association holds a unique cultural event in Pincher Creek, a thriving ranch community.

Cowboys and cowgirls from western Canada and the United States gather for a weekend devoted to poetry inspired by life on the range.

The highlight is the Saturday night gathering of poets at the Pincher Creek Community Hall. The poets recite works that evoke the hard work, romance, and traditions of the west.

On the same weekend, the community puts on an art show and auction along with a dance, fashion show, and Sunday rodeo.

Shopping

Dressing western can be as simple as picking up a pair of Levi's or Wrangler's, wearing a checked shirt or blouse and topping it off with a straw cowboy hat. Or, dress can be elaborate: exotic boots that cost hundreds of dollars, finely decorated satin shirts, and Stetsons elaborately decorated with feathers.

It is easy enough to find well-stocked western wear sections in the big department stores in summer, but it is often more fun to shop in the smaller specialty western shops in cities or small towns. There you are more likely to find the gear that ranchers actually wear.

Most shops have belt buckles and accessories such as hand-crafted jewelry. There are also finely worked saddles and other leather goods on display, such as chaps (leggings). Some western shops and specialty galleries also feature western paintings, prints, and bronze sculptures.

For native souvenirs, there are several outlets throughout Alberta. Moccasins and other leatherwork are among the favored souvenirs with authentic ceremonial masks and headdresses also available in a higher price range.

Alberta Indian Arts and Crafts Society
10105-109 Street
Edmonton AB T5J 1M8
Phone: 426-2048

k.d. lang

Few country singers can match the sensation created by the wildly energetic k.d. lang, of Consort, Alberta.

The dynamic singer from the Neutral Hills of east central Alberta has been extremely successful with albums like *Absolute Torch and Twang* and *Shadowland*. She's won Juno awards in Canada and Grammy's in the United States.

Still, she hardly fits the mold of a female country star. In her early days of performing, she wore cutoff cowboy boots with work socks, horn-rimmed glasses, and campy square dance dresses.

For a while, she suggested she was the reincarnation of Patsy Cline, a traditional country and western singer who died in a 1963 plane crash.

Now, lang makes a less garish fashion statement and downplays the spiritual link with Cline, although she can still bring an audience to its feet with her version of Walkin' After Midnight. With a strong influence of jazz and blues, lang and her band, the reclines, are also stretching the boundaries of country music and reaching a strong cross-over audience.

Chiniki Handicrafts
Box 31
Morley AB T0L 1N0
Phone: 881-2883

Cree-Ations Weaving Co.
P.O. Box 1117
Bonnyville AB T0A 0L0
Phone: 826-4640

Ermineskin Garments and Crafts
Box 369
Hobbema AB T0C 1N0
Phone: 585-3750

Kayas Cultural Centre
Fox Lake AB T0H 1R0
Phone: 659-3760

Montana Arts and Crafts
Box 70
Hobbema AB T0C 1N0
Phone: 585-3744

Peigan Crafts Ltd.
Box 100
Brocket AB T0K 0H0
Phone: 965-3755

Sarcee Arts and Crafts
3700 Anderson Road SW
Calgary AB T2W 3C4
Phone: 238-2677

Three Eagles Gift Shop
Box 64
Brocket AB T0K 1H0
Phone: 965-3738

Top: Cowboy hats come in a wide variety of styles from the plain and simple straw models to fancy felt Stetsons adorned with feathered bands.

Bottom: Cowboy boots are usually leather, although expensive styles made out of exotic materials such as snakeskin can be found.

Scenic Drive 5: To the End of the Range

Cochrane to Canmore

From a distance, it looks as if the lone cowboy atop the grassy hill could turn and ride off at any moment. Instead, the lone wrangler and his horse are frozen in time. The larger-than-life bronze *Men of Vision* statue overlooking the site of the old Cochrane Ranche, is an ideal starting point for a journey west across rolling grasslands and foothills dotted with stands of trembling aspen.

Highway 1A is an excellent alternative to the Trans-Canada Highway between Calgary and Canmore if you are not in a hurry and if you want to get a close look at the culture of natives and cowboys. Extra caution is required since Highway 1A is just two lanes wide and the shoulders are steep and narrow in places.

Cochrane

Cochrane can be reached by Highway 1A from northwest Calgary or by taking Highway 22 north from the Trans-Canada Highway. The area has been an important ranching centre since 1881 when Senator Matthew Cochrane leased 100,000 acres (40,000 ha) of prime rangeland for a penny an acre and staged a massive cattle drive north from Montana and Wyoming. The **Cochrane Ranche Provincial Historic Site (1)** on the west edge of town has a small interpretive centre with artifacts on display and a

short slide show. It's a place for picnics or strolls on the interpretive trail up to the "Men of Vision" statue. Interpretive staff answer questions and provide special programs throughout the summer.

The new **Western Heritage Centre (2)** to the north of the site has been designed to tell the history of the rodeo and the livestock industry, a little over a century old in the west. The $10 million centre (under construction in 1992) includes dioramas, a combined auction ring and theatre, and a variety of other displays

Malcolm Mackenzie's Men of Vision statue stands atop a rise in the foothills on the west edge of Cochrane. Ranching began in the area in 1881.

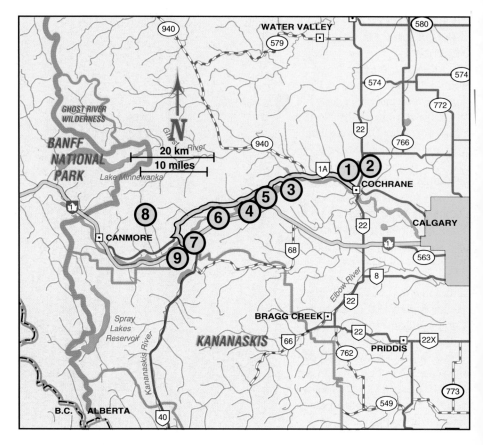

along with a library, restaurant, and exhibit hall.

The town of Cochrane itself is worth exploring. Several galleries and craft shops offer western paintings, bronzes, carvings, books, and other remembrances of the old west. Malcolm Mackenzie, the artist who created the "Men of Vision" statue, owns a gallery northwest of town (p. 85).

Highway 940, 13 kilometres west of Cochrane, heads north to some magnificent foothills guest ranches.

Cochrane to Canmore

Highway 1A runs along the north edge of the Bow River on gently rolling hills. A hydroelectric dam at the confluence of the Bow and Ghost rivers has created **Ghost Lake (3)**, a popular recreational area for windsurfers and power boaters.

At the west end of the reservoir, a picturesque white church stands out against the backdrop of the Rockies. The **McDougall Church (4)** was built in 1875 by Methodist missionary John McDougall.

By the time you reach the church, you are on the Stoney Indian Reserve and you remain on Native land for the next 30 kilometres.

Chief Goodstoney Rodeo Centre (5) offers occasional rodeos. In Morley, the administrative centre for the reserve, there is a handicraft store with moccasins, beads, necklaces, and other native products. A short sidetrip on the road through Morley leads to Chief Chiniki Restaurant, known for buffalo burgers, wild game, and other traditional meals.

Back on Highway 1A, the Stoney Indian Park offers camping and hiking. **Nakoda Lodge (6)** on Hector Lake is popular for Sunday brunch and includes an extensive collection of native art. The lodge is frequently used for conferences. Facilities include an indoor pool, sauna, and exercise room.

At **Seebe (7)**, the highway leaves the reserve and enters the Rocky Mountains. The imposing wall of limestone to the north is **Mt. Yamnuska (8)**, popular with experienced rock climbers.

McDougall Church, on the Stoney Indian Reserve west of Calgary, was built in 1875. Missionairies George M. McDougall and his son John C. McDougall ministered to natives for 77 years. The building is the second oldest in Alberta that is still standing on its original foundation.

The foothills west of Calgary provide prime ranch country. Western movies are occasionally filmed in the area. Alberta has about 4 million head of cattle and calves, about twice the size of the human population.

Yamnuska is Stoney for "end of the range."

Here, there are several choices. Before heading farther west, you can stop and camp at **Bow Valley Provincial Park (9)** near Seebe or stay at one of the local guest ranches. Or, you can stay on Highway 1A as it continues on to Canmore. There is good roadside fishing along the way. However, views are occasionally marred by a large cement plant and limestone quarry operations.

Or you may want to rejoin the Trans-Canada Highway and return to Calgary, or continue westward into the mountains.

Scenic Drive 6
High River to Fort Macleod

The foothills southwest of Calgary have provided prime ranching country for more than a century and attracted diverse characters. In 1882, John Ware hired on at the Bar U Ranch near Longview. The former slave was a rarity as one of the few black cowboys in western Canada, and he soon became a highly respected horseman. Another cowboy at the Bar U, the Sundance Kid, is better remembered for his days as an outlaw than for his work on the range. In 1919, Edward Prince of Wales travelled to Canada to visit veterans of World War I. He, too, fell in love with the rolling hills. The prince, who became King Edward VIII in 1937, bought the Bedding-

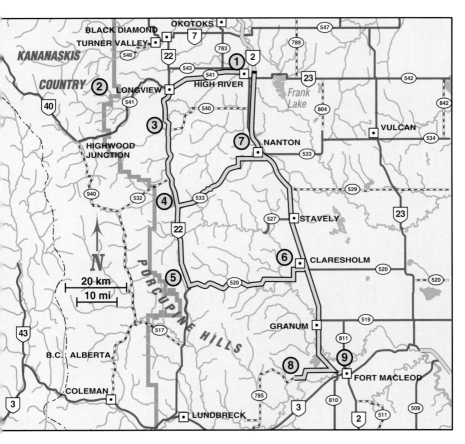

ton Ranch and renamed it EP for "Edward Prince." He visited the property before his brief reign as king, and he returned later with Wallis Simpson, the divorced woman for whom he abdicated the throne. The EP ranch was sold in 1962 to a local rancher.

Start your drive in High River, 56 kilometres south of Calgary. High River, a former, stop on the stage coach run between Calgary and Fort Macleod, has a local museum in a converted railway station. There is a display of railcars outside. Inside there are artifacts from the area's pioneer days. The Bronze Boot Art Gallery features western paintings and bronze sculptures. Eamor's Custom Saddlery and Olson's Silver and Leather can provide handcrafted western souvenirs. **George Lane Memorial Park (1)** is a lovely riverside spot for camping and picnicking.

Drive west out of High River on the Coal Trail that links up with Highway 541. Enjoy the panorama of the foothills and Rockies as you drive toward Longview.

Longview got its start, as "Little New York," during a brief oil

Railroad memorabilia are displayed in the former train station that has been turned into the Claresholm Museum. The old railway stations in Claresholm and High River look alike because they were both built from a single large station that was dismantled in Calgary. Both stations have been turned into museums.

boom in the 1930s when 2500 people lived there. Now there are less than 300 in the hamlet that was renamed to reflect the wide open spaces. The community serves as a gateway to the southern region of the **Kananaskis Country (2)** recreation area.

Turn south on Highway 22 and watch for the "horse neck" pumps that still extract crude from oilfields in the area. At the intersection of Highway 540, look for the original buildings of the **Bar U Ranch (3)** straddling Pekisco Creek.

Chain Lakes Provincial Park (4), at the intersection of Highway 533, offers good fishing and camping.

The **Porcupine Hills (5)**, which border the east side of the highway, were originally named by Natives who thought the evergreens resembled quills on the rolling slopes.

You can stay on Highway 22 all the way to Lundbreck near the Crowsnest Pass, but you can also head east at Highway 520 or 533 and travel through scenic ranch lands to **Claresholm (6)** or **Nanton (7)**. Both towns are regional agricultural centres serving grain farmers and cattle ranchers. Browse in the local western shops. Nanton has a restored Lancaster Bomber on display.

If the Claresholm museum building looks familiar, that's because it is also a restored railway building. In fact, the railway stations in both High River and Claresholm were built from salvaged material from a larger station that was torn down in Calgary.

Both Nanton and Claresholm are on Highway 2, the major north-south route in the province. It is a short drive south to **Head-Smashed-In Buffalo Jump Interpretive Centre (8)** and **Fort Macleod (9)**, or a quick trip north back to High River and Calgary.

Southern Alberta Pioneers and Their Descendants Association

Left to right: Clarence Davis, Lucille Togstad,
Joan Davis, Ted Togstad, Dora Armstrong
and Ralphine Locke

The association welcomes visitors to its log cabin with a splendid view of Calgary and the Rocky Mountains, at 3625 - 4th Street SW, Calgary. (Phone 243-3580) The Pioneers and Descendants have collected over 40 volumes of handwritten and typed history stories over the last 68 years. To be eligible to belong to the association, you have to be a direct descendant of somebody who lived in Alberta before 1890.

The Association's Dora Armstrong recommends: "going to the Glenbow Museum. There are many artifacts there, as well as archives, so you can look up the history of Alberta. Also, you should see Fort Calgary, which is the basis for Calgary's history."

Dora also recommends her grandfather's favourite place: "There wasn't a place so fair as the vale of the Bow and Elbow."

Other Association members tell us about the early days in their families:

Ralphine Locke:

My grandfather was trading between Winnipeg and Fort Edmonton in the 1870s. In 1879, he was hired to bring out a printing press from Winnipeg – a good three week trip. My grandfather got the press all the way to the North Saskatchewan River. In those days, they didn't have a bridge, so they used to put buckskin around the box of the Red River cart and take the wheels off and float it over. So he did this. But the press was too heavy and it sunk in the river, and they couldn't get it out. So my grandfather had to go back to Winnipeg for another press. Within the year, the first edition of the *Edmonton Bulletin* came out.

Pat Donahue:

My grandmother lived out at Priddis in a log house. She had seven children, aged six weeks to ten years old when her husband died. She used to have beer barrels, and she would put up pickles and strawberry jam and all the food in them. She had an open pit that was cool, and put all the barrels in there, so she could feed her seven children for the winter. Then, when the children had grown up, she bought the Midnapore Hotel, and ran it by herself for years.

Lucille Togstad:

My father was from Ontario of Irish descent. He homesteaded out at Elktown, west of Didsbury, and he started a sawmill. About 1910, all the the winter's timber was stored, ready for sawing in the summer. Then the flood came and washed everything right down the Red Deer River. So, my father was out of the sawmill business. But he had enough money to pay off his men. Then he farmed his homestead for a while, but in those days they did not have the kind of crops that would withstand frost. So he came to Calgary.

Mountains

"The scenery is wild and beautiful," Captain John Palliser wrote after exploring the Canadian Rockies in the 1850s. The mountain wilderness is equally impressive to modern visitors who are attracted by magnificent views such as this one along the Continental Divide west of Banff.

T he Canadian Rockies have made vivid and lasting impressions on visitors for thousands of years. Archeologists have found evidence of native hunters as far back as 11,000 years. They were attracted by plentiful deer, elk, and other game. They may have also been inspired by the spiritual aspects of the towering peaks and considered them sacred.

In a little more than 100 years, the Canadian Rockies have become internationally renowned for their wild beauty. Banff National Park now attracts more than four million visitors a year. Jasper National Park records over 1.3 million visits. Waterton Lakes National Park, and the recently developed Kananaskis Country provincial recreation area attract growing numbers each year.

In the Banff townsite there are times when it seems that all the visitors have arrived at once, and they are all crammed on to Banff Avenue. However, development in the mountains has been concentrated to keep the wilderness as undisturbed as possible. Ever since, Rocky Mountains National Park, (the forerunner of Banff

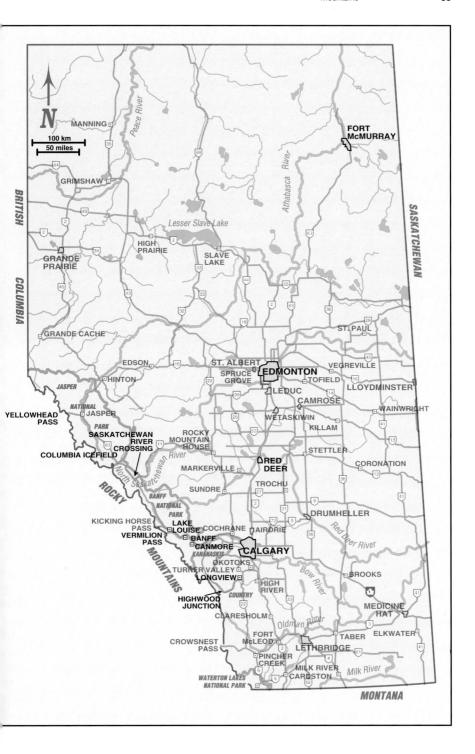

Bathers enjoy soothing hot springs water at the Cave and Basin pool and bathhouse in 1910. Railway workers found the mineral springs in 1883. The federal government established a reserve around the property in 1885, later to become part of Banff National Park.

National Park) was established in the 19th century, national park planners have struggled to serve increasing numbers of visitors while protecting the precious, fragile wilderness.

Banff National Park

History

The story of Canada's first national park is tied closely to the nation-building efforts of the first prime minister, Sir John A. Macdonald.

Railways

In 1871, British Columbia became part of Canada on condition that a railway would be built to the coast through the Rocky Mountains and other western ranges.

It was a formidable task, but surveyors picked out a route through the Yellowhead Pass near the fur-trading outpost at Jasper. The "National Dream" of a railway spanning the country soon turned to a nightmare for Macdonald. He was forced to resign, for accepting large political contributions from one of the groups seeking the lucrative contract to build the railway.

Macdonald later returned to office and won parliamentary approval to work with a new coalition of investors. They were interested in a more southerly route entering the Rockies through the Bow River valley west of Calgary. James Hector had already found a feasible route through the southern Rockies where his unfortunate encounter with a pack animal in August, 1858, led to naming of Kicking Horse Pass.

Major A.B. Rogers was given the job of pushing the route farther west. The surveyor had a relentless drive and little consideration for the toll on his men and their workhorses, as he pushed them to extremes. In 1882, he solved one of the toughest problems faced by the railway builders when he found a route through the Selkirk Mountains. As a reward, Rogers Pass was named for its discoverer. The tobacco-chewing pioneer with the broad moustache was also given a $5,000 bonus but he was so proud, he didn't cash the check and had it framed instead.

Railway construction proceeded quickly on the prairies and reached beyond Calgary in 1883. By the end of the year it had almost reached the Continental Divide, at a spot called Laggan.

Hotsprings
On November 8, 1883, railway workers took time off to prospect near the Siding 29 railway stop.

Section foreman Frank McCabe and two crewmen, William and Tom McCardell, found soothing hot springs on the flank of Terrace Mountain (later renamed Sulphur Mountain). The hot mineral water not only provided soothing relief for the railway workers.

It was also the beginning of Banff National Park. McCabe and the McCardell brothers thought they had found the true mineral wealth of the region. Only two years earlier, prospectors believed

Surveyor, Major A.B. Rogers played a key role in finding a route through the Rockies and other western mountain ranges for the Canadian Pacific Railway. He was so proud of a $5000 bonus check given for his work on the railway, he kept it framed rather than cash it.

they had found a rich vein of silver nearby. Silver City had quickly reached a population of more than a thousand but was abandoned just as quickly when the ore showed little worth.

McCabe and the McCardells put a fence around the hot springs and tried to stake their claim to the spot. A dispute soon arose when two American hunters pointed out that they had wanted to claim the springs in 1875. Others tried to get a piece of the action, and McCabe complicated matters further by trying to sell the group's interest in the springs without consulting his partners.

And other more influential railwaymen had plans for the area. Sandford Fleming and William Cornelius Van Horne were quick to see the potential for tourist development in the mountains. Sir John A. Macdonald was eager to see a profitable railway, and on November 28, 1885, his government established the 26 square

Distinctive Cave and Basin facilities were restored for centennial of Banff National Park in 1985. Swimmers can enjoy the pool in summer. Bathers can soak in the nearby naturally heated Upper Hot Springs pool open year-round.

kilometre Banff Hot Springs Reservation. A federal inquiry the following year resolved the dispute over ownership of the springs. They would become public property: "which promise to be of great sanitary advantage to the public." The inquiry ruled that Frank McCabe and William McCardell should each get $675 for the improvements they had made to the site.

Since then, the name of the park has changed several times. The park was known as Hot Springs Reserve and Rocky Mountains National Park before 1930 when Banff National Park was finally chosen. The boundaries have also changed. At its largest, the park covered 11,440 square kilometres. The present boundaries were set in 1964 and Banff

National Park now covers 6641 square kilometres.

How the hot springs work

The temperature of the Earth's core is extremely high and water that seeps down through layers of rock gets heated an average of one degree Celsius for every 33 metres of descent.

At 3000 metres below the surface, the water is close to boiling. As the hot water rises, it is generally cooled again. However, in some spots the crack systems in the rocks allow the water to rise quickly to the surface, before heat is lost.

The original Cave and Basin hot springs in Banff have an average temperature of about 33.5° C while the nearby Upper Hot Springs are a much hotter 47.3° C.

Radium Hot Springs in Kootenay National Park have an average temperature of 47.7° C while the steamy Miette Hot Springs in Jasper are hottest at 53.9° C.

The temperature fluctuates throughout the year and generally drops several degrees each spring when snow meltwater seeps into the rock layers and dilutes the hot water.

The hot water dissolves a variety of minerals including sulphur, which accounts for the rotten egg smell of untreated water. Much of the smell is caused by algae that metabolize the sulphur and create hydrogen sulphide. Some hot springs are also mildly radioactive due to natural nuclear reactions ocurring at great depth.

The radioactivity is not considered dangerous. In fact, hot mineral springs have long been considered to have healing properties. The extent of those powers is open to question, but there is no doubt about the soothing effect of the hot springs after a day hiking or skiing.

Cave and Basin and the Upper Hot Springs

Development of the park and the Cave and Basin hot springs went ahead quickly. Bathhouses were built in 1887 and customers lined up to pay 10 cents a swim. By 1912, the use had increased so much that architect Walter Painter was commissioned to design a lavish bathing complex which included the largest swimming pool in Canada. The structure was beautiful. But over the years, bathers were attracted to the warmer water at the nearby Upper Hot Springs pool, and the Cave and Basin facility was shut down in 1976.

In 1985, Cave and Basin was restored to its original glory for the centennial of Banff National Park and the Canadian Parks Service. A few things had changed over the years. The original construction project cost $200,000 in the early 1900s. The restoration work and development of an interpretive centre at the site cost $12 million. Bathers can still enjoy the warm water during the summer and can even rent vintage bathing suits for the occasion.

The Upper Hot Springs on Sulphur Mountain, which were first developed for public use in the 1930s are open year-round.

Banff Springs Hotel

From the beginning, the railwaymen were eager to encourage tourism. Their idea was to build a series of grand hotels to lure wealthy travellers into the Canadian wilderness. Banff got its name during one of the early meetings, convened to discuss the development of a mountain hotel near Siding 29. A railway land commissioner suggested a new name for the area after Banffshire, Scotland, birthplace of the first president of the CPR, Sir George Stephen.

Aside from approving the name, William Cornelius Van Horne also heartily endorsed the

Banff Springs Hotel has expanded and modernized several times since opening in 1887. Railroad vice-president William Cornelius Van Horne saw Banff tourism as a way to help pay for the new transcontinental railway. "Since we can't export the scenery, we'll have to import the tourists," he said.

construction of a chateau-like hotel as a way to bring badly needed revenue to the new rail line. "Since we can't export the scenery, we'll have to import the tourists," Van Horne said. Architect Bruce Price was commissioned to design the $250,000 resort to be built at the confluence of the Bow and Spray rivers.

Van Horne had the design changed when he discovered that the original building was oriented so that the kitchen staff had the best view of the river valley; the guest rooms overlooked a thick forest. With hasty modifications, the 250-room Banff Springs Hotel, the world's largest, opened on June 1, 1888. Room rates started at $3.50.

The hotel was an immediate success. The capacity was dou-

bled by 1903, but guests were still being turned away. Walter Painter, the CPR architect who designed the renowned Cave and Basin facility, also redesigned the Banff Springs Hotel. The $2 million Painter Tower was a striking addition as was the use of distinctive Rundle Rock facing. A variety of additions and renovations continued until 1928, including repairs after a major fire in 1927.

The hotel was expanded once again, in time for the 1988 Winter Olympics. Today it can accommodate 1100 guests in 578 rooms. The hotel has been used in all seasons for many years and accommodates skiers.

However in summer, it is packed to the limit. Visitors browse the shops or take in the view from the restaurants and

lounges, and play golf. The Banff Springs Hotel Golf Course is one of the most scenic in the world. The 6729 yard, par 71 course was designed by Stanley Thompson in 1927.

Banff Today

In 1990, Banff achieved unique status as a fully fledged town within the national park. For the 6000 residents, it meant gaining a greater voice in local issues, while working with the national park administration. Businesses and homeowners sign long-term leases and pay annual rental fees for use of the publicly owned land.

Most restaurants, motels, and shops are concentrated along Banff Avenue, and there is also activity on Bear , Wolf , and Caribou Streets.

Banff Avenue can be extremely congested on a summer afternoon, and the town has experimented with a free shuttle bus to lessen traffic. It is best to park in one of the free lots on a side street and stroll Banff Avenue to take in the sights.

It is easy to avoid the crowds. There are lovely riverbank pathways and it is possible to rent a canoe or bicycle to explore the surrounding area.

Banff Park Museum

The railway-style building on Banff Avenue by the Bow River is a throwback to the early days of wildlife viewing in the Rockies. At the turn of the century, a variety of animals were stuffed and put on display. Several other species were kept in an adjacent zoo. The

Banff Avenue shoppers can find anything from fudge to exclusive fashions. Commercial activities in Banff National Park are concentrated in the town of Banff. A smaller service centre is located at Lake Louise.

Viewpoint for Bow Falls lies between Bow River Bridge and Banff Springs Hotel. River is fed by meltwater from the Wapta Icefield, 90 km to the north.

zoo was closed in 1937 and the taxidermy policy was discontinued. The museum was restored in 1985 as part of the National Parks Centennial and early artwork and artifacts are on display.

Bow Falls
The waterfalls near the Banff Springs Hotel provided a dramatic backdrop for Marilyn Monroe in the film *River of No Return.* The Bow River gets its water from the Wapta Icefield on the Continental Divide north of Lake Louise. The best vantage point is off River Avenue.

The Banff Centre
The Banff Centre for the Arts began as a summer theatre school in 1933. Since then, it has grown into a multifaceted independent educational facility with an internationally renowned School of Management. It is also an important hub of cultural activities.

During the summer, the campus is alive with students taking part in courses ranging from creative writing and photography to ballet and ceramics. The Banff Festival of the Arts features performances of students and visiting artists throughout the summer. The Banff Television Festival and the Banff Festival of Mountain Films have both become important annual events at the Centre. Artwork is on display in the Walter Phillips Gallery.

Fenland Trail
The 1.5 km loop through mixed wetland and forest offers excellent birdwatching and wildlife

viewing opportunities. An interpretive brochure is available at the trailhead on the east edge of the Vermilion Lakes.

Whyte Museum
Peter and Catharine Whyte found boundless inspiration in the Canadian Rockies for their artwork. They were also devoted collectors, not only of other paintings, but also of artifacts and writings about the mounatins. In 1968, the Whyte Foundation opened the Whyte Museum of the Canadian Rockies. The museum also includes the Archives of the Canadian Rockies and the library of the Alpine Club of Canada. Extensive photographic collections include the works of Byron Harmon, the Vaux family, and other early photographers. Three exhibit areas are used for displays, including touring shows. Two heritage homes are also maintained on the grounds and are available for tours.

Beyond Banff
Bankhead
Despite the existence of the national parks, blatant intrusions into the wilderness occured in the

Sulphur Mountain Gondola provides a quick ride to a 2285 m (7497 ft) mountaintop with a panoramic view of Banff. Gondola rides take eight minutes. A switchback hiking trail can also be taken to the top.

Minnewanka is the only lake in Banff National Park where gas-powered motoboats are allowed. It's also popular for fishing, sailing, and scuba-diving. The Native name is translated as either "Lake of the Water Spirit" or "Devil's Lake."

early years. When coal was discovered on the flanks of Cascade Mountain, the coal-mining town of Bankhead quickly grew to a population of a thousand. The mine was active from 1903 to 1922 producing coal to power CPR steam engines. After the mine closed, the town was abandoned and the buildings demolished or hauled to nearby Banff or Canmore. New mining claims have not been allowed in national parks since 1930. A self-guiding interpretive trail has been developed at Bankhead on the Lake Minnewanka Road, 7.4 kilometres from Banff.

Cascade Mountain
2998 m (9836 ft)
Cascade Mountain is one of the prominent peaks in the Banff area, seen both from the town of Banff and on the eastern approach from the Trans-Canada Highway. It was named by James Hector in 1858 and is adapted from the Stoney name Minnehappa – "mountain where the water falls." Cascade is a popular spot for mountain climbers in winter when they can scale the frozen waterfalls.

Lake Minnewanka
This popular fishing spot is the only lake in Banff National Park that allows gas-powered boats. The reservoir was created in 1912 when the first of a series of dams was built. Water flowing out of the lake is used to supply hydroelectric power. The resort village of Minnewanka Landing was submerged as water levels rose be-

hind the successively larger dams. The underwater remains are a popular attraction for scuba divers. The lake offers excellent trout fishing and boat tours are available.

Mt. Rundle
2949 m (9676 ft)

Mt. Rundle is a massif that stretches 20 kilometres from Canmore to Banff along the southern edge of the Trans-Canada Highway. The mountain is named for Methodist missionary Robert Rundle who arrived in the Bow Valley in 1847 to bring Christianity to the Natives.

Sulphur Mountain Gondola
The gondola lift takes you to the top of Sulphur Mountain (2285 m) in eight minutes. There is also

Hoodoos near Tunnel Mountain were formed after erosion carried away surrounding glacial deposits. Exotic pillars were once sheltered from the rain by capstones. The natural umbrellas have toppled off, and these hoodoos are gradually wearing down.

Top: Bighorn sheep are commonly seen atop Sulphur Mountain. Sheep are accustomed to tourists and will approach looking for handouts. Park regulations prohibit feeding wild animals since it decreases their ability to fend for themselves.

a hiking trail up the mountainside. Either way, there are magnificent views from the summit including the town of Banff, Lake Minnewanka, and neighboring peaks such as Rundle and Cascade. There are several bighorn sheep that await handouts from visitors at the top. It is harmful to the animals if they learn to rely on humans for food. It is also against park regulations to feed them.

Tunnel Mountain Hoodoos
Don't bother looking for the tunnel. The mountain got its name in 1882 when a surveyor suggested a 275 metre rail tunnel be built to route the Canadian Pacific rail line through the Bow Valley. Railway builders decided to go around the peak but the name stuck. The hoodoos along Tunnel Mountain

Top: Sky over Mt. Norquay lights up with burst of fireworks on Canada Day (July 1).

Bottom: Banff Springs Golf Course is one of the most scenic in the world. The course lies along the banks of the Bow River and is surrounded by mountains such as Rundle and Cascade. Elk are frequently seen on the fairways.

Road were shaped by unique erosion patterns. Boulders act like umbrellas and keep rainfall from wearing down the cement-like material underneath. As the surrounding terrain is washed away, pillars remain even after the capstones fall over. Natives believed the hoodoos were either giants turned to stone or teepees that housed evil spirits.

Vermilion Lakes
The three shallow lakes on the western edge of town were formed by glacial deposits that blocked the Bow River.Until recent years, the parks service had maintained a dam to keep water levels high enough for fishing, windsurfing, and other recreation. The removal of the dam has restored a natural order to the lake system, which is fed by floodwaters from the Bow River each spring. Beavers continue to build their own dams in the area. Look for osprey and bald eagles in the area. The four kilometre drive along the lakeside is popular with joggers and cyclists. The lakes also offer excellent photo opportunities, with Mt. Rundle in the background.

Lake Louise
The Stoneys called it Lake of Little Fishes. Outfitter Tom Wilson named it Emerald Lake when native guides led him to its shore in 1882. The railway men, who had grand plans for the region, favored the royal treatment, And in 1884, the sparkling lake was named after Princess Louise Caroline Al-

Bighorn Sheep

Bighorn sheep are often seen in the Rockies grazing on mountainside grasses. They are also attracted to both natural and artificial mineral licks. Bighorn sheep can often be spotted licking minerals off the sides of parked cars.

They are extremely tolerant of humans and will congregate in areas where there are possible handouts. Park regulations prohibit feeding animals since it makes them dependent on artificial food sources and less able to fend for themselves.

Bighorn rams stand a little less than one metre at the shoulders and can weigh 135 kilograms or more. The females, or ewes, are 15 to 20 percent smaller. Bighorns are greyish brown with a lighter colored belly and a creamy white rump patch around a small brown tail.

Sheep have horns rather than antlers like the elk, moose, and deer. Unlike antlers, horns are not shed each year after the mating season. They continue to grow and the age of adults can be determined by counting the growth sections on the horns. Ewes have short horns, but the rams have impressive curling horns that can reach almost a full circle in the older animals. Horns have been measured at 115 centimetres along the front curve and have weighed over 35 kilograms.

The horns play an important role in the autumn mating rituals when males go head-to-head in butting contests to establish a hierarchy.

Top: Mount Victoria draped with the impressive Victoria Glacier provides a brilliant white backdrop to the blue-green water of Lake Louise, as seen from a rental canoe, the lakeside path, or from a lofty room in the Chateau Lake Louise.

Opposite: Chateau Lake Louise has been a landmark for over a century. Original accommodation was a log cabin built in 1886. Early wooden structures were destroyed by fire. Major renovations and expansion were completed for the hotel's centennial.

berta, the daughter of Queen Victoria and wife of Canada's governor general.

Lake Louise was originally part of a 132 square kilometre forest reserve established in 1892. But ten years later it was incorporated along with Banff and the Chateau Lake Louise into Rocky Mountains National Park.

The lake is 2.4 kilometres long and more than half a kilometre wide. Lake Louise is at an elevation of 1731 metres, 200 metres higher than the valley floor, location of the the CPR's Laggan Station. A winding road was built for carriages to work their way up toward the "Lakes in the Clouds" and the Lake Louise resort was steadily growing.

Chateau Lake Louise

The management of the Canadian Pacific Railway saw Lake Louise as another prime destination for tourists and built a small chalet by the lake in 1890.

There were setbacks, however. The original chalet burned to the ground in 1892. It was replaced by a split-level lodge with rustic accommodation for 12 guests. By 1900, two wings were added to increase the capacity to 200. Despite elements of Tudor and Victorian architecture, the hotel was called the Chateau Lake Louise to enhance its continental ambience. Architect Walter Painter, who had already made his reputation in Banff, designed a 94-room addition that was completed in 1913.

Lake Louise

In 1882, a Stoney guide, named either Edwin or Gold Seeker, led outfitter Tom Wilson toward "snow mountain above the lake of little fishes." Wilson had been packing supplies for the survey crew of the Canadian Pacific Railway near the confluence of the Bow and Pipestone Rivers. Wilson was intrigued by the sound of an avalanche crashing down from a distant peak and wanted to get a closer look.

Wilson became the first white man to see the sparkling waters now known as Lake Louise. Wilson decided to name it Emerald Lake for its brilliant color, but two years later it was renamed Lake Louise in honor of Princess Louise, wife of Canada's Governor General, the Marquis of Lorne. Wilson discovered another lake just across the Continental Divide near the present town of Field, British Columbia, that is still known as Emerald Lake.

The Canadian Pacific Railway knew Lake Louise could easily become a valuable tourist draw and quickly built a lakeside chalet. Several trails were soon built to the "Lakes in the Clouds" and in 1902, the area was incorporated into Rocky Mountains Park, later to become Banff National Park.

In 1924, another fire destroyed two older wooden wings at the Chateau, so a new concrete structure was added to the Painter Wing. The most significant change since then occurred in the 1980s when the hotel changed from a summer to a year-round operation. A major renovation and expansion project was completed for the hotel's centennial in 1990. The guest capacity is now 1000.

Lake Louise Today

The Lake Louise area encompasses: the lake on the western edge of the Bow Valley, the Chateau Lake Louise, and the village of Lake Louise in the valley bottom. The commercial area is much smaller than in Banff and most activity including the grocery store and liquor store is in the Samson Mall. The Post Hotel, which was built along the Pipestone River in the valley bottom, rivals the Chateau as the finest accommodation in the area. And its restaurant is certainly one of the best in the Rockies. The Lake Louise ski area is at Mt. Whitehorn, directly across the valley from the lake itself.

Lake Agnes

The 3.4-km hike from the shores of Lake Louise up to Lake Agnes is a steep excursion with an elevation gain of about 300 metres. However, the hike is worth it for the view and the treats served at a rustic teahouse, on the edge of Lake Agnes. The trail is a series of

switchbacks beginning in subalpine forest. Mirror Lake is a rest spot and Natives knew it as "the goat's looking glass." The teahouse is in a magnificent location near the top of Bridal Veil Falls. Lake Agnes is named for Lady Agnes, wife of Prime Minister Sir John A. Macdonald.

Lake Louise Gondola Lift
A 20-minute gondola ride lifts passengers from the base of the Lake Louise ski area to an elevation of 2010 m (6700 ft) on the slopes of Mt. Whitehorn. Restaurant service is available at the top and there are short hiking trails. In winter, Mt. Whitehorn is one of the most popular ski areas in the Rockies.

Beyond Lake Louise
Moraine Lake
"No scene has given me an equal impression of inspiring solitude and rugged grandeur," Walter Wilcox wrote in 1899 when he viewed the emerald-green lake 12 kilometres east of Lake Louise. The ten peaks rise to elevations more than 1000 metres above the lake along a ridge 15 kilometres long.

The scene is depicted on the Canadian twenty dollar bill. Services are available at Moraine Lake Lodge.

Mt. Temple
3543 m (11,626 ft)
Mt. Temple is the third highest peak in Banff National Park and is the tallest in the Valley of the Ten Peaks. It was named for Sir Rich-

Hikers are rewarded with wonderful views as well as tea and cake at Lake Agnes. It's a steep 3.4 km walk from the Chateau Lake Louise to the scenic lake, named after the wife of Canada's first prime minister. The lakeside teahouse operates in summer.

Moraine Lake and the Wenkchemna Peaks gained widespread recognition when they were depicted in a photograph on the back of Canada's twenty dollar bill. Mountaineer Samuel Allen used Stoney Native words for the numbers one to ten to name prominent peaks in the area southeast of Lake Louise. Wenkchemna is the native word for "ten."

ard Temple, the patron of a scientific expedition to the Rockies in 1884. The Macdonald Glacier at the summit is named after Canada's first prime minister.

Mt. Victoria
3464 m (11,365 ft)

Mt. Victoria provides a perfect backdrop for the one million visitors who stroll the flowered pathways on the edge of Lake Louise each year.

The Victoria Glacier is about 10 kilometres from the most popular vantage points along the north edge of the lake. It is almost 100 metres thick on the upper portion and 150 metres thick on the lower section.

Mountain climbers have been attracted to the Mt. Victoria area since 1893.

Plain of Six Glaciers

The shoreline around Lake Louise is a great spot for strolling, but there are some scenic rewards for those who take an extension of the Lakeshore Trail up past Victoria Glacier. There is a teahouse for those who make the 5.5-kilometre hike up from the chateau. There are also excellent views of Mt. Lefroy and the Lefroy Glacier. A lookout point above the teahouse offers a dramatic lesson in glaciology, with views of the deep crevasses. They are formed as the glaciers flow slowly down the mountain slopes. Large deposits of rocks, known as moraines, show how far the glaciers once extended. Off in the distance, there are sounds of falling rock from the action of the glaciers on the mountainsides.

Skoki Lodge

In 1930, skiers built a backcountry lodge in the Skoki Valley northeast of the Lake Louise ski area. The ski area has since taken over the management of the lodge. Year-round bookings for overnight accommodation are made at the ski area. The 15 kilometre journey to the lodge is for capable hikers or skiers only. Those who do travel in from the trailhead (near the Mt. Temple Day Lodge) are in for a memorable trip over Boulder and Deception passes. There is a small shelter on the way to Boulder Pass known as the Halfway Hut. The building is for day-use only. It is just as well since the building is rumored to be haunted by avalanche victims. Skoki Lodge is a good base for exploring some of the most scenic terrain in the Lake Louise area. "Skoki" is a native word meaning marsh.

Jasper National Park

Like Banff, the history of Jasper National Park is closely linked to the railway business. Jasper Forest Park was established in 1907 to provide a wilderness experience for travellers on Canada's second transcontinental rail line.

The Grand Trunk Pacific Railway (GTPR) had noted the success of the rival CPR railway route through Calgary, Banff, and over the Kicking Horse Pass. In 1902, GTPR began lobbying to establish a second line across Canada from New Brunswick to British Columbia. They would use a

Cougars

The cougar or mountain lion is the largest wild cat in Alberta. They are found in the mountains and foothills, but sightings are rare because there is only a small population of them and they are extremely wary of humans.

Males and females are similar in appearance, though females are smaller, averaging about 45 kilograms. Males average 75 kilograms but can weigh more.

Cougars are tawny brown with a lighter colored belly. Adult males can measure 1.5 metres in body length. The tail is an impressive 75 centimetres in length with a distinctive black tip.

Cougars occasionally hunt elk, small mammals, and birds but they most commonly prey on mule deer. They do not have the stamina for a long chase and prefer to pounce from close range.

The cougars are solitary animals and extremely territorial. A single animal may stake out a hunting ground from 100 to 300 square kilometres.

Females seek out mates every other year and usually gives birth to two to four kittens in summer.

The Jasper Tramway gives a lofty view of the Athabasca Valley and Jasper townsite. The Tramway climbs 937 metres to the upper slopes of The Whistlers. On clear days, Mt. Robson, the highest peak in the Canadian Rockies, can be seen from a distance of 80 km.

northerly route via Edmonton and over the Yellowhead Pass in the Rockies. The rail line was located near Jasper House, an old fur-trading supply stop.

That route was initially chosen by the CPR, but they saw more profit in a southern line. The federal government saw the tourist potential in a second route and helped finance the project by going into partnership with the GTPR.

In 1907, the 12,950 square kilometre Jasper Forest Park was established. Rail service didn't come for another five years. For a time, there were two rail lines through the park with the Canadian Northern Railway competing with GTPR. There were places where the parallel rail lines were just metres apart. The inefficiency was

obvious and the Canadian National Railway was established to consolidate the route. The surplus rail lines were shipped to Europe for use in World War I.

The divisional point and main stop in Jasper Forest Park was originally called Fitzhugh Station, after a railway man. However, that was replaced by "Jasper," the name of the new townsite and the park itself.

Jasper Hawes had run a fur trading outpost for the North West Company in the early 1800s. It soon became known as Jasper House and served as an important stopping point for early explorers.

In 1930, the park was enlarged to its present size, 10,878 square kilometres. Jasper is the largest of the four national parks on the

Continental Divide in the Canadian Rockies. Banff and Jasper, on the Alberta side of the Divide, and Kootenay and Yoho, on the British Columbia side, have been jointly designated as a World Heritage Site because of the valuable mountain wilderness.

Jasper Park Lodge

The planners for the Grand Trunk Pacific Railway wanted to build two hotels – one in the Jasper townsite and the other at Miette Hot Springs. The proposal for Chateau Miette included a 15 kilometre monorail to shuttle guests back and forth from the hotel to the hot pool. However, the Chateau Miette could not be financed.

On the other hand, Fred and Jack Brewster put up a less lavish resort – ten large tents along the shore of Lac Beauvert. They called it Jasper Park Camp, but it was better known as "Tent City" until 1921 when Canadian National Railways acquired the operation, and built 12 log bungalows and a spacious dining hall.

The main building was described as the world's largest single-storey log building. It was difficult to keep up with the tourist demand, and the lodge was enlarged in 1927 and 1928. On July 15, 1952, the historic structure was destroyed by fire.

A new central lodge was opened the following year. A few of the original bungalows are still in use, but several new cabins and suites have been added. There is also accommodation in the main lodge.

Jasper Park Lodge, on the shore of Lac Beauvert, traces its roots to a basic Tent City camp. Canadian National Railway began construction of the lodge in 1922 to compete with the Banff Springs Hotel and Chateau Lake Louise. All are now part of the chain operated by Canadian Pacific Hotels and Resorts.

A French-speaking missionary had trouble crossing a river near Jasper in 1846 and named the tributary Maligne — "wicked." A scenic lake and this deep canyon bear the same name. A series of walkways and bridges provide several viewpoints.

Canadian Pacific Resorts and Hotels bought the lodge in 1988 and undertook major renovations and some expansion. Much of the work was needed because of the recent switch to year-round use.

The present lodge covers 7000 square metres or about two acres. There are 58 cabins with an overall capacity of 800. One of the most charming aspects of the lodge is the long-standing tradition of delivering room service orders by bicycle during the summer.

The lodge's 18-hole golf course was designed by Stanley Thompson and opened in 1925.

Jasper Today

Jasper is a quieter townsite than Banff mainly because it is much farther from a major city. Banff is just 128 kilometres from Calgary and it takes less than 90 minutes to make the drive. Jasper is 362 kilometres from Edmonton and the trip is closer to four hours.

With fewer visitors, there is less variety in shopping and dining out, but there are fewer line-ups and less congestion on Miette Avenue and Connaught Drive.

Lac Beauvert

The translation is "beautiful green lake" and it is obvious why the Brewster brothers chose the spot on the shore of Lac Beauvert for the early visitors to Jasper. Lac Beauvert, along with nearby Edith and Annette lakes, are good places close to the townsite for fishing, picnicing, and wildlife viewing.

Jasper Tramway
The tramway lifts passengers 937 metres almost to the top of The Whistlers, 2464 m (8084 ft). The vantage point offers views of the townsite and the Athabasca and Miette valleys. On a clear day, Mt. Robson can be seen in the distance in British Columbia. At 3954 m (12,972 ft), Mt. Robson is the highest peak in the Canadian Rockies. Cafeteria and dining room service is available at the top of the tramway. There is also a hiking trail. Tramway passengers should be prepared for cooler and windier conditions than in the valley below.

Beyond Jasper
Maligne Lake
Maligne Lake, 48 km southeast of the townsite, is the largest natural

lake in the Canadian Rockies as well as one of the busiest. There is fishing, trail-riding, hiking, and boating. The lake is one of three in the mountain national parks that is open to power boats.

The glacier-fed lake was formed by an ancient rockslide that created a reservoir that stretches for 22 kilometres. A 90 minute boat tour of the lake is offered. There are also rentals of power boats, row boats, and canoes. Spirit Island is a much-photographed landmark with rugged peaks and glaciers providing a dramatic backdrop.

Maligne Canyon
In 1846, Jesuit Missionary Father de Smet had a difficult time trying to cross a turbulent mountain river. He named it Maligne, the

Maligne Lake is the largest natural lake in the Canadian Rockies and one of three in the mountain national parks open to motor boats. Scenic tours are available on the 22 km long lake. Picturesque Spirit Island is a prime destination.

Mt. Edith Cavell, one of the most striking peaks in Jasper National Park, has undergone several name changes. Natives knew it as "White Ghost". French-speaking fur-traders called it "La Montagne de la Grande Traverse" (mountain of the great crossing). It was briefly known as Mt. Fitzhugh before being renamed in honor of a nurse killed in the World War I.

French word for "wicked."

The Maligne River has carved an impressive canyon out of the limestone as it flows from Maligne Lake into the Athabasca River. The canyon that begins 11 kilometres east of the townsite, is up to 55 metres deep in places and is the most spectacular gorge in the Canadian Rockies. There are several self-guiding trails to excellent viewpoints.

One of the best hikes is a four kilometre walk starting at the Fifth Bridge. There is a teahouse that operates throughout the summer.

Guided hikes are offered on the frozen canyon floor in winter.

Miette Hot Springs
The Miette Hot Springs , 61 kilometres east of Jasper, are the hottest of the developed hot springs

in the Canadian Rockies. The average temperature of close to 54°C is almost seven degrees hotter than Banff's Upper Hot Springs.

The water also contains a much greater concentration of minerals including sulphur, and the smell is much more noticeable. Early development of the springs was done mainly by coal miners from nearby Pocahontas. Work progressed rapidly in 1919 when the miners had plenty of free time during an extended strike.

Modern bathing facilities were constructed in 1937, and the springs have been upgraded several times since then.

Mt. Edith Cavell
3363 m(11,033 ft)
On October 12, 1915, British nurse

Edith Cavell was shot by a German firing squad on a charge of assisting Allied prisoners of war to escape during World War I. The impressive Mt. Edith Cavell is 29 kilometres south of Jasper, at the end of a winding access road off the Athabasca Parkway (Highway 93A). The Angel Glacier is draped over a saddle along the northeast slopes of the mountain. For better views of the mountain and glacier, take The Path of the Glacier Trail from the Mt. Edith Cavell parking lot. The round-trip takes about an hour.

Columbia Icefield

There are 17 massive glacial areas in the Canadian Rockies that are classified as icefields. Naturally, the Icefields Parkway offers some of the best views of the thick ice sheets. The Columbia Icefield, about halfway between Lake Louise and Jasper, is the largest and most accessible of the icefields.

It is possible to drive up to the toe of the Athabasca Glacier and get out and feel the edge of a 320 square kilometre blanket of ice. There are guided walks onto the ice surface, and tours are provided even farther out onto the glacier in specially adapted buses. Balloon tires are used for traction on the frozen surface.

Glaciers are spectacular marvels of nature but they can also be very dangerous places. Deep cracks in the ice, known as crevasses, are particularly hazardous.

How Icefields and Glaciers Form

Glaciers form in areas where more snow accumulates than melts. There are several factors that make the Columbia Icefield and several other spots in the Rockies well-suited to glacial development.

First, there is a heavy snowfall. About 10 metres of snow falls on the Columbia Icefield each year. Cooler temperatures at higher elevation also preserve the ice. The Columbia Icefield has an average elevation of 3000 m (9845 ft). Flat or gently sloping terrain is also

Glaciers are the major source of the world supply of fresh water. Much of North America was covered by sheets of ice 12,000 years ago. Remnants of the ice age are now found at northern latitudes and in the high mountains.

Colorful fireweed springs up just a few hundred metres from the frozen edge of the Athabasca Glacier. Meltwater from the glacier feeds the Sunwapta River and eventually flows to the Arctic Ocean.

required. Snow simply avalanches off steep mountainsides.

As the snowpack builds up, ice begins to form in the bottom layers. The snow crystals gradually deteriorate and become compacted under the weight of new snowfall. Also, meltwater from the surface seeps down and freezes. Glacial ice begins to form when the compacted snow reaches a thickness of about 30 metres.

Color of Snow and Ice
There are some interesting colors in glacial ice and snow. On the surface, a glacier appears to be white because of air and impurities contained in the ice. As the ice becomes compressed in the lower layers, it turns blue primarily because most of the air is squeezed out.

Some snow found on glaciers has a reddish tinge. Watermelon snow is created by one-celled algae that thrive on impurities found in the snowpack. The algae are a good food source for snow worms, another species that makes its home in cold surroundings. You should avoid eating red snow.

How far do Glaciers Move?
The Columbia Icefield is one of the largest temperate icefields in North America. It covers 320 square kilometres and reaches a depth of up to 900 metres.

Eight glaciers fan out from the centre. Three are visible from the Icefields Parkway – the Dome, Stutfield, and Athabasca glaciers.

One of the most intriguing aspects of glacial ice is its ability to

flow downhill. Ice becomes elastic when put under enormous pressure. In a glacier, that means ice near the surface is brittle. But down towards the bottom, it becomes elastic and pliable under the weight of all those layers above.

Since the ice is on a slope, it slides downward, but the rate of movement varies a great deal in different parts of a glacier. In the Athabasca Glacier, ice flows at a rate of about 125 metres a year in the icefall section where the ice is on steep terrain. On the more gentle slopes halfway down the glacier, the rate is about 80 metres a year. At the terminus (end point), there is less momentum because of increased friction with the rocks, and the rate is just 15 metres a year.

It takes about 150 years for snowfall at the top of the Columbia Icefield to turn into ice and make its way to the toe of the Athabasca Glacier.

Why Glaciers Advance and Retreat

Despite the constant flow, most glaciers in the Canadian Rockies are in recession and appear to be retreating up mountainsides. The advance and retreat of glaciers is determined by long-term weather patterns. When the earth's climate was much cooler, nearly all of Canada was covered by glacial ice. A warming trend caused most of the ice sheet covering Alberta to melt away between 10,000 and 12,000 years ago.

A less dramatic warming trend over the past 120 years has caused

Glacial ice is formed from compressed snow. Enormous pressure causes it to flow down the mountainside. Meltwater creates intriguing ice sculptures. Caution is needed when exploring glaciers to avoid slipping into crevasses and other gaps in the ice.

Outfitter guides packhorses across the Saskatchewan Glacier on the way to the Columbia Icefield in the 1930s.

the Athabasca Glacier to retreat 1.6 kilometres. Between 1945 and 1964 the rate of recession was 20 to 37 metres a year. The retreat had slowed to a more moderate 1 to 3 metres a year by 1970.

Glaciers are a major source of fresh water throughout the world. Meltwater from the Columbia Icefield flows into three different oceans – the Atlantic, Pacific, and Arctic.

Athabasca Glacier

Length	6.5 km
Width	1 km average
Maximum thickness	300 m
Volume of ice	640 million cu m
Skyline elevation	2800 m
Terminus elevation	1900 m

Exploration of the Columbia Icefield Region

Native travellers would certainly have been the first to see the Columbiam Icefields.

European exploration was piqued by a mistake made in the early 1800s, by map-maker David Thompson. During his travels Thompson estimated that Athabasca Pass was 3350 m (11,000 ft) above sea level.

Thompson's error was compounded in 1827 when Scottish naturalist David Douglas crossed Athabasca Pass and climbed neighboring Mt. Brown. Based on Thompson's elevation, he estimated the height of Mt. Brown and nearby Mt. Hooker to be approximately 4900 m (16,000 ft).

Later, mountaineers were drawn to the area in search of the

gh peaks, but they could not
1d anything approaching the
evation estimate made by
ouglas. Norman Collie explored
e region north of the Saskatch-
van River Crossing in 1898. Al-
ough he did not find any 4900
etre peaks, he did find the
rawling icefield, ringed with
mewhat lower peaks.

Collie later solved the mystery
the exaggerated elevations of
ts. Hooker and Brown. He dis-
overed that Douglas had relied
1 Thompson's faulty informa-
on. Athabasca Pass is closer to
750m in elevation (and not the
350 metres estimated by
hompson). And Mt. Columbia is
e highest point in the area and
Alberta at 3747 m(12,293 ft.).
t. Columbia, along with Snow
ome, Mt. Alberta, and Mt.

Athabasca are among the most
popular peaks in the Rockies.

Exploring the Icefield Today
A new era of discovery on the Columbia Icefield began in 1952
when Bill Ruddy began a motor-
ized tour operation on the Athabasca Glacier. He equipped 14
Bombardier snowmobiles to handle the steep frozen terrain and
took passengers out onto the frozen slopes.

Brewster Transportation took
over in 1969 and brought in their
own fleet of specially adapted vehicles. Various refinements were
attempted before the company
turned to Canadian Foremost
Ltd., a Calgary company with ex-
pertise in transportation systems
for the oil industry.

Snocoaches wind
their way toward the
headwall of the
Athabasca Glacier
with balloon tires
adapted to give
traction over the ice.
Vehicles were
designed with the
help of technology
developed for oil
exploration in harsh
environments.

The result was the Snocoach, a 56 passenger bus with balloon tires that seems capable of handling everything from sand dunes to lunar landscape.

Brewster operates a fleet of 12 Snocoaches on 90 minute tours throughout the summer. The 19,500 kilogram vehicle is well-suited to the rough terrain. It is powered by a 210-horsepower diesel engine. It can reach a top speed of 42 kilometres per hour and can climb a 32 degree slope. However, the vehicles, which cost close to $350,000 each, are not pushed to their limit during the tours. Rides can be booked at an office adjacent to the interpretive centre.

The Columbia Icefield Interpretive Centre provides displays and a video program on glaciers. Restaurant service and accommodation are available at the Columbia Icefield Chalet.

Waterton Lakes National Park

Kootenai Brown called it a "land of dreams" when he ventured into the spectacular valley of the Waterton Lakes in 1865. The 526 square kilometre park in the southwest corner of the province encompasses an abrupt transition from prairie to mountaintops, as high as the summit of Mt. Blakiston, 2940 m (9645 ft), highest mountain in the park. The mountains at Waterton Lakes have another remarkable characteristic. Rock layers formed 1.6 billion years ago are stacked atop

relatively young 60-million-year-old shales. The anomaly was caused by movement on the Lewis Fault, a weakness in the Earth's crust. The mountains began to form as a folding pattern from pressure between land masses. The fault line marks the place where the older layers rode on top of the younger shales. The moving mass of older rocks is known as the Lewis Overthrust. The Lewis Overthrust crept along at about one centimetre a year, and covered a distance of up to 70 kilometres before the mountain-building was over. Erosion over the past 40 million years has worn off the young layers on the mountaintops to expose the Precambrian rock below.

History

Archeologists have found evidence of native activity in the region as far back as 8400 years ago. Kootenai Natives living west of the Rockies made frequent trips through the mountains to hunt in the area they called "Omok-se-kimi," which means beautiful waters.

Thomas Blakiston, a meteorologist on the Palliser Expedition, explored the region in 1858 as he searched for a southern transportation route through the Rockies. Blakiston named the picturesque chain of lakes he found after Charles Waterton, a renowned British naturalist.

John George "Kootenai" Brown had settled in the Waterton Valley in 1879, and by the early

1890s, he was concerned about the encroachment of settlers on the mountain wilderness (see box p 131). Brown and rancher F. W. Godsal lobbied the federal government and Kootenay Lakes Forest Park was established in 1895. Brown served as its first warden. And he became the first superintendent at the age of 71 when the forest became a national park in 1911. Brown's grave can be found alongside the main access road to the Waterton townsite.

Waterton-Glacier International Peace Park

In 1932, Waterton/Glacier International Peace Park was established primarily due to lobbying from Rotary International service club members in Alberta and Montana.

The first of its kind in the world, Waterton Lakes National Park and Glacier National Park are administered separately by Canadian and U.S. park authorities, but there is a great deal of co-operation in managing the wilderness.

It is possible to take a scenic boat cruise or to hike along the shore of the Upper Waterton Lake, and cross the international border for a quick trip to the United States. There are no border crossing formalities on the short return trips by boat or hiking trail.

Longer excursions into Glacier National Park are highly recommended, especially the scenic drive over Logan Pass on the Going-to-the-Sun Road. Regular customs and immigration checks are made at the Chief Mountain Highway crossing.

Prince of Wales Hotel overlooks the Upper Waterton Lake, which straddles the border between Alberta and Montana. The Waterton valley and lakes are named for 19th century British naturalist Charles Waterton.

The International has been cruising the Upper Waterton Lake for more than 60 years. The tour boat crosses the border between Canada and the United States halfway down the lake. Passengers can get off for a stroll in Goat Haunt, Montana, before returning to the Waterton marina.

Peace Park celebrations are held each summer from July 1 (Canada Day) to July 4 (Independence Day in the U.S.).

Waterton Lakes and Glacier National Parks are listed as international biosphere reserves with UNESCO. As biosphere reserves, researchers look at the relationship between the national park lands and the surrounding areas where agriculture and resource development are permitted.

Waterton Park Townsite
Waterton gets only a fraction of the visitors that Banff or Jasper do. But the townsite can be very crowded in July and August. Accommodation can be scarce in motels and the campground. Even during the busy season, it is common to see bighorn sheep and mule deer wandering through town.

Cameron Falls is a picturesque spot on the edge of the townsite.

The steep, 1.2 kilometre hike up the Bear's Hump, behind the park information centre, provides a lofty view of the town and the lake.

There's an 18-hole golf course overlooking the Middle Waterton Lake and a heated swimming pool in the townsite. The lake is too cold for swimming, but a sunken paddlewheeler in Emerald Bay is popular with scuba divers.

Most of the restaurants and shops are clustered along Waterton Avenue and Mount View Road.

Spring and fall are becoming more popular with tourists. In winter, most of the townsite is shut down with just a few services for year-round residents and cross-country skiers. The Kilmorey Lodge provides accommodation and restaurant service year-round.

Prince of Wales Hotel
Once again, a railway builder financed a landmark hotel in the middle of mountain wilderness.

Unlike Banff or Jasper, the Prince of Wales Hotel was built to serve rail passengers on the U.S. side of the border. Louis Hill of the Great Northern Railroad saw Waterton Lakes as ideal for an addition to the chain of grand hotels built for visitors in Glacier National Park, Montana.

Construction began in 1926 on a seven-storey, gabled resort.

Kootenai Brown

Like thousands of other fortune hunters, John George Brown set out for the Cariboo goldfields of western Canada in the 1860s. Like thousands of others, he didn't find much gold but saw plenty of other opportunities on the frontier.

The former British army officer led an adventurer's life in the New World becoming a Pony Express rider, buffalo hunter, whisky trader, Rocky Mountain Ranger, scout, oilman and the first superintendent of Waterton Lakes National Park. He had more than his share of close calls along the way. After one unsuccessful venture as a prospector in the Cariboos, Brown set out for the supposed rich fields in Edmonton. Along the way, he and his companions were attacked by Blackfoot Natives and he was shot in the back with an arrow. Two Natives were killed in the

skirmish and Brown survived with the aid of some turpentine to disinfect the wound. Years later as a mail rider, he was captured by Chief Sitting Bull. Brown and his partner were stripped by their Sioux captors and held prisoner while the Indians decided their fate. The men managed to escape in the night and turned up at a nearby U.S. army post without clothes but with their scalps.

Brown earned his nickname through his association with the Kootenai Indians. He was once a relentless hunter of buffalo and wolves but gradually turned into an avid conservationist.

He pressed the federal government to set aside a wilderness reserve on the southern edge of Alberta and got his wish in 1911 when the Kootenay Forest Reserve was turned into Waterton Lakes National Park.

There were some difficult challenges for builders since the closest rail stop was 60 kilometres away. Massive boilers had to be delivered by horse team and sled because they were too heavy for wagons on the rough road. High winds blew the wooden structure off centre several times. Cables were installed from the upper floors down to buried anchors to reinforce the building.

The 81 room hotel opened in 1927 and quickly became popular on both sides of the border. The hotel has undergone renovations in recent years. As well, Glacier Park Incorporated upgraded its fleet of vintage touring buses which transports passengers between the Prince of Wales Hotel and the rest of its chain of resorts in Montana.

Beyond Waterton
Upper Waterton Lake
When the Prince of Wales Hotel opened, the *International* cruise boat was launched to provide tours the full 11 kilometer length of the Upper Waterton Lake. The *International* is over 60 years old, but still cruises throughout the summer. Stopovers can be made at Goat Haunt, Montana, at the south end of the lake. Boat service can also be used to reach the start of the Crypt Lake Trail, a steep but rewarding day hike.

The lake is the deepest in the Rockies at 152 metres (500 ft) and is extremely cold, too cold for swimming. The high winds attract sailboarders. Private powerboats are allowed on the Middle and Upper Waterton lakes. Fishing is allowed but a national park fishing permit is required.

Cameron Lake
The Akamina Parkway is a scenic 16 kilometre drive from the townsite to Cameron Lake. Look for deer and bighorn sheep along the way. There is also a marker at the spot where Alberta's first oil well was drilled in 1902.

Cameron Lake is not open for power boating, but canoes, row boats, and paddle boats can be rented. Take a stroll on the level lakeside trail.

Hikers and boaters should avoid the southern edge of the lake. Grizzly bears are frequently spotted on an avalanche slope above the lake. (See box p. 209.)

Red Rock Canyon
There is a high concentration of iron in a rock known as argillite, found throughout the park. The rock is red in areas where the iron has oxidized and is green where the iron remains unoxidized.

Red Rock Canyon, 17 kilometres northwest of the townsite, provides a colorful example of oxidized argillite. A short interpretive trail winds along the canyon.

Another short trail leads to a scenic lookout by Blakiston Falls. Deer and bighorn sheep are quite common in the area.

Kananaskis Country

In the 1970s, Alberta Premier Peter Lougheed was in the fortunate position of leading a government that had surplus revenue. Royalties from the booming oil and gas business were used to establish the Alberta Heritage and Savings Trust Fund, a multibillion dollar stockpile. Money was channeled into industrial diversification, medical research, and a variety of long-term investments as a hedge against bad times.

Lougheed also used the opportunity to create Kananaskis country, a sprawling recreation area in the foothills and mountains southwest of Calgary.

Kananaskis Country is an alternative destination to the mountain national parks. It is 4250 square kilometre area set aside as a multiple-use region, with an emphasis on providing as many opportunities for different kinds of recreation as possible. Activities are restricted to specific areas so that cross-country skiers, downhill skiers and snowmobilers all have their own areas for enjoyment. Similarly, some places like the McLean Creek area in the foothills are open to off-highway motor vehicles. The more sensitive mountain environment is restricted to quieter pursuits such as hiking and bicycling.

Ranching, logging, and natural gas extraction are also carried on in parts of Kananaskis Country.

History

The bountiful wildlife in the Kananaskis Valley attracted Stoney, Blackfoot, Cree, and other Natives for centuries before white explorers arrived in the 1850s. Captain John Palliser learned of a particularly grim encounter between warring tribes when he travelled through the area in 1858. According to legend, a Native warrior had been hit in the head with an axe and apparently died. But the warrior named Kananaskis, came back to life and Palliser named a high mountain pass in his honor. A churning mountain river and the 88 kilometre valley surrounding it also took the same name.

Resource development came to the Kananaskis area soon after the arrival of the railway in 1883.

Iron deposits in shale (known as argillite) can be green or red. Red Rock Canyon shows argillite that turned a deep red when it oxidized under intense heat caused by pressure during shifts in the Earth's crust.

Beaver

The beaver is the largest rodent in Alberta with a weight of 20 kilograms and a length that can exceed one metre. The brown thick-furred mammal is also Canada's national emblem.

Beavers are strong swimmers with webbed toes and a large flat tail used as a rudder. A beaver also uses its tail, which accounts for almost half its length, to slap the water as an alarm when predators are near. It can dive and travel great distances underwater and stay beneath the surface for up to 15 minutes.

Beavers have a significant impact on their environment. With sharp teeth and powerful jaws, they can make quick work of bringing down large riverbank trees. In wetland areas, they use sticks, logs, mud, and roots to build lodges and dams. Families of beavers build the dams to create ponds and establish a secure transportaion system. The animals are slow-moving on land and don't like to stray too far from water where they can easily escape predators.

Beavers feed on the inner bark of deciduous trees as well as shrubs, saplings, and aquatic plants. They are nocturnal and are most likely to be spotted in the evening as they glide through the water creating a small wake.

The Eau Clair and Bow River Lumber Company began logging operations to serve the building industry in Calgary. Coal mines were started in Canmore and on the flanks of Mount Allan. Calgary Power dammed the Kananaskis Lakes in 1932 and regulated the flow of the Kananaskis River through its generating station at the confluence with the Bow River. Cattlemen leased large tracts of grazing land along the edge of the foothills and grasslands.

Depression-era workers opened up the area in the 1930s when they cleared fire roads. Their camp at the forestry research station near Barrier Lake was later used to house German prisoners during World War II.

Kananaskis Today

The last coal mine in the area closed in 1979, and logging operations have been cut back substantially. TransAlta Utilities still controls the flow of water on the Kananaskis River. Kayakers check with the power company to find out when conditions are best for whitewater paddling and a slalom course has been developed.

Recreational use has increased in Kananaskis Country in recent years. There are 2000 auto campsites as well as remote sites for backpackers. Some campgrounds are adapted for equestrians. Others are set aside mainly for off-highway vehicle users. The Mount Kidd Recreational Vehicle Park has a hot tub, sauna, and a variety of other amentities for motor homes. Camping sites are in demand all summer. Reservations are advised.

Accommodation is available in Canmore, on the north edge of Kananaskis Country or in Kananaskis Village. The William Watson Lodge was built to cater to the needs of Alberta's handicapped and seniors.

There are three provincial parks in the region – Peter Lougheed Provincial Park, Bow Valley Provincial Park, and Bragg Creek Provincial Park(Scenic Drive 1 and 9).

The 36-hole Kananaskis Country Golf Course ranks as one of the best in the country. The Nakiska downhill ski area on Mount Allan and the Canmore Nordic Centre were developed for the 1988 Winter Olympics.

The wildlife that attracted the original natives to the region still flourishes. Grizzly and black bears, elk, deer, cougar, and a variety of birds and other animals are found in the valleys and on the mountain slopes. Hunting is strictly regulated and restricted to specific areas. See Listings.

Nakiska was built for downhill skiing but attracts hikers and sightseers in summer. The Calgary Philharmonic Orchestra performs an outdoor concert at the base of the ski hill once a year.

don't want to make the drive out to the mountains. Bragg Creek Provincial Park is a popular day use area along the banks of the Elbow River.

Highway 66 southwest of Bragg Creek leads to scenic foothills campgrounds, hiking trails and the McLean Creek off-highway vehicle zone. There are popular equestrian areas and campgrounds off Highway 549 west of Millarville and off Highway 546 west of Turner Valley.

Kananaskis Area Highlights

BraggCreek/East Kananaskis
(Scenic Drive 1)
Bragg Creek, 50 kilometres southwest of Calgary, is a popular hamlet for summer day trips with several art galleries and craft shops along with a few casual restaurants. The Wintergreen downhill ski resort offers runs on foothills terrain mainly for Calgarians who

Peter Lougheed Provincial Park
(Scenic Drive 9)
This 508 square kilometre park is the heart of Kananaskis Country. It encompasses the Upper and Lower Kananaskis Lakes, a variety of hiking trails and six campgrounds. There are also paved trails for bicycles and wheelchairs.

Canmore had its start as a coal mining town, but the mountain community east of Banff National Park has turned to tourism for its future. The town gained international recognition in 1988 when it hosted the cross-country skiing and the biathlon competition during the Winter Olympics.

The upper and lower lakes allow fishing and power boating but like most mountain lakes, they are too cold for swimming.

Canmore and Spray Lakes
(Scenic Drive 5)
Canmore got its start as a coal mining soon after the arrival of the railway in 1883. By 1888, there were 450 people in town, and a one-man detachment of the North West Mounted Police was established. The old outpost is still standing but the coal mines are long gone.

The mountain town of about 5000 serves as a gateway to both Banff National Park and Kananaskis Country. Canmore lies just outside the national park gates on the Trans-Canada Highway and is only 22 kilometres from the town of Banff. For years, it served as a bedroom community for Banff, and few visitors ventured beyond the strip of gas stations along the highway.

Times have changed, espe-

cially since the Winter Olympics. The Canmore Nordic Centre is still used for international events and training camps, but is also well-used by recreational skiers. Cyclists and hikers take to the trails in summer.

Canmore has a thriving artistic community with paintings and crafts available at a variety of outlets. The town has an impressive variety of restaurants.

A steep gravel road on the south edge of town leads to the Smith Dorrien/Spray Trail and access to several good trails for hiking and cross-country skiing. Mount Engadine Lodge, south of the Spray Lakes Reservoir, provides meals and accommodation.

Highwood Pass and
Cataract Creek
(Scenic Drive 6 and 9)
The southern section of Kananaskis Country has equestrian trails in the Etherington Creek area. There is also hiking, camping, fishing, hunting, and snowmobiling in winter. Highway 541 west of Longview is the main access road to the southern end of the Kananaskis Trail.

Kananaskis Village
(Scenic Drive 9)
Kananaskis Village is a main accommodation centre with three hotels located near the Nakiska ski area, the Kananaskis Country Golf Course, and the Fortress Mountain ski area. There are also nearby trails for hiking, cycling, and horseback riding.

Scenic Drive 7: Bow Valley Parkway

Banff to Lake Louise

The Bow Valley Parkway (Highway 1A) is the leisurely alternative to the Trans-Canada Highway for the journey between Banff and Lake Louise. The parkway is reached by the Lake Louise overpass or off the Trans-Canada Highway, 7 kilometres west of Banff. The speed limit is 60 kilometres per hour for most of the route and a nonstop drive takes about an hour. Allow extra time to visit the interpretive displays, picnic spots, campgrounds, and hiking trails along the way.

The original road, built in 1920, served as the route between Banff and Lake Louise until the Trans-Canada Highway was completed. Roadside displays to interpret the area's natural features and human history were placed along the Bow Valley Parkway in the 1980s.

The winding route lined with trembling aspen and spruce is popular with cyclists even though there are more hills than on the Trans-Canada. There is an opportunity to see deer, elk, and even the occasional moose.

The Bow Valley has been created over millions of years with the Bow River carving a route through the main range and front range of the Rockies. During glacial advances and retreats from 75,000 to 11,000 years ago, ice gouged out the valley, changing it from a V-shape into a U-shape. As the ice retreated, massive deposits were left, most noticeably near **Storm Mountain (8)**. The

Yellow buttercups blanket the valley floor with Castle Mountain dominating the skyline near the midpoint of the Bow Valley Parkway. The gently winding road offers a leisurely alternative to the Trans-Canada Highway between Banff and Lake Louise.

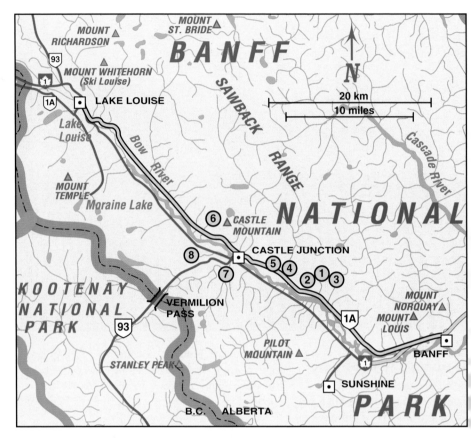

Bow River itself, is formed by melt-water from glaciers in the Wapta Icefield.

There are places where the two-lane parkway splits to go around obstacles. In one place between Banff and Castle Junc-tion, a few metre long **island of greenery (1)** was created to pro-tect a tall white spruce. The park superintendent of the day may have insisted that the spruce be saved. Another explanation is that a road foreman napped in the shade of the tree, and workers didn't want to disturb him as they cleared a right-of-way. In any

event, the tree blew down in fierce storm in 1984.

A significant division in the road occurs at the nearby **Hillsdale Slide (2)**. The rockslide occurred 8000 years ago and the mound has become overgrown.

Look for a gaping **hole-in-the-wall (3)** on the side of **Mount Cory (3)**, 11 kilometres west of Banff. The hole, 600 metres above the valley floor, was created by melt-water from the Bow Glacier that once filled the valley. The cave is just 30 metres deep.

Johnston Canyon (4), 26 kilo-metres west of Banff, is a popular destination with a walkway system built right into the canyon walls. The 15 metre lower falls are just one kilometre from the trailhead with the 30 metre upper falls 1.6 kilometres farther. The trail continues beyond the canyon to the Inkpots, 5.8 kilometres from the trailhead. Sediment in the water gives the mineral spring pools a deep blue-green color.

Silver City (5), 27 kilometres west of Banff, was a boom town of 2000 in 1884 when prospectors heard of vast silver deposits on the flanks of Copper Mountain. They found low-grade copper, but not much silver, and the town was abandoned within two years. **Castle Mountain (6)**, at an elevation of 2766 metres (9128 ft), was named by James Hector of the Palliser Expedition in 1858. It's a classic example of a main range peak. The sedimentary rock layers are horizontal rather than tilted like those in the front range. Erosion creates the appearance of a castle. The name was changed to Mount Eisenhower after World War II, but after years of protest, the original name was restored in 1979. The most southerly tower is named Eisenhower Peak.

At **Castle Junction (7)**, motorists can continue on to Lake Louise or take Highway 93 to Radium Hot Springs and Kootenay National Park in British Columbia.

Scenic Drive 8: Icefields Parkway

Lake Louise to Jasper

During the depths of the Great Depression, work crews carved a narrow dirt road along the rugged crest of the Continental Divide. Only daring drivers attempted the Banff-Jasper Road when it opened in 1940. Since then, the 230 kilometre, twisting mountain roadway, The Icefields Parkway, through Banff and Jasper National parks has been brought up to modern standards with wide shoulders that are popular with cyclists in summer. The Icefields

Johnston Canyon is one of the most popular hikes in Banff National Park. A suspended walkway follows the canyon past two waterfalls.

Peyto Lake gets its distinctive turquoise color from rock powder suspended in the water. The finely ground material is created by abrasion from glaciers. The best viewpoint for the lake is from a platform on the Bow Summit interpretive trail.

Parkway (Highway 93) ranks as one of the most scenic drives in the world with views of more than a hundred glaciers along with turquoise lakes and jagged peaks. The Parkway is maintained year-round and can be breathtakingly beautiful in winter. Naturally, extra caution is needed in winter and snow tires are essential. On the route there are several national park campgrounds as well as a chain of low-cost hostels operated by the Southern Alberta Hostelling Association. Grizzly bears and other wildlife are frequently seen along the highway. The animals should not be approached. Highlights are noted by distance from the south end of the Parkway followed by the measurement from Jasper.

Hector Lake (1), at Kilometre 16 (214 km from Jasper), is a typical glacial meltwater-fed lake. The unusual green-blue color comes from rock flour ground by the ice and left suspended in the water. Mountain lakes are generally too cold for swimming. Avoid drinking the water since the rock dust can cause diarrhea, and occasionally there are parasites in the water that can cause gastro-intestinal problems. Mount Hector, at an elevation of 3394 m (11,135 ft), is named for James Hector of the Palliser Expedition of 1857-60. (See p. 55.)

The **Crowfoot Glacier (2)**, at Kilometre 33 (197 km from Jasper), was once shaped like a three-toed crow's foot. One of the toes has receded over the years but the name remains. A picnic site is located one kilometre farther

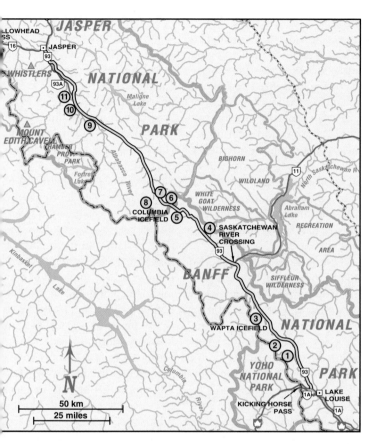

north on the shores of Bow Lake, source of the Bow River. The Wapta Icefield is draped over the mountains to the west. At the north end of the lake is Num-ti-jah Lodge built in the 1920s by colorful outfitter Jimmy Simpson. The lodge has a restaurant, accommodation, and a small gift shop. Num-ti-jah is the native word for marten, a member of the weasel family.

At Kilometre 40 (190 km from Jasper), the highway climbs to **Bow Summit (3)** the highest point on the parkway at 2069 m (6788 ft). A pulloff leads to interpretive exhibits and a lofty viewpoint overlooking Peyto Lake. The lake is named for Bill Peyto, a pioneer outfitter in the Canadian Rockies.

At Kilometre 77 (153 km from Jasper), Saskatchewan River Crossing marks the junction with the David Thompson Highway (Highway 11). It's the major service centre on the parkway. The David Thompson Highway is an access route into the scenic Kootenay Plains west of Rocky Mountain House.

The **Weeping Wall (4)** at Kilometre 117 (125 km from Jasper) is drenched in summer with seeping water from snowmelt high on Cirrus Mountain. In winter, a thick crust of ice builds up and attracts ice climbers who scale the wall using specialized ice axes and spiked footwear (crampons).

Parker Ridge (5) at Kilometre 117 (113 km from Jasper) offers an excellent opportunity to see delicate alpine flowers. It is a short steep hike up the ridge to a panorama of the Saskatchewan Glacier. Stay on the established trail to avoid damaging the fragile vegetation.

The parkway crosses the boundary between Banff and Jasper National parks at **Sunwapata Pass (6)**, at Kilometre 122 (108 km from Jasper). At 2023 m (6676 ft), the pass is the second highest point on the parkway. Mount Columbia, 3747 m (12,294 ft), is the highest peak in Alberta.

For a close look at the **Athabasca Glacier (7)**, stop at the Icefield Centre, at 127 km (103 km from Jasper). The Athabasca Glacier drains part of the **Columbia Icefield (8)**, a 325-square-kilometre area of ice up to 300 metres thick. An interpretive centre provides information about the awesome power of glaciers as they flow gradually down the mountainsides.

A trail leads to the edge of the Athabasca Glacier. Glacier tours are available in specially-designed fat-tired vehicles onto the ice. *Caution is needed on the glacier since hidden crevasses and holes carved by swirling water can be dangerous.*

Snow Dome, 3520 m (11,549 ft), on the northwest edge of the Athabasca Glacier, is a watershed boundary. Water flows from its flanks into three oceans – the Arctic, via the Athabasca and Mackenzie rivers, the Atlantic via the North Saskatchewan River and Hudson's Bay, and the Pacific via the Columbia River.

Sunwapta Lake at the toe of the Athabasca Glacier marks the source of the Sunwapta River. The Icefields Parkway follows the river past the Stutfield Glacier, named for Hugh Stutfield who accompanied Norman Collie during his explorations of the Columbia Icefield from 1898 to 1903.

At Kilometre 175 (55 km from Jasper), a short trail leads to **Sunwapta Falls (9)**. "Sunwapta" is Stoney for turbulent river. The Sunwapta and Chaba rivers meet just west of the falls and form the Athabasca River.

With the help of glaciers, the Athabasca River has formed a broad, forested valley. **Goats and Glaciers Viewpoint (10)**, at Kilometre 191 (39 km from Jasper) offers a panorama of the valley and the glaciers on Mts. Fryatt, Brussels, and Christie. Mountain goats are also readily seen in the area.

Athabasca Falls (11) at Kilometre 199 (31 km from Jasper), provides a picnic spot and a short interpretive trail.

Scenic Drive 9: Kananaskis Trail

The 105 kilometre drive through the heart of Kananaskis Country provides access to popular attractions such as the Nakiska Ski Area and Kananaskis Golf Course.

It also winds through a beautiful stretch of the Front Ranges and crosses the highest driveable pass in the country, Highwood Pass. It is 82 kilometres south of the Trans-Canada Highway and 2227 m (7306 ft) above sea level. Highwood Pass is almost 300 m higher than Bow and Sunwapta summits, the two highest points on the Icefields Parkway.

Kananaskis Trail (Highway 40) heads south from the Trans-Canada Highway, 73 kilometres west of Calgary. The **Barrier Lake Information Centre (1)**, eight kilometres south of the Trans-Canada Highway, provides information on facilities and trail conditions in Kananaskis Country.

The roadway parallels the Kananaskis River, a popular kayaking area for experienced whitewater paddlers. *The flow of the Kananaskis River is controlled by a series of dams to produce hydroelectricity. The information centre can be contacted to find out when water will be released.* There is a **viewpoint (2)** to watch slalom racers just north of the information centre.

Barrier Lake (3) is open for boating and fishing; it is too cold for swimming. **Wasootch Creek (4)**, just south of the reservoir, leads to a popular rock-climbing area.

The **forest research station (5)**

Beavers are extremely active in the Kananaskis Valley with dams and ponds found in several spots alongside Kananaskis Trail (Hwy 40). Mt. Kidd rises in the background.

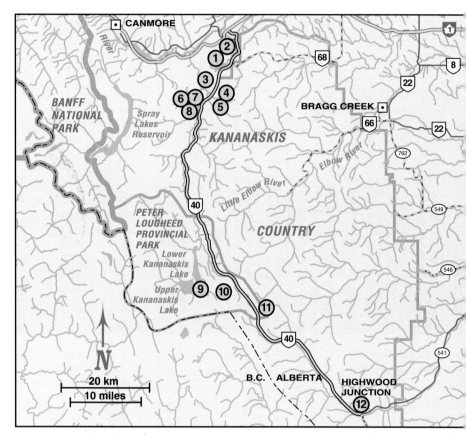

on the east side of the highway was used to house German prisoners during World War II. A short interpretive trail provides information on forest management and the camp's role of the camp during the war.

The most popular recreation facilities in Kananaskis Country are clustered in the Ribbon Creek area. The **Nakiska downhill ski area (6)** was built on the slopes of Mt. Allan for the 1988 Winter Olympics. The peak was named after John Allan, the first professor of geology at the University of Alberta.

Several other peaks in the Kananaskis region were named after military figures and battleships in World War I including *Foch, Black Prince, Indefatigable,* and *Warspite.*

Aside from downhill skiing, Nakiska has served as a unique venue for outdoor concerts by the Calgary Philharmonic Orchestra.

The nearby 36 hole **Kananaskis Country Golf Course (7)** is very popular. Tee times are booked months in advance.

Nearby **Kananaskis Village (8)** has three hotels and a small visitor centre.

On leaving the village, the highway enters **Peter Lougheed Provincial Park (9)**, named for Alberta Premier Peter Lougheed who was instrumental in establishing Kananaskis Country. The 509 square kilometre provincial park encompasses the Upper and Lower Kananaskis lakes, interpretive trails, paved bicycle trails, and a variety of picnic spots and campgrounds. Most of the facilities are reached by road, the **Kananaskis Lakes Trail (10)**.

A gate just south of the Kananaskis Lakes Trail turnoff is used to close a section of the highway from December 1 to June 15, to protect sensitive winter habitat for elk.

The highway begins a long steep climb up to **Highwood Pass (11)**. Ptrarmigan Cirque is a lovely short hike from the top of the pass with a wide variety of alpine flowers on display. The highway descends parallel to the Highwood River. The Kananaskis Trail ends at **Highwood Junction (12)** on the eastern edge of the Rockies.

Motorist can continue east on Spitzee Trail (Highway 541) through the foothills to Longview and High River.

Kananaskis Trail is the loftiest highway in Canada where it crosses the Highwood Pass. The highway is closed in the area of the pass during winter to protect sensitive elk habitat.

Urban Alberta

The best views of Edmonton are found along the banks of the North Saskatchewan River. An extensive park system is located on both sides. The city centre lies north of the river.

Officially, Alberta has 16 cities but Edmonton and Calgary are by far the largest centres in the province, and they have had a rivalry dating back before the province was established in 1905.

There are still some hard feelings in Calgary that its sister city to the north was chosen as the provincial capital. Now, however, the feelings are most heated when it comes to competition between the Edmonton Oilers and Calgary Flames on the ice and the Edmonton Eskimos and Calgary Stampeders on the football field.

There is a good natured rivalry between the two cities but there are also deep feelings of pride in the separate identities of Calgary and Edmonton. Edmonton has developed as a service centre for the province's resource industries, primarily oil and natural gas. Calgary has kept pace as an administrative centre for the same industries. The head offices of many energy companies are based in Calgary.

Both cities have long outgrown their frontier town image and each has gained stature for hosting international events. Calgary

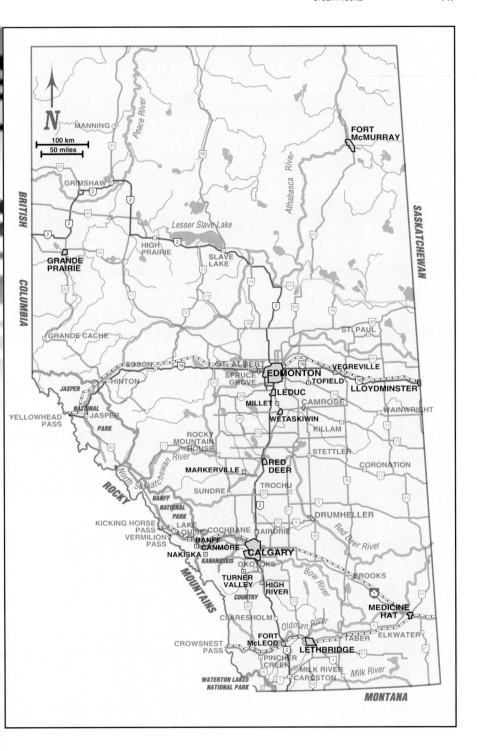

is well known for the 1988 Winter Olympics, and Edmonton is well known for the 1978 Commonwealth Games and the 1983 World University Games.

Although Edmonton and Calgary are the best known cities in Alberta, there are also smaller centres that offer their own rewards.

EDMONTON

Edmonton is looking boldly toward the future and has already billed itself as the Official Host City for the Turn of the Century. Residents of the Alberta capital have good reason to expect significant events as another century approaches.

In 1795, William Tomison established Fort Edmonton on the banks of the North Saskatchewan River. The Hudson's Bay Company trading post was ideally located on the frontier, to attract Cree hunters from the north, who brought in beaver, otter, martin, and fox pelts. From the south, Blackfoot Indians came with buffalo meat, muskrat pelts, and other natural resources.

Fort Edmonton thrived as a commercial centre and profited from another significant event in 1897. The Yukon gold rush was on and fortune seekers were looking for an all-Canadian route to the north. Fort Edmonton was established as a staging point for the long journey into the rugged Klondike. Unfortunately, the actual route was impractical, and most prospectors turned back before getting anywhere close to the goldfields. Many stayed in Edmonton to seek more reliable employment, and by 1904, the city was incorporated with a population of 9000. A year later, it was chosen over Calgary, Banff, and Vegreville as the capital of the new province of Alberta.

Today, with a population over 600,000, Edmonton is again looking for major developments as the turn of the century approaches. In fact, the Official Host program is primarily a way of promoting the city's readiness to stage events from the annual Klondike Days celebration of the gold rush era

John Rowand

The son of a Montreal doctor, John Rowand joined the North West Company as a fur-trader at the age of 14. He made a name for himself overseeing the trading posts in the territory of Saskatchewan before being named chief factor at Edmonton House in 1823.

Rowand made the outpost profitable. He also introduced refinements, including the first glass windows in the territories and a horse-breeding operation.

His success led to an early construction boom in the area that would one day become the capital city of Alberta.

and the eclectic Fringe Theatre Festival to international celebrations.

The city, which was built on the strength of primary resources – first furs and later agriculture and oil – has become much more diversified in recent years. Cultural facilities have been established as well as that mecca of shopping and fantasy – The West Edmonton Mall.

Edmontonians are enthusiastic about sports. The Oilers of the National Hockey League provide the main winter attraction at the Northlands Coliseum, and the Eskimos of the Canadian Football League entertain the fans at Commonwealth Stadium in late summer and fall. The crowds are at their noisiest when the archrivals from Calgary are in town.

There are excellent recreational facilities in Edmonton especially around the scenic natural areas lining the North Saskatchewan River valley.

Edmonton Facts
Population: 605,538
Elevation: 668 metres (2192 ft)

Visitor Information
Information centres are located at the Edmonton Convention Centre, 97th Street and Jasper Avenue; Gateway Park, Highway 2 on the south edge of the city; at the international airport; and on the Yellowhead Highway (Highway 16) on the east and west edges of the city.

Write or phone: Edmonton Convention and Tourism Authority #104, 9797 Jasper Avenue, Ed-

Edmonton has maintained an abundance of parkland particularly along the banks of the North Saskatchewan River. Capital City Recreation Park stretches for 28 km along both sides of the river.

monton AB T5J 1N9(403-988-5455).

Alberta Tourism has a centre for province- wide information at 10155-102nd Street (427-4321).

Name

Fur trader William Tomison named Fort Edmonton after Edmonton, England, birthplace of Sir James Winter Lake, deputy governor of the Hudson's Bay Company.

Highways

Located on the major east-west route, Highway 16 (the Yellowhead Highway) and Highway 2, Alberta's primary north-south route. Edmonton is close to the geographic centre of Alberta 294 kilometres north of Calgary, 514 kilometres north of the U.S. border.

City Streets and Avenues

There are some areas with named roads but most streets and avenues are progressively numbered starting from the southeast corner of the city. Streets run north and south and avenues run east and west.

Transportation and Tours

Air Service: Edmonton International Airport. 29 kilometres south of the city; reached by taxi or shuttle bus.

Edmonton Municipal Airport. just north of the city core; reached by taxi.

Rail Service: Via Rail. Part of the passenger rail line that passes through Toronto, Winnipeg, Saskatoon, Jasper, and Vancouver.

Public Transportation: Edmonton Transit, 100A Street and Jasper Avenue (421-4636), operates both buses and and light rail transit system. Maps and schedules are available at the above address. In summer, the transit system also operates Route 123 on Sundays and holidays, with stops at many of the city's most popular attractions.

Greyhound Bus Lines, 10324 - 103rd Street (421-4211), are part of a national network and offers routes to communities throughout Alberta.

Royal Tours (424-8687) offers sightseeing tours of the city ending at West Edmonton Mall.

Northland Helicopters (447-4534) provides an aerial view of Edmonton with 20 minute flights.

Windship Aviation (438-0111) has early morning and evening hot-air balloon flights.

High Level of Fitness Equipment Ltd. (439-0227) runs half-day and full-day bicycle tours along the river valley.

Landing Trail House Carriage Tours (961-3370) offers rides in horse-drawn carriages.

Rental Cars: Those listed are available at the two airports and downtown. Others are listed in the telephone directory Yellow Pages.

Avis, downtown (424-0223), international airport (890-7596), municipal airport (451-6866). Budget, downtown (428-6155), international airport (890-7560), municipal airport (454-5894). Hertz, downtown (423-3431), international airport (890-4435), municipal airport (452-3616). Tilden, downtown (422-6097), international airport (890-7232), municipal airport (453-3667). Rent-a-Wreck, downtown (423-1755), international airport (434-3468), municipal airport (423-1755).

Media

The *Edmonton Sun* and the *Edmonton Journal* are the two local daily newspapers. There are 18 local AM and FM radio stations. There are local stations for both the CBC and CTV television networks as well as ITV (independent) and two local cable outlets, with cable service providing the major U.S. networks.

Emergencies

Dial 911 for emergency police, fire, ambulance, poison centre, or other medical assistance.

Edmonton Sexual Assault Centre (423-4121).

Suicide Distress Line (424-4252).

The Alberta Legislature Building was completed in 1912 on the former site of Fort Edmonton. Edmonton was chosen as the capital of the new province in 1905, despite competition from rivals including Calgary and Banff.

Pyramids on the prairies contain a variety of floral displays. Three of the four glass structures of the Muttart Conservatory contain representative vegetation from arid, temperate, and tropical regions of the world. The fourth is used for shows that are changed monthly.

Museums, Galleries and Historic Sites

Edmonton is a young city with a strong sense of its heritage. Along with special interest museums for everything from toys to schools to police work, there are fascinat-

ART WALK

The Gallery Walk Association of Edmonton represents seven galleries clustered in the downtown area near Jasper Avenue and 124th Street. Works include those by Native and local artists as well as national and international pieces. Hours are 9:30 am to 5 pm, Tuesday to Saturday. Admission is free. Phone 482-5471 for participating galleries.

ing exhibits for those interested in modern science and the frontiers of space.

The **Provincial Museum and Archives of Alberta**, 12845 - 102nd Avenue (427-1786), is the place to start, to get a view of the earliest days of settlement in the region. Dioramas and exhibits trace the development of the province from the era of dinosaurs through the Ice Age to the arrival of the Natives and the white settlers. Films, lectures, and other special events are scheduled throughout the year. Open year-round Tuesday through Sunday,. 9 am - 8 pm from Victoria Day (late May) to Labour Day (early September), and 9 am to 5 pm the rest of the year.

Fort Edmonton Park, off Whitemud Drive and Fox Drive

(428-2992), focuses on the progress of Fort Edmonton, from its origin as a fur-trading post in the 1800s to the gold rush days of the 1880s and its establishment as the provincial capital, Edmonton, in 1905. "The Fort" shows the city's fur-trading origins along with a recreated Native campsite from the early 19th century. A display called "1885 Street" shows the boom in growth around the time of the Klondike Gold Rush. At "1905 Street," Edmonton is depicted as the capital when Alberta became a province. The city's growth as a business centre during the Roaring Twenties is shown at "1920 Street."

There are plenty of activites on site including wagon rides, pony rides, canoe rides, and a streetcar, as well as a 1919 steam locomotive.

At the **Alberta Railroad Museum**, 24215 - 34th Street NW (472-6229), the glory years of railroading in Western Canada (1877-1950) are celebrated with displays of steam and diesel locomotives, passenger and freight trains, and specialized equipment. Open mid-May to early September, phone for the schedule of dates for trains to run on a two kilometre track. Admission charge.

Canada's Aviation Hall of Fame in the Edmonton Convention Centre, 9797 Jasper Avenue (424-2458), depicts the pioneer days of flying in Canada with artifacts, scale models, and films and videos. Open Mon. to Fri., 10 am to 5 pm; Sat., Sun., and holidays, noon to 5 pm. Admission charge.

Ten Tips for Kids

1. Ride the slides at Wild Waters Aquatic Park, 21515 - 103rd Avenue. Phone 447-3900.
2. Check out the Siberian tigers at the Valley Zoo, 134th Street and Buena Vista Road. Phone 483-5511.
3. Take out a Go Kart at the Whitemud Drive Amusement Park, 7411 - 51st Avenue. Phone 465-1190.
4. Get a glimpse of the past at Fort Edmonton Park. Phone 428-2992.
5. Get a glimpse of the future at Edmonton Space and Science Centre. Phone 451-7722.
6. Take a ride in a model submarine or have a look at a replica of the 500-year-old *Santa Maria* at the West Edmonton Mall.
7. Get acquainted with mother nature at the John Janzen Nature Centre, Whitemud Drive and Fox Drive. Phone 428-7900.
8. Take part in the International Children's Festival in May.
9. Enjoy the great outdoors. There is plenty of parkland especially along the North Saskatchewan River. Phone the River Valley Outdoor Centre, 428-3033, for special events.
10. Visit a museum devoted to toys. Old Strathcona Model and Toy Museum, 8603 - 104th Street, has a fascinating collection of models and toys made entirely of paper. Phone 433-4512.

The Edmonton Space and Science Centre offers a fascinating look at the unverse. The Margaret Zeidler Star Theatre and Devonian Theatre with its four-storey tall IMAX screen provide a wide variety of shows. Look for a moon rock and interactive displays in the exhibition rooms.

Edmonton Art Gallery, #2 Sir Winston Churchill Square, 99th Street and 102A Avenue (422-6223), displays works ranging from historical to contemporary, with more than 30 exhibitions each year. There is a children's gallery and a variety of special events. Open year-round. Mon. to Wed., 10:30 am to 5 pm; Thurs. and Fri., 10:30 am to 8 pm; and Sat., Sun., and holidays, 11 am to 5 pm. Admission charge.

Edmonton Police Museum, 9620 - 103A Avenue (421-2274), is for those interested in the history of law and order in the city. Open Tues.-Sat., 10 am to 3 pm. Free admission.

Edmonton Space and Science Centre, Coronation Park, 11211 - 142nd Street (451-7722), is one of the most sophisticated facilities

of its kind in Canada. The four-storey IMAX movie screen in the Devonian Theatre offers breathtakingly realistic views of life or Earth, while the Margaret Zeidler Star Theatre takes spectators or voyages througout the universe There are interactive displays and intriguing artifacts including a moon rock. Special events include laser light shows, concerts, and live theatre. Open Sun.-Thurs., 10 am to 10 pm; Fri.-Sat., 10 am to 10:30 pm. Closed Mondays. Ad mission charged.

Rutherford House, 11153 Saskatchewan Drive (427-3995), was built in 1911 by A.C. Rutherford Alberta's first premier. Guides in period costume lead tours and offer demonstrations of home life in the early 20th century. There is a tearoom and gift shop. Open daily 10 am to 6 pm, from mid-May to early Sept.; and noon to 5 pm in winter. Admission by donation.

Old Strathcona Model and Toy Museum, 8603 - 104th Street (433-4512), features toys and models made of paper or card. The displays include models of everything from castles and skyscrapers to birds, planes, trains, spaceships, and animals. Victorian era card games are also shown along with reproductions of paper dolls from the 18th and 19th centuries. Open Wed.-Fri., 1 pm to 9 pm; Saturdays, 10 am to 6 pm; and Sundays, 1 to 5 pm.

George Chrunik
Ukrainian Dancer/ Choreographer/ Instructor

I have been a Ukrainian dance instructor for more than 16 years. I started out Ukrainian dancing at the age of nine. Both my parents are Ukrainian and they placed me in the local dance organization in Two Hills, just east of Edmonton. In our area every town has its dance group. That is why there are so many Ukrainian dancers in Alberta; between 3000 and 5000. And most of them are in the northeast.

Ukrainian dance is very, very energetic, very demanding. It can be acrobatic. The males are always doing the squatting steps we call *preshitku*, which people want to see. As a result most people miss the intricate movements by the female dancers in the background, and they are a delight to see. Actually, I think the lady dancers really work harder than the men. But unfortunately it goes unnoticed. In Ukrainian dance there are many kinds of solo movements. But to me, the most important part of the dance is the corps part, to be part of an entire unit.

The costumes in Ukrainian dance come from the customs of the different regions of the Ukraine. There are also certain costumes within a region which show whether a woman is married, a teenager, and so forth. A highlight of my dance career was performing at Lviv in the Ukraine, in front of relatives who still live there.

The most influential annual Ukrainian festival in Alberta is the Pysanka Festival in Vegreville. Dance groups come from all over Canada to perform there. In addition, there are the year-end Ukrainian dancing school concerts that take place on spring weekends in many communities. And there is also the Ukrainian Day at the Ukrainian Cultural Heritage Village east of Edmonton where performers include dancers, singers, choirs, and bands, all from Alberta. The Heritage Village is a model of a pioneer Ukrainian village, with actors portraying aspects of a pioneer's daily life on the prairies.

Western Boot Factory leaves no doubt about the goods for sale inside. The 12 metre tall (40 ft) concrete, steel, and fibreglass landmark cost $250,000 and weighs 35 tonnes.

Admission by donation.

The Telephone Historical Information Centre, 10437 - 83rd Avenue (441-2077), traces the history of the telephone in the city since 1885 with hands-on exhibits and a multimedia show in the Alex Taylor Theatre. Open Mon.-Fri., 10 am to 4 pm; Sat.-Sun. noon to 4 pm.

Ukrainian Canadian Archives and Museum of Alberta, 9543-110th Avenue (424-7580), includes artifacts, photographs, and other materials reflecting the important contribution of Ukrainians to the development of the west. Open May to Sept., Mon.-Sat., 1pm to 4 pm; Oct. to April, Tues.-Sat., 1 pm to 4 pm. Admission by donations.

Ukrainian Museum of Canada, 10611-110th Avenue (483-

5932), displays costumes and other crafts from various regions of the Ukraine. Free admission.

On Stage
The Northern Alberta Jubilee Auditorium, 87th Avenue and 114th Street (427-9622), hosts a variety of touring performance as well as productions by the Edmonton Opera, Edmonton Symphony Orchestra, and the Alberta Ballet Company.

Major concerts are also held in the **Northlands Coliseum** and the **Edmonton Convention Centre**.

Edmonton has a thriving theatrical scene with 13 professional theatre companies in the city. Alternative theatre is alive and well with the enormously popular **Fringe Festival** in August. (see Festivals for details).

The **Citadel Theatre** complex, 99th Street and 101A Avenue (425-1820), features four individual theatres. **Stage Polaris**, 85th Avenue and 101st Street (432-9483), offers family entertainment. The **Nexus Theatre**, McCauley Plaza, 100th Street and Jasper Avenue (429-3625), caters to the lunch hour crowd. Dinner theatre fans have a choice of **Stage West**, 166th Street and 109th Avenue (483-4051), or **Mayfair Dinner Theatre**, 10815 Jasper Avenue (428-8900).

Restaurants and Clubs

Edmonton's cultural diversity is well represented in the wide selection of restaurants offering everything from renowned Alberta beef to French, Ukrainian, and Russian cuisine.

The city has close to 2000 restaurants. Look for variety in the downtown area around the Boardwalk Market, near the art galleries at High Street and 124th Street and in the Old Strathcona Historic Area.

Shopping

Naturally, the West Edmonton Mall is *the* destination for shoppers. (See p. 160).

There are, however, plenty of other areas in Edmonton for browsing on a smaller scale. The Edmonton Centre, Eaton Centre, ManuLife Place, and McCauley Plaza are all within easy access in the downtown core.

The Boardwalk Market, 102nd Avenue and 103rd Street, has an

eclectic collection of shops in two converted warehouses.

High Street and 124th Street is a good area for fashion hunting and browsing art galleries with some book shops and distinctive restaurants thrown in for variety.

Look for specialty shops centred on Strathcona Square, formerly the "Old Post Office," in the Old Strathcona Historic Area, around Whyte Avenue and 105th Street.

The Sporting Life

There's plenty of action for sports fans with four professional teams sharing the limelight.

The *Edmonton Oilers* practically owned the National Hockey League's Stanley Cup when Wayne Gretzky led the team in the 1980s. Even without the Great One, the Oilers continue to rank among the top clubs. They play in the Northlands Coliseum, 118th Avenue and 74th Street (471-2191), from September to May but tickets can be scarce.

Shoppers at the downtown Eaton Centre can take a break for mini-golf. The Pedway network of enclosed pedestrian walkways links most downtown office buildings and shopping centres.

The *Edmonton Eskimos* have also had their share of glory in the Canadian Football League and take to the field from June to November at Commonwealth Stadium, 111th Avenue and Stadium Road (429-2881).

The *Edmonton Trappers*, a farm team for the *California Angels*, play ball from April to September in John Ducey Park, 96th Avenue and 102nd Street (429-2934).

Racing fans can bet on their favorite thoroughbreds in summer and harness racers in the spring and fall at Northlands Park, 112nd Avenue and 74th Street (471-7378).

Festivals

Edmonton is a city of festivals, starting at the stroke of midnight on the first day of the year and peaking in summer with seven major festivals packed into nine colourful weeks.

The **First Night Festival** has become a popular family-oriented, alcohol-free New Year's Eve celebration spread out over 16 downtown venues. There is music, theatre, street performances, and film presentations. The countdown to midnight is focused on Churchill Square with a fireworks display.

In May, events are aimed at the younger set. The **Teen Festival of the Arts** held early in the month. Teenagers show their talents in band competitions, plays, art shows, and literary events. Later in the month, the **Interna-** tional Children's Festival features entertainment from around the world.

The summer begins with the **Jazz City International Festival** and **The Works: a Visual Arts Celebration**, both launched in late June. City clubs and concert halls bring in top acts for 10 days of upbeat entertainment. There are also workshops and free outdoor performances. The entire city turns into an art gallery for the two-week Works festival. Exhibitions are found throughout the city in parks, office buildings, and downtown sidewalks, as well as the regular galleries.

The **Edmonton Street Performers Festival** brightens up the scene for 10 days in mid-July. Magicians, musicians, jugglers, clowns, mimes, and other entertainers perform throughout the city.

Klondike Days are when Edmontonians turn the clock back and celebrate their gold-rush heritage. The 10-day event kicks off with a parade in mid-July. Festivities are focused on the Edmonton Northlands Exhibition Grounds but there are also pancake breakfasts and other events throughout the city. Locals dress the part: women wear turn-of-the-century dance-hall outfits and men are decked out in the finery of the day, or occasionally dressed as prospectors. They get to show off their costumes in the Sunday Promenade. There is also a wild and wet World Championship Sourdough Raft Race on the

North Saskatchewan River.

The city celebrates its ethnic and cultural diversity during the first weekend of August with the **Edmonton Heritage Festival**. There are craft displays, music performances, and demonstrations in more than 40 pavilions throughout William Hawrelak Park.

The following weekend in August is devoted to music from blues to bluegrass. The Edmonton **Folk Music Festival** runs for three days in Gallagher Park.

Edmonton's most distinctive festival turns the city upside down for the last two weeks of August. The **Fringe Theatre** event officially runs for nine days starting in mid-August, but the hottest productions in the alternative theatre extravaganza are usually held over as encores. The festival is a theatre-goer's fantasy. More than 1000 performances of 150 productions in 14 theatres are centred in the Old Strathcona District. Don't look for traditional stage plays in this offbeat collection. It is called Fringe Theatre after all. For advance ticket orders and program details, contact Chinook Theatre, 10329 - 83rd Avenue, Edmonton AB T6E 2C6 (448-9000).

The *Santa Maria* is an exact replica of the ship used by Christopher Columbus on his historic voyage in 1492. It was hand-carved and painted in Vancouver, BC and trucked through the Rocky Mountains before being launched in the West Edmonton Mall.

Mindbender roller coaster is a triple-loop, 14-storey-tall ride in West Edmonton Mall. The 37,160 sq m indoor Fantasyland Amusement Park has 24 rides and attractions.

West Edmonton Mall

This is more than a city unto itself. It could almost be an independent country. The Guiness Book of World Records lists West Edmonton Mall as the largest shopping complex in the world.

The sprawling mall is much more than a huge shopping centre. It may be hard to find much time for browsing a mere fraction of the 800 stores, considering the other diversions spread over 483,000 square metres (5.2 million square feet), or the equivalent of a hundred Canadian football fields. The mall, which cost more than $1 billion to build, stretches from 170th to 178th Street between 87th and 90th Avenue.

Consider the Fantasyland Amusement Park, the world's largest indoor facility of its kind. **The Mindbender**, a roller coaster with a triple loop, stands 14 storeys high. **The Drop of Doom** gives a

---

West Edmonton Mall Facts

• The mall was built in three phases at a total cost of $1.1 billion. The first phase opened in 1981, the second in 1983, and the third in 1985.

• There are over 800 stores, 19 movie theatres, 5 amusement areas, 1 night club, 1 casino, 1 bingo hall, and 1 chapel.

• There's enough parking for 20,000 cars.

• There are 15,000 people employed at the mall.

• There are 58 entrances.

• An 18-hole miniature golf course is patterned after the Pebble Beach Course in California, complete with sand traps and waterholes.

• A time capsule was buried in the Fantasyland Amusement Park and will be opened in September 2033.

• There are 25 sharks in the Sea Life Caverns.

• The replica of the *Santa Maria* was built in Vancouver, British Columbia, and pieces were hauled through the western mountain ranges on flatbed trucks.

• The four submarines were built in Port Moody, British Columbia.

• One water fountain is modelled after a design at the Palace of Versailles in France. Two others are dancing water fountains.

• The bird aviaries contain pheasants, peacocks, African crowned cranes, and a variety of other species.

• The Ice Palace, built at a cost of $5 million is used by the Edmonton Oilers hockey club, a seniors skating club, figure skaters, and the general public (but not all at the same time).

13-storey free-fall ride. There are 24 rides and attractions in all.

You can also strap on a pair of skates and glide around the rink where Wayne Gretzky practised while he was an Edmonton Oiler. The Oilers still periodically use the NHL-sized ice surface for practices throughout the season.

One of the most unique attractions in the mall is the **Deep Sea Adventure** submarine ride. The mall boasts that with four genuine submarines, it has more than the Canadian Navy. The 24-passenger self-propelled submarines are capable of reaching a depth of 46 m (150 ft) but you don't have to go that deep to explore the indoor lake that is 122 m (400ft) long and up to 6 m (20ft) deep. The 35 minute ride offers view of 200 different species of marine life including sharks and sting rays along with an assortment of animated surprises.

If you want to see a more traditional vessel, there is an astonishingly accurate replica of the *Santa Maria*, the ship that carried Columbus to the New World in 1492.

The **Dolphin Lagoon** features four Atlantic bottle-nosed dolphins. Maria, Mavis, Gary, and Howard can jump up to 6 m (18 ft).

For those who want to get into the water themselves, the mall's waterpark provides a year-round spot for surfing, swimming, sliding, and even sunbathing. There is the powerful **Blue Thunder** wave pool along with 22 water slides. **The Twister** and **The Screamer** are both more than 24 metres (80 ft) high. There is an outdoor deck for soaking up the

The West Edmonton Mall's waterpark includes the Blue Thunder Wave Pool and the Twister and Sky Screamer waterslides. The 2 ha (5 acre) enclosed park is kept at a constant 30°C (86°F).

There are displays and artwork throughout the mall including replicas of the crown jewels of Great Britain, as well as rare Ching Dynasty vases, a two-metre high hand-carved Ming Dynasty pagoda, and a model of the Canadian Rockies.

Bourbon Street offers a touch of New Orleans, with 13 dining rooms and bars, and **Europa Boulevard** houses fashion boutiques in an old-world setting.

There is no need to return to reality at the end of the day. Fantasyland Hotel and Resort in the southwest corner of the Mall has 125 theme rooms. Rooms are patterned in a variety of motifs from Roman, Arabian, or Polynesian, to a Victorian Coach or pickup truck. There are about 200 other rooms that are traditional in decor.

The Sourdough Raft Race during Klondike Days pays tribute to the spirit of early prospectors. Fortune hunters who travelled to Edmonton at the turn of the century had little luck in their search for a route to the northern goldfields.

sun in summer and an indoor one with sun lamps for use when the snow is swirling outside.

A variety of admission packages are available for the attractions from all-inclusive day passes to individual ride tickets.

If you do get around to shopping, there are 210 fashion shops for women, 35 for men, 55 for shoes, and 35 for jewelery, along with four major department stores. Shopping hours are 10 am to 9 pm, Monday through Friday; 10 am to 6 pm, Saturday; and noon to 6 pm, Sunday.

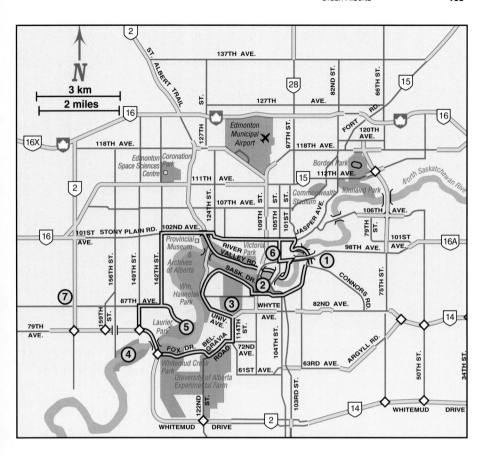

Scenic Drive 10: Edmonton

Edmonton, like most prairie towns and cities, looks best along its river valley. Here trees and shrubs line the banks and birds and wildlife find a home amid the urban landscape.

The most scenic spots in Edmonton, as well as several major attractions, are found along a route that loosely parallels the North Saskatchewan River.

Start at the **Muttart Conservatory (1)** off 98th Avenue and 96A Street. The four glass pyramids are easy to spot. Each structure houses a different floral collection including arid, temperate, and tropical. The fourth pyramid features changing displays. It is a wonderful oasis especially in winter. Phone 428-5226 for information.

Follow Saskatchewan Drive along the south edge of the river. The **High Level Bridge (2)** is one of the most prominent landmarks on the river. The 8000 tonne bridge is 755 metres long (nearly half a mile) and 53 metres above the river. The 1913 structure is held together by 1.4 million riv-

Calgary sparkles under a full moon. Clear skies are common in the rainshadow of the Rocky Mountains. The Calgary Tower once dominated the skyline. Downtown is now crowded with skyscrapers built during successive oil booms.

ets. Since 1980, the bridge has also been used as a manmade waterfall, designed by Edmonton artist Peter Lewis. The taps are turned on for the Great Divide Waterfall during holiday weekends and special events like the Sourdough Raft Race during Klondike Days.

Saskatchewan Drive skirts the edge of the **University of Alberta (3)**. With 30,000 students, it is Canada's second largest English-speaking university.

Head south on University Avenue and 114th Street to Belgravia Road and Fox Drive. **Fort Edmonton Park (4)**, off Whitemud Drive and Fox Drive, is another worthwhile stop with its series of streets depicting different eras of the city's history. Call 428-2992 for information.

The **Valley Zoo (5)**, just across the river at 134th Street and Buena Vista Road, is entertaining and educational. The zoo has expanded beyond its original storybook theme to include more sophisticated exhibits of African wildlife and birds of prey. Phone 483-5511 for information.

Take 142nd Street and 102nd Avenue to either Jasper Avenue for a tour of downtown Edmonton or River Valley Road for views from the north side of the river.

End the tour at the **Alberta Legislature Building (6)**, 109th Street and 97th Avenue. It was opened in 1912 on the original site of the trading fort built by the Hudson's Bay Company. Tours of the legislature and the government greenhouses are available.

A side trip can be added to the **West Edmonton Mall (7)**, which lies between 170th and 178th streets and 87th and 90th avenues.

CALGARY

For most of the year, Alberta's largest city is eager to present itself as a friendly, modern, cosmopolitan centre, more sophisticated than it used to be in its cowtown days. However, if you happen to arrive in early July, be prepared to celebrate Calgary's western heritage. Everyone in the city turns into a 10-day cowpoke for the **Calgary Exhibition and Stampede**. The colorful rodeo and chuckwagon races have been an international symbol for Calgary for more than 70 years.

In 1988, the city staged one of the most elaborate winter sports festivals in history, the Winter Olympics, and inherited impressive facilities, including the **Olympic Saddledome**, now home of the National Hockey League's *Calgary Flames*. As well, there are the ski jumps and the bobsled and luge runs in **Canada Olympic Park**. There is also a speed skating oval at the University of Calgary. International competition is still featured at some venues and there are opportunities to tour the facilities. It is even possible to lace on some speed skates and skate on the oval or hop on the back of a bobsled for a pricey but thrilling ride.

Since its early days, Calgary's economy has been closely tied to of the oil industry. The prosperous times of the late 1970s created a massive building boom. Downtown, skyscrapers were constructed at a staggering rate. As the new buildings went up, city planners designed a network of enclosed pedestrian walkways

A large flame is lit atop the Calgary Tower for special events. The tower was turned into a huge Olympic torch during the 1988 Winter Games. The Olympic Saddledome with its distinctive sloping roof is now home to the *Calgary Flames* of the National Hockey League.

known as **Plus 15s** since they are about 15 feet above ground. It is possible to walk for several blocks through shopping concourses linked to office towers without having to go outdoors, a decided advantage in the depths of winter.

While Calgarians take full advantage of the winter for skiing and other outdoor pursuits, they do enjoy reminders of warmer cli-

Sam Livingston

Sam Livingston was a man who was always looking ahead but it's doubtful he was thinking about his own future when he was asked to decide the fate of a cattle rustler.

Livingston was hauling freight in the 1860s between Fort Macleod, Alberta, and Fort Benton, Montana. Six American vigilantes had caught the rustler and convened a hasty trial. They had a split vote on whether or not the man was guilty and should hang from the nearest tree.

Livingston was enlisted to break the tie and had enough doubt to opt for letting him go. It was almost a fatal mistake. A year later, the same outlaw and his gang trapped Livingston and his crew of freighters. They were close to shooting the men when the leader recognized Livingston as his benefactor and he called off the robbery.

The Irish-born frontiersman travelled a long and winding trail to become Calgary's first settler. He tried his hand in the goldfields of California and British Columbia before crossing the Rockies and becoming a trader and freighter.

He eventually built a trading post west of present-day Calgary and later started farming near the North West Mounted Police fort, the settlement area that grew into Calgary.

Livingston's success in growing oats, vegetables, and even fruit was important in showing others about the vast agricultural potential of the western plains.

mates. The fourth floor of the Toronto Dominion Square (8th Avenue and 3rd Street SW) is an extensive indoor park, **Devonian Gardens** contains 20,000 tropical and local plants representing 138 species, and sculptures and other artwork. Occasional concerts are held there.

The ever-rising skyline has encroached on the lofty domain of the **Calgary Tower**, a 190-metre tall concrete landmark at the foot of Centre Street. The Tower offers a bird's-eye view of the city and mountain panorama to the west, from a revolving restaurant and an observation deck. The Tower took on special significance during the 1988 Winter Games when a rooftop flame was lit with an Olympic torch. The flame is still set ablaze for special occasions.

The prosperity of the oil booms have also led to some magnificent public facilities. The **Calgary Centre for the Performing Arts** is an impressive complex that is home to the Calgary Philharmonic Orchestra, Theatre Calgary, and a variety of other groups. The downtown centre has helped the nightlife at the city's core. There was a time when downtown streets seemed incredibly quiet after the office towers emptied out each day. The Olympic Plaza, Performing Arts Centre and a revitalized Stephen Avenue Mall have all helped keep people downtown after dark.

There are family-oriented leisure centres throughout the city with indoor waterslides, swimming pools equipped with wave-making devices, and a variety of other recreational facilities.

Calgary Facts
Population: 692,885
Elevation: 1049 metres (3341 ft)

Visitor Information
The Calgary Convention and Visitors Bureau operates year round booths at the Burns Building, 237-8th Avenue SE; Canada Olympic Park at Trans-Canada Highway and Bowfort Road; Calgary International Airport, arrivals level; and 6220-16th Avenue NE. A booth is also operated during summers in the South Centre Mall. Phone 262-2766 and 1-800-661-1778.

Alberta Tourism operates a booth in the McDougall Center, 455-6th Street SW. Phone: 1-800-222-6501 within Alberta; 1-800-661-8888 outside Alberta.

Name
James Macleod, Assistant Commissioner with the North West Mounted Police, suggested the name for Fort Calgary in 1875 when the force established an outpost at the junction of the Bow and Elbow Rivers. The fort was likely named after his family's ancestral home, Calgary on Skye. There is some question whether the original Gaelic meaning for Calgary is "clear running water" or "preserved pasture at the harbor."

Bob Edwards

"Now I know what a statesman is. He is a dead politician and what this country needs is more of them."

The editor of the *Calgary Eye Opener* and numerous other Alberta newspapers had no difficulty expressing his opinions when it came to politicians, socialites, and other easy targets for satire.

The feisty and witty Scottish-born journalist started his first newspaper in Wetaskiwin, near Edmonton in 1894. His irreverent style was obvious from the start when he wanted to call the paper the Wetaskiwin Bottling Works but settled on the *Free Lance*.

Edwards wore out his welcome in several small towns including Strathcona and High River partly because of his fondness for alcohol and his tendency to make up society notes.

He started the *Calgary Eye Opener* in 1904 and found greater acceptance for items such as: "The many friends of Mrs. T. Tinglebuster of Elbow Park, who recently underwent an operation for appendicitis, will be glad to learn that she is dead. She was an awful bore."

Edwards didn't hesitate to include himself among the targets and once put his own name in twice when he listed the top three liars in the province. The third was Alberta Premier A. L. Sifton.

Highways
The Trans-Canada Highway (Highway 1) passes through Calgary becoming 16th Avenue North, inside the city limits.

Highway 2, the province's major north-south highway, enters Calgary from the south and becomes Macleod Trail. It becomes Edmonton Trail north of the Bow River.

City Streets and Avenues
Calgary is divided into four quadrants with streets running north and south and avenues running east and west. The streets and avenues are progressively numbered starting from Centre Street and the north-south division at the Bow River. It is important to remember whether an address is in the northwest, northeast, southwest or southeast. Downtown driving can be challenging since streets are mainly one way.

Subdivision addresses can also be confusing since they tend to all sound alike. It is important to know whether you are going to Rundlehill Road, Rundlehill Drive, Rundlehill Way or Rundlehill Place.

Transportation and tours
Air Service: Calgary International Airport is off Barlow Trail north of McKnight Boulevard, about 25 minutes to downtown by taxi or Airporter bus.

Rail Service: Regular passenger service is no longer available through Calgary, but rail sightseeing packages are available. Contact Brewster Gray Line Transportation and Tours (221-8242).

Public Transportation: Calgary Transit (276-7801) operates both buses and Light Rail Transit. Maps and schedules are available from the information centre at 206 - 7th Avenue SW (opposite The Bay).

Greyhound Bus Lines, 850 - 16th Street SW (265-9111), provides transportation to communities throughout Alberta as well as across Canada.

Sightseeing packages are offered by Thanks for the Memories Luxury Tours (292-0300), White Stetson (274-2281), and Brewster Gray Line Transportation and Tours (221-8842 or 1-800-332-1419).

Rental Cars: Avis, downtown (269-6166) and airport (221-1700)

Budget, downtown (263-0505) and airpor t(221-1710)

Hertz, downtown (221-1300) and airport (221-1676)

National, downtown (263-6386) and airport (221-1690)

Thrifty, downtown (262-4400) and airport (221-1961)

Tilden, downtown (263-6386) and airport (221-1690)

Media
The *Calgary Herald* and the *Calgary Sun* newspapers are both published mornings. There are 16 local AM and FM radio stations. And there are outlets for both the CBC and CTV networks in Calgary as well as CFAC (independent). Major US networks and special interest channels are available on cable.

Emergencies
Dial 911 for police, fire, or other emergencies.

Deaf persons emergency
(233-2210)

Poison Centre (670-1414)

Sexual Assault Centre (244-1353)

Suicide Crisis Line (266-0700)

Distress/Drug Centre
(266-1605)

Veterinary care (250-7722)

Museums, Galleries and Historic Sites
The **Glenbow Museum**, 130 - 9th Avenue SE (264-8300), is the major showpiece for art and historic artifacts in the city. It Is the largest museum in Western Canada. The collection represents the eclectic tastes of philanthropist oilman Eric Harvie who gathered treasures from around the world.

Visitors can get a taste of the way of life in a frontier town at Heritage Park in southwest Calgary. Historic buildings from throughout southern Alberta have been moved to the park. Rides are available on a steam engine train, vintage carousel, and paddle-wheeler that cruises the adjacent Glenmore Reservoir.

Olympic Plaza next to Calgary City Hall is used for lunchtime sunbathing in summer and skating in winter. The plaza was the site for medal presentations during the Winter Olympics.

The Glenbow Museum features a comprehensive and entertaining display of western Canadian history from the original Native culture to the arrival of the European explorers, fur traders, North West Mounted Police, settlers, and railway builders. Rockhounds can browse the mineral specimens on the fourth floor. There are also exhibitions displaying the work of regional, national, and international artists. Open year round, 10 am to 6 pm, Tuesday to Sunday. Admission charge.

Alberta's western traditions are brought to life at **Heritage Park**, 14th Street and Heritage Drive SW (255-1182). Historic buildings have been restored and assembled in a frontier town setting, with staff engaged in blacksmithing and other pioneer activivities. A restored steam engine offers short rides on the grounds. There are even restored amusement rides as well as a saloon for the older crowd.

The 200 passgenger S.S. *Moyie* paddlewheeler cruises the adjacent **Glenmore Reservoir**. Open mid-May to mid-October. Admission charge.

There's not much left of the original stockade but **Fort Calgary**, 750 - 9th Avenue SE (290-1875), shows the place where the North West Mounted Police established their outpost in 1875. The outline of the fort is shown with sections of logs. An interpretive centre details the early history of the city and the settlement near where the Bow and Elbow rivers meet. Open daily. Admission by donation.

For a broad view of the universe, **Alberta Science Centre and the Centennial Planetarium**, 7th Avenue and 11th Street SW (221-3700), combines displays of vintage aircraft along with hands-on science exhibits and astronomical shows. The Pleiades Theatre is used for a variety of stage shows and other performances. Open daily from 1 pm to 9 pm, throughout the summer; 1 pm to 9 pm, Wed.-Sun., the rest of the year. Admission charge.

There are also restored aircraft on display at the **Aerospace Museum**, Hangar 10, 64 McTavish Place NE (250-3752). Open 9 am to 4 pm, Mon.-Sat.; noon to 4pm, Sun. Admission charge.

Energeum, 640 - 5th Avenue W (297-4293), provides a look at Alberta's energy-related indus-

tries. Exhibits and models trace the development of coal, electricity, oil, and natural gas. Computers and other interactive displays help tell the story. Open daily, June to Aug.; and weekdays the rest of the year. Admission free.

The **Grain Academy**, in the Round-Up Centre on the Stampede Grounds (263-4594), is a small museum offering a look at one of the province's key agricultural industries. Open weekdays, year-round; and Saturdays, from April to Sept. Admission free.

The **Museum of Movie Art**, 3600 - 21st Street NE (250-7588), contains Hollywood nostalgia, with a collection of 4000 star photographs and film posters. Open Tues. to Sat.

The **Museum of the Regiments**, 4520 Crowchild Trail SW

The Olympic Saddledome cost almost $100 million to build and seats about 20,000. The landmark with the sloping roof is filled to capacity for most National Hockey League games.

(220-7674), traces the history of four Calgary-based regiments – Lord Strathcona's Horse (Royal Canadians), Princess Patricia's Canadian Light Infantry, the King's Own Calgary Regiment, and the Calgary Highlanders. Open year-round.

The **Nickle Arts Museum**, at the University of Calgary (220-7234), displays about 20 exhibitions a year, of national and international artists. Open Tues. to Sun. Admission charge.

There is a wide selection of private specialized galleries

Eric Harvie
Oil man and philanthropist

Calgary lawyer Eric Harvie may have made as much as $100 million in the five years after Leduc #1 signalled the discovery of a vast reserve oil reserve southeast of Edmonton in 1947.

Harvie had made a few modest investments in the Turner Valley oil field in the 1920s and 1930s. He was more ambitious in 1944 when he bought the mineral rights to 200,000 square kilometres (500,000 acres) surrounding Leduc. There are some estimates that the rights that made him a multimillionaire cost less than $5,000. But he quickly began giving millions back to Albertans through a variety of charitable projects.

His most visible project is the vast collection of art and artifacts at the Glenbow Museum and Archives in CalgaryHarvie roamed the world for two decades collecting everything from suits of European armour to Amazonian feathered headdresses. He had a special fondness for western Canadiana. He not only acquired works of art and handicrafts but also commissioned a variety of works.

He used other techniques to expand the collection of the Glenbow Foundation, which he established in 1954. He bought entire museums and sent professional collectors to remote corners of the world in search of objects such as carved ivory from China and ceremonial masks from Africa. In the 1960s, he gave family members and senior staff $1,000 each, and sent them out with the challenge to buy something for the Glenbow. The acquisitions included wood carvings, a collection of animal traps, artifacts from African bushmen, and a prefabricated western pioneer home.

In 1966, the Harvie family turned over the collection along with $5 million to the people of Alberta. Exhibitions were held initially in a former automobile warehouse. The Glenbow Museum was built in 1976 to house the still-expanding collection. In 1979, the Harvie family turned over an additional $20 million worth of art and other collectibles.

throughout the city, for example: Gainsborough Galleries, 509 - 2nd Street SW, western Canadian art; Guild Gallery, 910 - 8th Avenue SW, international art; The Sojourn, Penny Lane, 8th Avenue and 5th Street SW, Inuit art and handcrafts; and Kensington Paperworks, 817 - 17th Avenue SW, Canadian paintings and graphics on paper.

Olympic Venues
Olympic Plaza, 8th Avenue and Macleod Trail, was the setting for medal presentations during the Olympic Games. Now, it's a reflecting pool in summer and skating rink in winter. If you see people staring intently at the sidewalk, don't be alarmed. Olympic organizers raised money by selling commemorative sidewalk bricks, and donors try to find their personalized inscriptions from among thousands.

The **Olympic Saddledome** at Stampede Park (261-0400) is home to the *Calgary Flames* of the National Hockey League. It is used for major concerts. The building itself, with its unique cable suspended roof, is a city landmark.

The Olympic Oval, on the University of Calgary campus (220-7954), was the scene of speed-skating events at the Games and is still used for international competition. Visitors can rent speed skates and try out the 400 metre surface.

McMahon Stadium, adjacent to the University of Calgary (289-

0205) pre-dates the Olympics, but was used for the opening and closing ceremonies. It is used by football teams: *University of Calgary Dinosaurs* and *Calgary Stampeders*.

Canada Olympic Park, on the Trans-Canada Highway on the west edge of the city, is the most prominent Olympic venue. The twin towers for ski jumping stand out on the horizon. Guided tours are available that include a stop at the top of the 90 metre jump. The Olympic Hall of Fame traces the history of the winter games with over 1500 exhibits spread over three floors.

The Olympic park is also available for budding Olympians to get a taste of the winter sports. The park is open for downhill skiing in winter. There are also times throughout the year when it is possible to hitch a very fast ride on a bobsleigh (about $100) or a much less expensive short run on the luge track.

It is far from being an Olympic

Pedestrians shared the sidewalk with sculptures on the Stephen Avenue Mall. "The Conversation" by William McElcheran is an eyecatcher near 1st Street SW.

sport but bungee jumping has also been offered at Canada Olympic Park.

For the sedate, the Naturbahn Teahouse offers panoramic views of the city. In addition to the regular menu, there are three sittings for Sunday brunch.

Ten Tips for Kids

1. Watch the polar bears play at the Calgary Zoo, off Memorial Drive NE. There are 1400 other animals in the zoo which ranks as Canada's second largest. There's also an intriguing display of dinosaurs in the zoo's Prehistoric Park section. The zoo is open year-round. Prehistoric Park is open from late May to mid-Nov. Phone 232-9372.

2. Ride the slides at Bonzai Water Slide Park, Macleod Trail and Heritage Drive SW. Open June-Sept. Phone 255-3426.

3. Try the Mountain Scrambler, Corkscrew Coaster, or Ocean Motion rides at Calaway Park, 10 kilometres west of the city on the Trans- Canada Highway. There are also live performers and a petting farm, as well as a driving range and campground. Open daily from mid-June to early Sept; weekends only, from mid-May to mid-June and from early Sept. to early Oct. Phone 240-3822.

4. Ride the rails at Heritage Park, 1900 Heritage Drive SW. Or you can ride a vintage paddlewheeler or old-fashioned carousel. Watch craftsmen perform traditional skills in an authentic historic setting. Open daily, mid-May to early Sept; weekends from early Sept. to early Oct. Phone 255-1182.

5. Hit the surf at the leisure centres. Pools at the multipurpose leisure centres in the city are equipped with high-powered wave machines. There are also water slides, skating rinks, racquet courts, and other facilities. Open year round.

Family Leisure Centre, 11150 Bonaventure Drive SE (278-7542); Southland Leisure Centre, 19th Street and Southland Drive SE (251-3505); or Village Square Leisure Centre, 2623 - 56 Street NE (280-9714).

6. Hit the beach at Sikome Lake in Fish Creek Provincial Park on the south edge of the city. The artificial lake can be crowded on a hot summer day, but it's a good place to cool off. Fish Creek also has a riding stable, restored ranch house, and plenty of trails for hiking and cycling.

7. Hug the curves at Kart Gardens International, 9555 Barlow Trail NE. Various go-karts and tracks are designed for drivers aged four and up. Open April to Oct. Phone 250-9555.

8. Enjoy twisted fairy tales and other plays for kids, presented by the Loose Moose Theatre Company. Phone 291-5682.

9. Paddle a canoe at the Bowness Lagoon, 48th Avenue and 90th Street NW. There are amusement rides for kids and there are picnic grounds. The lagoon is also a great spot for skating in winter.

10. Take part in the International Children's Festival in late May. Special events are held throughout the city.

For further information, phone 247-5404 (tours), 247-5452 (skiing and snowboarding), 247-5490 (bobsleigh), 247-5490 (luge), and 247-5465 (teahouse).

The two other major Olympic venues are about an hour's drive west of Calgary. **Nakiska**, on Highway 40 in Kananaskis Country, was built for the downhill ski events and has become a popular recreational ski resort. **Canmore Nordic Centre**, on the edge of Canmore, near Banff, was used for the cross-country ski event and the groomed trails are excellent for both recreational skiers and racers.

On Stage
The **Calgary Centre for Performing Arts**, 205 - 8th Avenue SE (294-7444), which opened in 1985, houses three different theatres and the acoustically renowned 1800-seat Jack Singer Concert Hall. The concert hall features the Calgary Philharmonic Orchestra as well as touring artists. Special lunchtime performances are held throughout the summer on the towering Carthy organ, which was built for the centre.

The Max Bell Theatre is the home of Theatre Calgary, and the Alberta Theatre Projects has taken up residence in the Martha Cohen Theatre. The One Yellow Rabbit Theatre Company is in the Secret Theatre.

The **Southern Alberta Jubilee Auditorium**, 1415 - 14th Avenue NW (297-8000), is less intimate than the Jack Singer Concert Hall

The Calgary Tower

On February 19, 1967, construction began on a strange looking space-age structure in the heart of downtown Calgary. When it opened on June 30, 1968, the Calgary Tower stood tall above the downtown skyline and became the most dominant landmark in the city. Since then, the city's skyscrapers have grown up around the tower, but it is still a good spot to see the layout of the city and the panorama of the Rockies to the west.
A few facts:
• The tower is 190.8 metres (626 ft) tall.
• The observation deck is 1228.2 metres (4,030 ft) above sea level.
• It takes 48 seconds to reach the top by elevator.
• There are 762 steps in each of the two staircases for use in emergencies.
• The dining room makes a complete rotation once an hour.
• A rooftop flame turned the tower into a huge torch during the 1988 Winter Olympics and is still used for special occasions.
• Open year round. Phone 266-7171.

Flamingos greet visitors to the Calgary Zoo. The zoo is the second largest in Canada with more than 300 species of animals. Botanical gardens are maintained indoors. Prehistoric Park on the north edge of the zoo grounds contains replicas of dinosaurs.

Lunch Box Theatre, Bow Valley Square, 205 - 5th Avenue SW (265-4292), offers short performances aimed at the lunchtime crowd. The season runs from late Sept. to mid-May.

Pumphouse Theatre, 2140 - 9th Avenue SW (263-0079), features a wide variety of performing arts groups in a unique historic building.

Loose Moose Theatre Company, 2003 McKnight Boulevard NE (291-5682), is credited with starting the innovative Theatresports event pitting improvisational actors in head-to-head competition. Adaptations of fairy tales and other stories are also presented for kids.

Restaurants and Clubs

There was a time when the only choice for diners in Calgary seemed to be whether to have their beef rare, medium or well-done. The city still has an excellent selection of steak houses and prime rib is justly featured on the menus but there are also plenty of other choices from Thai to Californian to French and Italian.

Shopping

Calgary doesn't have anything like the West Edmonton Mall for shoppers and some people are very grateful for that. There are several distinctive shopping districts scattered throughout the city.

Kensington, at 10th Street NW and Kensington Road, is an entertaining blend of cafes and

but can handle larger productions such as *Cats* and *Les Miserables*. The 2713-seat auditorium is also well-suited to medium-sized concerts and ballet. The hall was built to commemorate the 50th anniversary of Alberta becoming a province and opened in 1957. The 231-seat Dr. Betty Mitchell Theatre on the lower level is used for small-scale productions.

Dinner theatre fans have their pick of **Stage West Dinner Theatre** (243-6642), which brings in well-known television performers, or **Glenmore Dinner Theatre** (279-8611), which features local talent.

specialty shops and a few galleries. A British flavour is enhanced by the imported phone booths. The shopping is diverse with a health food store, kitchen supplies, bookstores, the crowded Roasterie coffee bar, and both new and used clothing outlets.

The stretch of 17th Avenue SW between Centre Street and 14th Street has also become a popular specialty area. Most of the activity is focused around 8th Street and 17th Avenue SW. **Mount Royal Village** has nearly 40 upscale shops emphasizing on women's fashion, jewelry, and accessories. There are also several cafés, a bakery specializing in bagels, a wine boutique, and bookstores.

Some of the best shopping is in the heart of **downtown** with several major department stores linked by the Plus-15 walkway system, starting at The Bay at 7th Avenue and 1st Street SW and heading west to Holt Renfrew and the Calgary Eaton Centre and Banker's Hall.

The Sporting Life

With mountains nearby, Calgarians love outdoor recreation. But they also find time to support a wide variety of professional sports, from rodeo and football to motorcycle racing and show jumping.

For personal fitness, there are great drop-in facilities at The Eau Claire YMCA, 101- 3rd Street SW (269-6701), and the Lindsay Park Sports Centre, 2225 Macleod Trail S (233-8393).

The **Calgary Flames** of the National Hockey League have become the biggest draw in the city and games at the Olympic Saddledome are frequently sold out. There is a long waiting list for season tickets, but some seats are available before each game. Phone 261-0475.

The **Calgary Stampeders** of the Canadian Football League rarely fill McMahon Stadium, but still play an entertaining brand of football in summer and fall. Phone 289-0258.

The **Calgary Cannons** of the Triple A Pacific Coast League are a farm team for the Seattle Mariners, and many of the players are on the verge of making it to the big leagues. Phone 284-1111.

The **Calgary 88's** have earned a solid reputation in the young World Basketball League and have attracted growing crowds at the Olympic Saddledome for the past several summers. Phone 264-3865.

Race City Speedway, 114th Avenue and 68th Street SE(236-7223), holds stock car and motorcycle races as well as other special events.

Stampede Park, 14th Avenue and Olympic Way SE (261-0214), is used for thoroughbred and harness racing throughout the year.

Spruce Meadows, on the southwest edge of the city off Marquis of Lorne Trail (254-3200), has become one of the world's best show jumping facilities.

The 57 square kilometre (140

The *Calgary Flames* attract sellout crowds throughout the National Hockey League season. Most seats are held by season's ticket holders but a few hundred tickets go on sale a few days before each game. The rivalry with Edmonton Oilers is one of the best in hockey.

acre) complex with training and breeding facilities has been built as a labor of love by Ron and Marg Southern. There are several major events held each year including The National in early June, the Queen Elizabeth Cup in late June, the North American in early July, and the Masters in early September. Spruce Meadows has grown to offer some of the richest prizes on the international circuit and regularly attracts the world's finest riders and horses.

The Southerns have remained committed to promoting the sport to as wide a spectrum of fans as possible and have kept admission prices quite low. They also welcome visitors free of charge to enjoy the grounds on non-event days.

Festivals

Like many other North American cities, Calgary promotes an alcohol-free start to the New Year with a family-oriented **First Night Festival** (276-5145). The festivities are spread throughout the city with the countdown to midnight focused on the Olympic Plaza.

Calgarians rekindle their fond memories of the Winter Olympics with the **Calgary Winter Festival** (268-2688) in mid-February. Events are held throughout the city with an admission charge for some.

The **Calgary International Children's Festival** (294-7414) stages special attractions aimed at the younger set for six days in late May. There are puppet shows, and performances by musical, theatrical and dance groups.

The week-long **Carribbean Festival** (292-0310) in mid-June has been celebrating Calgary's island connection for over a decade with a carnival parade, reggae music, and dance performances.

The music heats up for a week in late June with the **International Jazz Festival** (268-5203). Clubs and stages throughout the city feature local and international talent.

For 10 days each July, Calgary turns into a wild west town for the **Calgary Exhibition and Stampede** (1-800-661-1260). The rodeo and chuckwagon races run daily on the Stampede grounds along with of live entertainment, agricultural displays, and a midway. Nearly a million visitors pack the grounds each year and there is also plenty of action and entertainment throughout the city.

The **Calgary Folk Festival** (233-0904) brings in groups for a week of performances on Prince's Island and throughout the city.

Calgary is an ideal place for hot- air balloon pilots and they take to the skies at the **Balloon Festival** (240-5800) in mid-September.

Scenic Drive 11: Calgary

It's relatively easy to find the starting point for this drive. The **Calgary Tower (1)** is the city's most distinctive landmark. Start at the foot of the tower at 9th Avenue and Centre Street SW. Head east (it is the only way you can go on 9th Ave.) and you will quickly be out of the downtown core. On the way, you will pass the **Calgary Convention Centre (2)** and **Glenbow Museum (3)**. The **Calgary Centre for the Performing Arts (4)** is next to the Glenbow at Macleod Trail. The **Olympic Plaza**

Spruce Meadows attracts the world's finest equestrians. The show jumping facility on the south edge of Calgary opened in 1975 and now hosts three major events each summer: the National in early June, the Invitational in early July, and the Masters in early September.

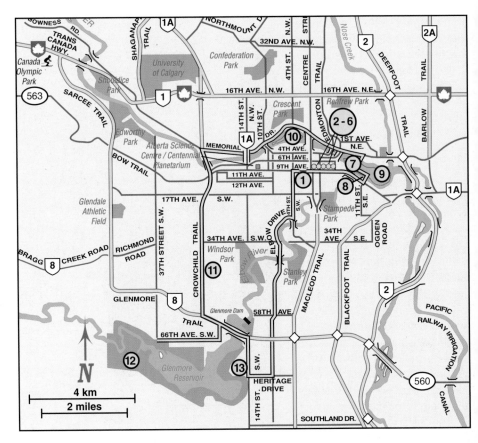

(5) and Calgary's old sandstone **city hall** (6) and new municipal building are on Macleod Trail just north of 9th Avenue.

Keep heading east on 9th Avenue to **Fort Calgary** (7) where the city began. It was here, at the confluence of the Bow and Elbow Rivers, that the North West Mounted Police built the stockade that sparked settlement in the area. The outline of the fort has been re-created with log sections and there is an interpretive centre to trace the city's early history.

The Deane House (8), just across the Elbow River from the fort, was built in 1906 for the post commander and has been restored as a teahouse.

Continue on 9th Avenue through Inglewood, the city's oldest district, and head north at 12th Street. The road winds past the southern boundary of the **Calgary Zoo** (9). The zoo was established in 1920 but has undergone several modernization programs including development of the popular polar bear complex. A prehistoric park has also been created with replicas of many of the dinosaurs that once roamed the area.

Head west on Memorial Drive

back toward downtown. Memorial Drive, lined with tall trees planted in honor of the city's war casualties, follows the Bow River. Just past the Centre Street bridge, there is parking and an overhead walkway for a detour to **Prince's Island Park** (10), a lovely spot for strolling on the edge of downtown.

Continue west on Memorial Drive and head south on Crowchild Trail. At 33rd Avenue S, Crowchild Trail passes Canadian Forces Base Calgary. The **Museum of the Regiments** (11), at 4520 Crowchild Trail SW, provides a look at the city's military traditions.

You can stay on Crowchild until it ends at **Glenmore Park** (12), one of the largest green areas in the city with some great hiking trails in the Weaselhead Flats natural area.

Or, head east on Glenmore Trail off Crowchild Trasil and cross the Glenmore Reservoir, which was built to supply drinking water for the south half of the city. Turn south on 14th Street and head south again to **Heritage Park** (13). The park has restored buildings and exhibits are from the turn of the century.

To return downtown, take Heritage Drive to Elbow Drive and turn north.

You meet the strangest creatures on the pathways of Prince's Island Park. University of Calgary dinosaur mascot greets visitors to the Calgary Folk Festival. Prince's Island can be reached by a pedestrian overpass off Memorial Drive or from the end of 3rd Street SW on the north edge of the downtown core.

Clear skies and wide open spaces around the city make Calgary an ideal spot for hot air balloon rides. Pilots gather for an annual festival in mid-September.

High level bridge stands up to 94 metres above the Oldman River on the west edge of Lethbridge. The Canadian Pacific Railway bridge was completed in 1909 and stretches 1.6 km over the river and coulees. The gold pendulum in the foreground pokes fun at Lethbridge's reputation as a windy city. The fake wind indicator notes that it isn't time to worry until the chain on the ball breaks.

LETHBRIDGE

Population: 60,614

Elevation: 914 metres (2999 ft)

Lethbridge, has been an important transportation and commercial centre for about a century. The windy city traces its roots to a dubious whisky-trading era, but has since become known as an agricultural centre. It is also known for some very distinctive manmade structures.

In 1869, American whisky traders began to head north from Fort Benton, Montana, to exploit the Natives by providing them with firewater. They found a well-protected spot along the banks of the Oldman River and built the notorious Fort Whoop-Up. The whisky traders' reign over the territory lasted only until 1874 when the North West Mounted Police brought law and order. However,there was no showdown in Lethbridge, since the whisky traders cleared out when they heard of the approaching lawmen.

Visitor Information

Brewery Hill Information Centre, 1st Avenue South off Highway 3 on the west edge of the city.

Scenic Drive Information Centre at Scenic Drive and Mayor Magrath Drive (320-1222).

Transportation

Time Air, 2nd floor, 1921 Mayor Magrath Drive (329-0355)

City Transit (320-3885)

Carefree Express (bus), 403 Mayor Magrath Drive S (327-7200)

Emergency and Medical (911)
City police (328-4444)
Royal Canadian Mounted Police
(329-5010)
Ambulance (327-3340)
Lethbridge Regional Hospital,
9th Avenue and 18 Street S
(382-6111)
St. Michael's General Hospital,
9th Avenue and 13 Street S
(382-6400)

Recreation
Bridge Valley Golf Course, on
Highway 3A west of the city
(381-6363)
Henderson Lake Golf Course,
South Parkside Drive
(329-6767)
YMCA, 515 Stafford Drive South
(327-9622)

Lethbridge celebrates its colorful heritage with the week-long **Whoop-Up Days** festivities the first week of August. The activities are focused on the Lethbridge and District Exhibition Grounds/Whoop-Up Park off Parkside Drive on the east edge of the city (328-4491). There is a casino, midway, craft shows, and a rodeo, of course. The park is also used for thoroughbred and quarter-horse racing from July to October as well as special events throughout the year.

However, the **Fort Whoop-Up Interpretive Centre** is on the other side of the city, along the banks of the Oldman River in Indian Battle Park (329-0444). The park itself is named after a clash among the Plains Natives in October 1870.

Displays at the Galt Museum depict the region's heritage with art and artifacts focusing on agriculture, mining, and other historic aspects. The museum building was originally a hospital for miners.

The Crees, aided by Assiniboines, attempted a surprise attack against the Blackfoot, Blood, and Peigan Natives along the river in what is now Lethbridge. The aggressors were almost completely wiped out in what is described as the last of the major intertribal battles among North American Natives. The interpretive centre includes a replica of the original whisky trading post along with an audiovisual presentation on the region's early history. The centre is open from May to early September.

Indian Battle Park has lovely tree-lined pathways on the riverbank and offers an impressive view of one of the city's most notable landmarks, the High Level Bridge. The Canadian Pacific Railway constructed this marvel of engineering in 1909. It is 96 metres high (314 feet) and 1623 metres long (5327 feet).

The **Helen Schuler Coulee Centre**, at the west end of 3rd Avenue South (320-3064), provides information on the nature preserve maintained along the riverbank near the base of the bridge. There are displays on the natural features along with self-guided trails. The Centre is open year-round.

In 1882, Sir Alexander Galt financed a mining venture by founding the North Western Coal and Navigation Company. The company hospital was built in 1885 at the west end of 5th Av-

enue South. The mines are long gone and the hospital has been turned into the **Sir Alexander Galt Museum** (320-3898). The four galleries and 2100 square metres (23,000 sq ft) of display space includes art and artifacts from the city's early days. The museum is open year-round.

The **University of Lethbridge**, on the west side of the Oldman River south of 6th Avenur S (329-2111), is another distinctive landmark in the city. Arthur Erickson designed the building to fit into the deep coulee on the river's edge. The university is an important cultural and entertainment focus for Lethbridge. The Performing Arts Centre includes a recital hall, theatre, and gallery. The gallery collection, which includes an Andy Warhol portrait of Wayne Gretzky, is so extensive, curators have been looking for additional space to show even a fraction of the work.

The **Southern Alberta Art Gallery**, 601 - 3rd Avenue S (327-8770) has display space used for regional, national, and international shows and is open year-round.

Genevieve E. Yates Memorial Centre, 10th Street and 4th Avenue S (320-3845), is used for ballets, operas, concerts, and other performances.

The **Nikka Yuko Japanese Garden**, off Mayor Magrath Drive near 9th Avenue S (328-3511) features another one of Lethbridge's

unique structures. The pavilion and other buildings in the 1600 square metre (4 acre) garden are made of cypress, hand-crafted in Japan and shipped to Canada to celebrate the country's centennial in 1967. The garden is designed as a spot for quiet reflection with pathways, streams, shrubs, and manicured trees. The garden is open from mid-May to late October.

RED DEER

Population: 57,000
Elevation: 860 metres (2822 ft)

Visitor Information

Chamber of Commerce Tourist Information Centre, 3017 Gaetz Avenue (347-4491)

Name

The first Europeans who saw the impressive elk herds grazing beside a picturesque river in central Alberta thought they must be related to the red deer of Scotland. Any relationship between the elk and red deer is a distant one at best, but the name has stuck for both the river and the city that has grown up on its banks.

Sylvan Lake, 15 km west of Red Deer, is one of the most popular water playgrounds in Alberta. The beach can be crowded on hot summer days but there's time for quiet evening walks as well.

Emergency and Medical

Ambulance, fire, police
emergency (911)
Hospital emergency (343-4422)
Royal Canadian Mounted Police
(346-1161)

Recreation

River Bend Golf Course
(343-8311)
Red Deer Recreation Centre
(342-6100)
Canyon Ski Area (346-5588)

Although, the Red Deer River attracted early explorers as a means of transportation, it is now important for conservation and recreation.

Waskasoo Park stretches more than 11 kilometres through the city and encompasses nearly 1000 square kilometres (2500 acres) of riverbank green space. The park system includes many of the city's most popular attractions including Fort Normandeau, Heritage Ranch, River Bend Golf Course, and Kerry Wood Nature Centre. There is a trail network for cycling and strolling in summer and cross-country skiing in winter. "Waskasoo" is the Cree word for elk.

Fort Normandeau, west of Highway 2 off 32nd Street (347-7550), is a replica of the post built during the turbulent era of the Riel Rebellion in the late 1800s. The interpretive centre details the early settlement of the area and its role as a stopping point between Calgary and Edmonton. Open May to Sept.

Heritage Ranch, at the west end of Cronquist Drive, offers trail rides and pond fishing and has a restaurant and picnic area. It is open all year. Phone 347-8058 (ranch) or 347-5595 (restaurant).

Cronquist House Multicultural Centre, off Kerry Wood Drive (345-0055), overlooks the well-stocked Bower Ponds fishing area. The restored 1911 Victorian-style building has a small gallery and shop for ethnic arts and crafts. Lunches and tea served. Open year-round.

Kerry Wood Nature Centre, 63rd Street near 45th Avenue (345-2010), outlines the natural history of the area. The centre, named for a prominent local conservationist and author, provides displays and audiovisual presentations. There are also trails leading to the nearby **Gaetz Lakes Sanctuary**, a Canadian Wildlife Service refuge for migratory birds. Naturalists have recorded 28 species of mammals and 128 species of birds in the marshy area. The centre is open all year.

Red Deer and District Museum, 47th Avenue and 45th Street (343-6844), provides details on the region's history including native and agricultural displays. It is also the starting point for a walking tour of the historic downtown buildings such as the Old Court House built in 1931 (and now a community arts centre), the Saint Luke's Anglican Church, and the Canadian Pacific Railway Station. Open year-round.

Heritage Square, between the museum and the Red Deer Recreation Centre, is a collection of some of the city's historic buildings. The square also includes the Aspelund Laft Hus, a replica of a 17th century Norwegian farm house with a sod roof.

There are two notable modern buildings in Red Deer, designed by two of Canada's leading architects. **St. Mary's Catholic Church**, 39th Street and Mitchell Avenue, is one of the early works by Douglas Cardinal. The exterior lines are flowing and organic. The interior is based on a spider web pattern with the altar at the centre and aisles radiating out from it.

Red Deer College Arts Centre (342-3520), designed by Arthur Erickson, contains rehersal halls and studios as well as the Centre Stage Theatre for student and professional productions.

In mid-July, Red Deer kicks up its heels with **Westerner Days**, an agricultural show that dates back more than 100 years. There is a downtown parade and special events at Westerner Park on the south edge of the city including a rodeo and chuckwagon races, midway, and casino.

The action is all in the sky for the first weekend of August with the **Red Deer International Airshow** (340-2333). The two-day event at Red Deer Industrial Airport has grown steadily over the past decade. Watch for aerial acrobatics, skydivers, high-performance aircraft, and hot-air balloons.

Stephansson House in Markerville, 30 km west of Red Deer, was home of renowned Icelandic poet Stephan Stephansson. The prolific writer, 1853-1927, wrote of his homeland and life in western Canada. Tours of the home are conducted. The Markerville Creamery Museum also shows the influence of Icelandic settlers.

MEDICINE HAT

Population: 43,000
Elevation: 668 metres (2192 ft)

Visitor Information

South East Alberta Travel and Convention Association, Box 605 Medicine Hat, AB T1A 7G5 (527-6422)

Tourist Information Centres on Bomford Crescent and off the Trans-Canada Highway at Southridge Drive (527-6422)

Name

There are two versions of the legend that gave Medicine Hat its unusual name. In the first, a starving Blood Native was approached by a giant serpent that emerged from a hole in the ice in the South Saskatchewan River. The snake demanded that the brave sacrifice his wife in exchange for a Saamis or Medicine Hat that would give him magical powers. The Native reluctantly agreed and went on to become a powerful medicine man.

There is even more tragedy associated with the other tale. According to native lore, the Cree and Blackfoot were battling along the riverbank long ago. The decisive moment came when the Cree Medicine Man fled the battle and lost his headdress, as he escaped across the river. The Cree warriors took it as a bad omen and were massacred when they lay down their weapons.

Aside from its unusual name, the city gained further international recognition in 1907 when Rudyard Kipling came out with his famous description that Medicine Hat had "all hell for a basement." The metaphor was inspired by the vast reserves of natual gas in the region discovered in 1883 by railroad builders who were drilling in search of water.

Transportation

Time Air, Medicine Hat Airport,
Flight information (526-6633),
reservations (1-800-372-9508)
Greyhound Bus Lines (527-4418)
Medicine Hat Transit (529-8214)

Emergency and Medical

Police Emergency (527-4111)
Medicine Hat Police (529-8400)
Royal Canadian Mounted
Police (527-8181)
Fire Alarm (527-5555)
Ambulance (529-8888)
Medicine Hat Regional Hospital,
665 - 5th Street SW (529-8000)

Recreation

YMCA/YWCA, 150 Ash Avenue SE
(527-4426)
Crestwood Recreation Centre,
1701-21st Street SE (529-8320)
Connaught Golf Club (526-0737)
Medicine Hat Golf and Country
Club (527-8086)

Museums and Historic Sites

Based on the natural gas, an, inexpensive source of power, Medicine Hat and its local industry thrived, most notably **Medalta Potteries**. The stoneware manufacturing company took advantage of plentiful Saskatchewan clay to mass-produce high quality china. It was used by the major

railway company hotels in Canada. The china was also extremely popular in homes and restaurants in the 1920s and 1930s, and was used by Canadian forces during World War II. Declining sales forced the company to close in 1954, but Medalta products remain highly prized by collectors.

The downdraft kilns and other remnants of the production facilities have been designated a national historic site. There is a small **Clay Products Interpretive Centre** in the National Porcelain Warehouse, Medalta Avenue Phone 529-1070 for tour information.

For an overall view of the region's history, start at the **Medicine Hat Museum and Art Gallery**, 1302 Bomford Crescent SW.

Phone 527-6266 (museum) or 526-0486 (gallery). There are displays on the roles played by the plains Natives, mounted police, railway builders, ranchers, and industrialists. There is also exhibition space used for the gallery's permanent collection as well as a variety of shows brought in as part of the National Exhibition Centre network. The museum and gallery are open year round.

The city's architecture has been well-preserved and can easily be surveyed in a walking tour of the downtown historic area. **St. Patrick's Catholic Church** with its 51-metre high spires is an impressive landmark on the edge of the South Saskatchewan River. Built in 1913, the church is an example of Gothic Revival architecture.

Clay Products Interpretive Centre in Medicine Hat displays artifacts from the 1930s when Medalta pottery was widely distributed. The prized stoneware was used in hotels and railways across Canada. The kilns and production facilities have been declared a national historic site.

South Saskatchewan River winds through Medicine Hat. An extensive riverbank park system has been maintained.

Other notable buildings include the 1919 **Court House**, and the 1887 **Victorian Ewart-Duggan residence**. The city's heritage has also been kept alive with the installation of 227 vintage street lights powered by natural gas. The city has a free brochure for a self-guided tour of the historic buildings available from the Tourist Centre off the Trans Canada Highway at Southridge Drive (527-6422).

The huge **teepee** near the tourist centre was imported from Calgary after the Winter Olympics. The 65 metre high structure was built to honor the role of natives in the history of southern Alberta.

Medicine Hat's **City Hall** dates back only as far as 1986, but it, too, has become an important landmark, recognized with a national award for architecture.

Festivals, Sports, and Recreation

For live entertainment, the **Cultural Centre, Medicine Hat College**, on College Avenue (529-3882), just off the Trans-Canada Highway, hosts touring shows as well as local talent. There is also a gallery with varying shows of fibres, paintings, ceramics, and other works.

The **Medicine Hat Exhibition and Stampede** (527-1234) enlivens the city for four days in late July. Cowboys have been gathering in "The Hat" since 1887, and the rodeo has grown into the second highest paying in the country, next to the Calgary Stampede. Approximately 100,000 spectators cram into the exhibition and stampede grounds for the rodeo and chuckwagon races. There are also country music performances and agricultural exhibits.

There is Class A baseball throughout the summer at **Athletic Park** (526-0404) where the Medicine Hat Blue Jays play. The farm team for the Toronto Blue Jays takes on teams from Montana, Idaho, and Utah.

Medicine Hat has an extensive riverbank park system with nearly 40 kilometres of trails for strolling, cycling, or skiing. **Echo Dale Park**, eight kilometres west of the city on Highway 3, has a pioneer farm display as well as horse rides. There is also swimming, fishing, and boating on the South Saskatchewan River. In winter, the river is good for skating and ice-fishing.

Police Point Park (529-6225), off Parkview Drive, has about 160 square kilometres (400 acres) of woodland. There are cycling and walking trails as well as an interpretive centre outlining the area's natural and human history.

Riverside Park, along 1st Street and 6th Avenue, is a pleasant downtown green space with formal gardens and a sculpted mural and statue by local artist Jim Marshall. The **Riverside Amusement Park** (529-6812), where the Trans-Canada Highway crosses the South Saskatchewan has 12 water slides, a go-kart track, and mini-golf. It is open weekends from mid-April to mid-June; daily from mid-June to September.

ST. ALBERT

Population: 41,000
Elevation: 672 metres (2205 ft)

This city, on the Sturgeon River northwest of Edmonton, is named after the patron saint of Father Albert Lacombe. Father Lacombe came west in 1852 to help Natives cope with the encroachment of white men. He struggled to combat the ravages of alcoholism and other diseases, like smallpox, that were inflicted on the Natives.

He also worked as a negotiator between the Natives and the railroad builders, as well as between rival nations such as the Blackfoot and the Crees.

Father Lacombe Chapel (427-2022), is on 7th Street and Vital Avenue just west of Highway 2. It was built in 1861. Guided tours of the restored log cabin are available from late May to early September.

Vital Grandin Centre (459-2116), 5th Street and Vital Avenue was the home of Alberta's first Catholic bishop. The church and residence are still in use. A main floor wing has been turned into a museum with the restored living quarters and chapel of Bishop Vital Grandin. Tours are available from late May to early September.

St. Albert Place, on the banks of the Sturgeon River, is a multiple-use area with city hall, a performing arts centre, and riverbank park.

Heavy equipment used to excavate oil-laden soil is shown at the Oil Sands Interpretive Centre in Fort McMurray. Natives once used tar sands to patch their canoes. Modern technology has been developed to extract oil from the sand.

FORT MCMURRAY

Population: 34,000
Elevation: 300 metres (984 ft)

Fort McMurray was founded in 1790 as a fur-trading post and later became an important salt-producing centre but today this northern city is the centre for the development of the massive oil sands plants.

The **Oil Sands Interpretive Centre** (743-7167), Highway 63 and Mackenzie Boulevard, details the elaborate process of extracting oil from the sticky tar sands. It is open year-round.

Tours from the centre can also be arranged to the Syncrude and Suncour plants (791-4336) in July and August.

For a look at the region's early history, visit **Heritage Park** (791-7575) on the banks of the Hangingstone River on Tolen Drive. The reconstructed village includes several historic buildings and a small museum.

GRANDE PRAIRIE

Population: 28,000
Elevation: 655 metres (2149 ft)

This northern city is not only a popular stopping point on the way to the Yukon and Alaska, but s also an agricultural centre for the Peace River region.

The **Pioneer Museum** (532-5482) in Muskoseepi Park displays artifacts from the early development of the region, and is the start for a walking tour of historic buildings, bridges, and other landmarks. The **Grande Prairie Regional College** building on 106th Avenue is a unique design by Alberta architect Douglas Cardinal.

LLOYDMINSTER

Population: 17,000
Elevation: 649 metres (2129 ft)
Lloydminster has a split personality: half the city is in Alberta and the other half is in Saskatchewan. British clergyman Isaac Barr led hundreds of his countrymen to the region in 1903 to start an agricultural settlement. The Barr colonists were ill-prepared for the rigors of the prairie winters and the hardships of homesteading. They persisted with the help of Chaplin G. E. Lloyd, and the grateful settlers named their community after him.

The **Barr Colony Heritage Centre** (825-3726) in Weaver Park displays artifacts from the turn of the century as well as a collection of paintings amassed by regional artist Count Berthold Von Imhoff.

Bud Miller All Seasons Park, 59th Avenue and 29th Street, features wilderness trails and a formal garden and maze. It also has Canada's largest sundial.

Forests and wetlands surrounding Grande Prairie provide important habitat for waterfowl and big game animals. The northern city serves as a gateway to the Alaska Highway.

Recreation

Fly-in lodges at Grist Lake and other northern destinations provide excellent sport fishing opportunities. Lake trout, northern pike, Arctic grayling, and other prized species can be found in the scenic waters.

Alberta has tremendous opportunities for recreation and adventure. The Rocky Mountains are the prime attraction. Some of the world's finest downhill ski resorts are found in Banff, Lake Louise, Jasper, and Kananaskis Country.

In summer, the mountains are a breathtaking setting for hiking, camping, fishing, golfing, canoeing, whitewater rafting, and other outdoor pursuits. There are activities to suit everyone from the extreme challenge of mountain climbing to more relaxing endeavors, such as a leisurely sight-seeing float trip down a quiet stretch of river.

The fun and excitement is not restricted to the mountains, however. More than 200 golf courses are scattered throughout the province. There are some great beaches and lakes for sunbathing and sailing. In both Calgary and Edmonton, there are even pools with man-made surf.

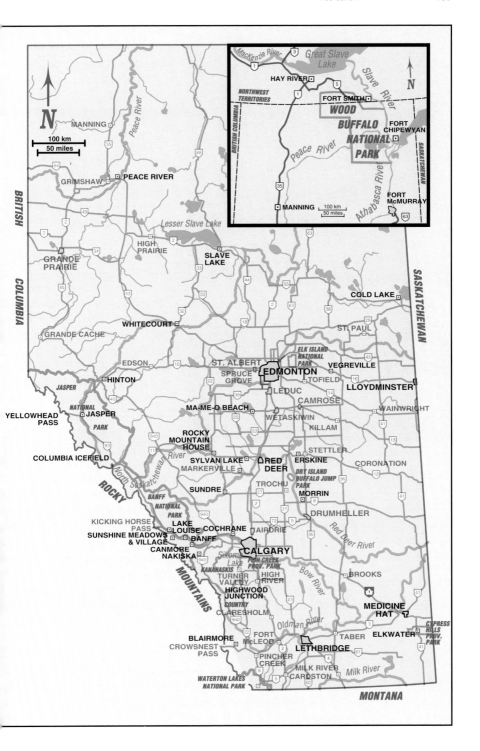

Cyclists on the Icefields Parkway near Bow Lake enjoy views of soaring peaks and sparkling glaciers at a leisurely pace. Tough climbs over high passes are rewarded with long downhills stretches.

Bicycling

The wide, well-paved roads that cross Alberta are well-suited to cyclists. There is nothing like reaching the top of a high mountain pass in the Rockies and then coasting for kilometer after kilometer past pristine lakes and towering peaks. Bikes are also useful for leisurely exploring Calgary and Edmonton. Both cities have extensive pathways along riverbanks. When planning long trips, keep in mind that the winds tend to be from the west.

Mountain bikes have become extremely popular in Alberta and there are several designated trails in the mountain parks that are open to backcountry riding.

Helmets should be worn ever when riding on city bike paths High visibility vests are also a good idea.

SuperGuide recommends:
Banff to Jasper (advanced)
The 290 kilometre ride between Banff and Jasper on the Icefields Parkway is the classic tour in the Rockies and one of the finest scenic routes found anywhere (Scenic Drive 8).

You can see more than 100 glaciers draped over the rugged mountains that line the route. There are picturesque waterfalls and opportunities for short hikes to see delicate wildflowers. One of the best side trips is the stroll up to the alpine meadows on Parker Ridge eight kilometres south of the Columbia Icefield.

Cyclists take three or four days to ride the route one way, and they do not agree on the best direction to travel the parkway. The hill climbs are more gradual if you start at Banff, but there is a greater chance of cycling into a headwind. No matter which way you travel, it takes stamina to tackle the steep climbs up to Bow Summit (2088 m) and Sunwapta Pass (2042 m). But the views are worth it.

There are several campgrounds, inexpensive hostels, and a few hotels along the way. Rocky Mountain Cycle Tours, Box 1978, Canmore AB T0L 0M0 (678-6770).

offers guided tours of the route with accommodation either in campgrounds or hotels. The tour company also offers a tempting one-day trip where guides drop off cyclists at the top of Bow Summit, and then it is a long downhill cruise to Lake Louise.

Kananaskis Trail over the Highwood Pass (intermediate)
It's a 57 kilometre ride on Highway 40 from the Kananaskis Lakes Trail junction to Highwood Junction (Scenic Drive 9). The highway, with wide paved shoulders, climbs gradually for 17 kilome-

Laurie Skreslet
Mountain Guide
First Canadian to
Climb Mt. Everest

What's most important to me is that I am a Mountain Guide – that's what I consider my profession. My secondary work is that I speak about it.

You know that when you're focusing on something serious and it's got all your attention, then the other things drop by the wayside. I've had clients say to me: I've forgotten how enjoyable it is to be hungry again, or thirsty again, or to be sore after a day of activity that was worthwhile. That's why I enjoy guiding, it allows me to put people back in touch with the wilderness. You can't tell people about wilderness – you've got to get the people out there experiencing it, then they will fight for it because they care.

If you are capable physically, I would suggest an overnight guided trip – one or two nights out where you would have to hike into an area that's a bit secluded, to get a sense of the wilderness. In Alberta, the wilderness is close by. It's right outside the city.

It seems to me that the land has memories in it, the land speaks to you, that's what I've been able to find out. No one has ever told me this, but it's what I feel. Deep in the mountains, certain areas, such as the Columbia Icefield, are very energetic. Other areas are very expansive – Head-Smashed-In Buffalo Jump, for example. The area down there around the Oldman River – it's like I go back in time when I'm down there. I climb up some of the bluffs and the hills; I fish, I search through the foothills, and it's peaceful. It's like you're in a time machine going back. If you calm yourself, it's almost like the hills speak to you.

If I had only one day to see Alberta, I'd try to take in two things. One would be the mountains, and the other, one of the prairie areas where you could see the evidence of dinosaurs.

For example, from Calgary you could drive up through the foothills to Canmore in the morning and take a helicopter flight over the Rockies for a short time. In the afternoon you could drive across the prairie to the Tyrrell Museum area.

Campers can pitch tents in popular campgrounds or find solitude by backpacking into wilderness sites.

tres to the 2206 m Highwood Pass. And there is a long gradual descent to Highwood Junction on the other side. There is a wonderful short hike at the pass to Ptarmigan Cirque and its lovely alpine flowers.

Kananaskis Trail highway over Highwood Pass is closed to motor vehicles from December 1 to June 15, to avoid disturbing wintering elk herds. Cyclists can take advantage of the closure in spring and have the road to themselves.

There is also a network of paved bicycle trails between Kananaskis Village and the Ribbon Creek Recreation Area and the Peter Lougheed Provincial Park visitor centre.

Calgary to Cochrane

This 38 kilometre ride (each way) on Highway 1A is a popular day trip with views of the mountains as you ride west (Scenic Drive 5). There is a wild downhill ride to the small town of Cochrane where cyclists frequently stop for ice cream before heading back to Calgary. The Cochrane hill is a steep climb cycling east, but a tail wind often helps. And it is easy enough to walk if cycling gets too difficult. You can also take a rest half way up the hill and watch the hang-gliders taking off from the top.

Edmonton to Miquelon Lake

It is best to take two days round-trip to ride the 60 kilometres out to Miquelon Lake Provincial Park on Highways 14, 21, and 623 (Scenic Drive 3). There is the reward of a sandy beach and cool swim at the end of the day's ride. Reserve a campsite if you are planning to stay overnight, especially on summer weekends. (See Camping.)

Camping

One of the best and most inexpensive ways to see Alberta is with a tent, trailer, or recreational vehicle. There is a range of facilities for camping, from roadside pull-offs (picnic tables, a pump for well water, outhouses) to fully equipped RV parks (hot tubs, satellite TV hookups, and tennis courts).

For a detailed list of campgrounds, Alberta Tourism publishes a free booklet, "Campgrounds in Alberta." Here are the six different types of campgrounds. Overnight fees are priced according to amenities offered.

National Parks

Alberta's national parks – Banff, Jasper, Waterton Lakes, Elk Island, and Wood Buffalo – all have excellent camping facilities. Fees vary depending on the amenities.

Since there are no reservations allowed at the national park campgrounds, it is best to find a spot early in the day during the months of July and August, as well as on weekends from late spring to early autumn.

In addition to the drive-in sites, there are also several camping spots designated for backcountry use. Permits are required, but there is no charge

There is a charge for bringing a motor vehicle into a national park, whether you intend to camp or not. One-day, four-day, and annual passes are available.

Provincial Parks

There are more than 100 campgrounds in the provincial parks and recreation areas scattered throughout Alberta. Some are

A recreational vehicle cruises Moraine Lake Road with stunning vistas of Wenkchemna Peaks. Most campgrounds are equipped to handle tents or recreational vehicles.

small and basic, but others, such as the popular mountain spots in Peter Lougheed Provincial Park, rival anything found in the better known national parks.

Campsites can be reserved at many provincial parks. Contact Alberta Tourism toll free at 1-800-222-6501 (within Alberta) or 1-800-661-8888 (elsewhere in Canada and the US)

Alberta Forest Service

Vast tracts of land along the eastern slopes of the Rockies and foothills are managed by the provincial forest service. There are several spectacular campgrounds along Forestry Trunk Road 940. It is mainly unpaved and stretches for more than a thousand kilometres along the edge of the mountains. Services are basic – no power, water, or sewer hookups. But there are less restrictions about recreational pursuits in the forestry area, and some areas are designed to promote activities such as horseback riding or off-road vehicle driving.

Alberta Transportation and Utilities

The province has 93 roadside campgrounds with basic services. No RV hookups are available but many campgrounds are equipped with sewage disposal facilities.

Municipal and Regional Campgrounds

Many Alberta towns and service groups operate small campgrounds adjacent to community parks. Fees are generally low and there is often a golf course, pool, or other recreation facility nearby.

Private Campgrounds

There is a wide range of services offered at the more than 200 privately operated campgrounds in the province. The Alberta Private Campground Owners Recreational Society (APCORS), Box 26, Erskine AB T0C 1G0 (742-5661), represents 27 operators and can be contacted to arrange reservations.

SuperGuide recommends:

Mount Kidd RV Park, in Kananaskis Country has just about everything you could ask for. There is a hot tub and sauna, tennis court, wading pool, and hookups include satellite TV. The 229 sites are surrounded by spectacular peaks and located next to the 36-hole Kananaskis Country Golf Course. The RV Park is open year-round and is privately operated. Reservations: P.O. Box 100, Exshaw AB T0L 2C0 (591-7700).

Tunnel Mountain Campground, in Banff National Park, is crowded, but it is near Banff. There are more than 1000 sites in three adjacent campgrounds.

Two Jack Lake, is in Banff National Park, 13 kilometres from Banff on Lake Minnewanka Road, and it is quieter.

Johnston Canyon, is halfway between Banff and Lake Louise, and is a nice spot, close to a lovely short trail into the canyon.

Columbia Icefield Campground is in Jasper National Park, halfway up the Icefields Parkway. It is in a breathtaking setting, but can get chilly at night, even in midsummer.

Whistlers is the major campground for visitors to the town of Jasper.

Canoeing and Kayaking

Canoes have been popular with visitors to Alberta since the fur-trading journeys of French-Canadian voyageurs. The province's rivers and lakes are ideal for modern paddlers. You can find everything from a leisurely float on the lower Red Deer River through the stark badlands surrounding Drumheller to whitewater challenges on the Kananaskis River.

All paddlers are required to use government-approved flotation jackets. Wetsuits are recommended for whitewater paddling.

Rivers in Alberta peak in June although some rivers such as the Kananaskis are controlled by power dams. Flow information is provided by phoning toll free 1-800-661-8917.

Two of Alberta's major rivers provide a unique way to tour the province's largest cities. The North Saskatchewan River flows through Edmonton and the Bow River winds through Calgary.

There are several places to rent canoes for short sightseeing outings such as Lake Louise, Cameron Lake in Waterton National Park, and a quiet stretch of the Bow River upstream from the Banff Avenue bridge in Banff.

Red Deer River offers leisurely paddling through prairies. The river is much wilder in the foothills and mountains, where kayakers and rafters challenge the whitewater.

Fishermen try their luck at Lundbreck Falls near the Crowsnest Pass. The Crowsnest River tumbles over a 12 metre drop as it flows eastward.

However, most canoeing in the province involves river travel and should only be undertaken by experienced paddlers or those who travel with qualified guides. Rivers in the province are fed by glaciers and are cool especially in the mountains and foothills. The Peace and Athabasca rivers are both well-suited to multi-day expeditions through the northern wilderness.

SuperGuide recommends:
Bow River
Banff to Canmore (intermediate)
This 21 kilometre, half-day trip offers a breathtaking view of Mount Rundle. There are some small rapids and a few places where sweepers must be avoided. Look for deer and elk along the way.

Calgary (novice)
Further east, the Bow River provides a unique way to see Calgary for those with basic skills. There is excellent fishing on the Bow River downstream from Calgary.

Red Deer River
Dry Island Buffalo Jump Park to Morrin Bridge (novice)
This 37 kilometre day trip is ideal for novice paddlers. It winds gently through the prairies and provides a view of the beginning of the badlands and its distinctive hoodoos. Watch for great blue heron, large graceful birds that patrol the river for fish.

Mountain Aire Lodge
The Upper Red Deer River near the Mountain Aire Lodge, west of Sundre, offers several whitewater

stretches favored by advanced canoeists and kayakers.

Kananaskis River (expert)
The Kananaskis is a wild mountain river ideal for whitewater enthusiasts. A slalom site has been developed for kayakers. The river is controlled by a power dam and paddlers should check with TransAlta Utilities or the nearby Barrier Lake Information Centre for flow rates.

North Saskatchewan River at Rocky Mountain House (guided)
Voyageur Adventure Tours offers a unique way to paddle the scenic North Saskatchewan. Half-day and full-day excursions are available in 10-passenger voyageur canoes. Guides provide details

about the region's fur-trading history. Contact the tour company at 4808 - 63 Street, Rocky Mountain House AB T0M 1T2 (845-7878).

Fishing

Alberta is an angler's paradise with world-renowned flyfishing on the Bow, Crowsnest, and other southern rivers. There are many stocked lakes and ponds in the mountains and prairies, and a selection of fly-in lodges across the north.

There are two basic fishing licences required, depending on your destination. A national park license is needed for fishing in Banff, Jasper, Waterton Lakes, Wood Buffalo, and Elk Island national parks. Permits are available from national park offices and

Kananaskis River offers challenging rapids for kayakers. National championships are held on a course near Barrier Lake Information Centre in Kananaskis Country. The information centre also has information on changes in river flow which is controlled by a power dam.

T5K 2G6, or from regional fish and wildlife offices. There are mandatory catch and release requirements in some regions, and the practice is encouraged throughout the province to protect fish populations.

The guide includes a list of about 150 lakes and ponds that are stocked with a variety of trout, grayling, whitefish, perch, or walleye.

Regional fishing conditions are available on hotlines operated by The Fishin' Hole in Edmonton (475-7777) and Country Pleasures in Calgary (278-1815).

SuperGuide recommends:
Bow River downstream from Calgary. Close to a dozen guides offer float trips on this renowned flyfishing river. Rates range from $200 to $300 a day. See Listings, for members of the Bow River Angling Outfitters Association.

Alpine forget-me-nots are found in subalpine and alpine meadows of the Rocky Mountains. The delicate pale purple or flowers have bright yellow centres.

some sporting good shops and concessionaires.

A provincial license is needed for fishing in the rest of the province except for children under 16. Special licences are required for sturgeon and fishing in trophy waters. Licences are available from provincial fish and wildlife offices, some sporting good outlets, hardware stores, and tackle shops.

Fishing regulations are available in "Alberta Guide to Sportfishing" (free), available from Fish and Wildlife Division, Main Floor, North Tower, Petroleum Plaza, 9945 - 108th Street, Edmonton AB

Lake Minnewanka, Banff National Park, has excellent trout fishing. Boats are available for rent. Guide services are offered.

Maligne Lake, Jasper National Park, is a prime spot for rainbow trout. Boats are available for rent. Guide services are offered.

Lakes of Northern Alberta. Several outfitters offer fly-in trips with an abundance of pike, whitefish, walleye, and other trophy fish. See Listings for members of the Alberta Fly-in Fishing Lodge Operators Association.

The largest rainbow trout caught in Alberta was 9.2 kilograms (20 lb 4 oz) taken from Maligne Lake in 1980. The record for lake trout is 23.8 kilometres (52 lb 8 oz) caught in Cold Lake in 1929. The record for northern pike is 17.2 kilograms (38 lb) caught in Keho Lake in 1983.

Golf

There are more than 200 golf courses in Alberta.

Three of Canada's finest courses are nestled in the mountains – Banff Springs, Jasper Park Lodge, and Kananaskis.

Wolf Creek, in Ponoka (near Red Deer) is also ranked as one of the best in the country.

Both Calgary and Edmonton have many courses but it is difficult to get tee times, especially on weekends. It is often easier to play on one of the smaller community courses.

Gliding

The puffy white clouds of spring mark the beginning of the prime season for hang gliders. Much of the hang gliding in Alberta is focused on a windswept hill overlooking Cochrane, northwest of Calgary. Several record-setting flights have been launched from this hill. Instruction is available from Muller Hang Gliding (932-6760) in Cochrane.

The hill is also used to teach the new sport of paragliding, which involves using a specially designed parachute to take flight from steep hillsides. Contact: Par-agliding Canada Inc. (932-4653).

Strong thermal air currents in Alberta are also ideal for traditional glider pilots, and many of the small municipal airports are used by local gliding clubs.

Hiking

Hiking in Alberta can be as easy or as strenuous as you want to make it. For those with strong legs and stamina, there are hundreds of kilometres of trails through the national and provincial parks and the designated wilderness areas. Those who just want to stretch their legs can enjoy several short strolls where the paths are easy, and the views are magnificent.

Staff at the national and provincial parks can provide information for those who want to head out on overnight adventures.

Hikers who are interested in strenuous guided hikes can contact Skyline Hikers of the Canadian Rockies, P.O. Box 3514, Postal Station B, Calgary AB T2M4M2. This nonprofit group organizes six-day outings in the Rockies from a base camp where meals and tent accommodation are provided.

For those who want a quick trip to the high country, there are several heli-hiking operators based primarily in Canmore. Trips vary from short sightseeing flights to mountaintop picnics to alpine hikes in Kananaskis Country. Longer customized tours are also available.

You don't even have to leave

Mountain Goat

Mountain goats and bighorn sheep share a fondness for steep terrain. Goats can be distinguished from sheep by their pure white shaggy coats. Bighorn sheep are dark to greyish brown.

Adult males, billies, stand a little more than one metre at the shoulder and weigh from 70 to 135 kilograms. Females, nannies, are slightly smaller. Both male and females have black horns that are curved slightly to the back, and the horns on the nannies are a little shorter. All adults have tufts of chin hair that form a distinctive beard.

Mountain goats have an amazing ability to climb onto extreme slopes to avoid predators, to find clumps of grass or bushes, or to reach mineral licks. They can negotiate narrow ledges with the help of hooves that are well-suited to mountain climbing. The bottom of the hoof is a soft pad surrounded by a hard shell. And goats have the ability to get traction on rock surfaces with the pads, or to lever themselves with the hard shell.

Goats are usually found well above timberline, although they venture down to lower elevations to get salt and other treats at natural mineral licks.

Mountain goats can escape most predators by seeking high ground. They are extremely alert to danger from below and occasionally fall prey to attacks from above by cougars and eagles. Eagles attempt to knock young goats off balance and feed on the carcasses after they fall.

the cities to get out for a scenic stroll. Edmonton, Calgary, and smaller cities such as Medicine Hat, Lethbridge, and Red Deer have all developed riverbank pathways that offer pleasant escapes from the concrete and pavement.

SuperGuide recommends:
SHORT HIKES
Banff National Park
Sunshine Meadows is a spectacular spot for viewing alpine wildflowers. There is a fee to ride the gondola up to the ski area in summer, but it quickly takes you above treeline to scenic hiking territory. Short interpretive trails wind around Rock Isle, Laryx, and Grizzly lakes. They will also take you to lofty viewpoints and through colorful meadows. Special care is needed to avoid disturbing the fragile environment.

Parker Ridge (Scenic Drive 8), on the Icefields Parkway, 41 kilometre north of Saskatchewan River Crossing, is a readily accessible alpine meadow. There are a series of switchbacks on a short, steep trail up to the ridge. But the 250-metre elevation gain is worth it to see the lovely alpine flowers and a stunning view of the Saskatchewan Glacier.

The Bankhead Trail is just 7.4 kilometres from the town of Banff on the Lake Minnewanka Road. The trail winds through the sparse remains of an abandoned coal mining town.

Lake Louise Lakeside (Scenic Drive 7), beside the Chateau Lake

Louise, is a level path that skirts the picturesque lake. There are fine views of the chateau and the Victoria Glacier. For those who want to hike there is a four kilometre trail (one-way) that rises from the edge of Lake Louise to Lake Agnes where a rustic teahouse provides snacks.

Larch Valley (Scenic Drive 7), reached from the end of Moraine Lake Road, is another short steep hike, particularly rewarding in the autumn when the larch trees turn a brilliant gold.

Jasper National Park

Maligne Canyon, on the Yellowhead Highway just east of Jasper townsite, is an extremely popular trail. The path winds along the edge of a narrow canyon with views of the roaring Maligne River.

There are also several scenic trails on the edge of Maligne Lake southwest of the townsite.

Valley of the Five Lakes, off the Icefields Parkway and 9 kilometres south of the Yellowhead Highway junction, contains a series of small, brilliant green lakes.

Mt. Edith Cavell, off Highway 93A and south of Jasper townsite, has a pleasant short interpretive trail near the hanging Angel Glacier. There is also a 3.8 kilometre trail up to Cavell Meadows to see alpine wildflowers and an even better view of the Angel Glacier.

Lac Beauvert, beside Jasper Park Lodge, offers a lakeside stroll with the opportunity to observe elk.

There are also pleasant lakeside walks beside nearby Lakes Edith and Annette.

Hikers pause to enjoy the wildflower display along the trail to Helen Lake in Banff National Park.

A short steep hike up the Bear's Hump offers one of the best views in Waterton Lakes National Park. The peak behind the park information bureau overlooks Upper Waterton Lake, which extends across the United States border into Montana.

Waterton Lakes National Park
The Bear's Hump, just west of the park information office, is a short steep climb, but there is a terrific view of the townsite and the lakes southward to Montana.

Cameron Lake, 16 kilometres up the Akamina Parkway, is a popular day-use area. A level trail circles the west side of the lake. Hikers with keen eyes may be able to spot grizzlies off on a distant scree slope at the south end of the lake.

Waterton Lakeshore Trail along the west edge of the Upper Waterton Lake is relatively level.

Ambitious hikers can walk 13 kilometers to Goat Haunt, Montana. National park staff lead interpretive hikes on this international route. It is also possible to take one of the regularly scheduled boat trips between Waterton Park Townsite and Goat Haunt, and combine it with a hike.

Kananaskis Country
Ptarmigan Cirque, from the Highwood Pass parking lot, is a lovely short hike that can be combined with a scenic drive along Kananaskis Trail (Highway 40). There are beautiful alpine flowers and fine views of the Kananaskis Range.

Canadian Mount Everest Expedition Trail, between the Upper and Lower Kananaskis lakes in Peter Lougheed Provincial Park, was named in honor of the Canadian expedition ascent of Mt. Everest in 1982. The trail provides a vantage point for the scenic lakes created by power dams in the Kananaskis Valley.

Peter Lougheed Provincial Park has a variety of other short interpretive trails and paved pathways suitable for wheelchairs. Self-guiding brochures are available at the park information centre.

Bears: If You Go Into the Woods Today ...

Your chances of running into a black or grizzly bear in the mountain parks are slim. And it is much less likely that the encounter will result in an attack. A few basic precautions will help keep you and the bears a safe distance apart:

• Before going into the backcountry, check with park staff about recent bear activity. Watch for notices at the trailheads.

• Keep your campsite clean. Whether you are in a campground or in the backcountry, do not leave food, garbage, or dirty dishes out in the open. Store food and utensils in your car trunk or if you are in the backcountry, hang a storage bag from a tree well away from your tent.

• Never attempt to feed a bear or approach one on the roadside to get a good photograph. Use a telephoto lens and stay in your vehicle.

• If you see a bear cub, leave the area immediately. Female black bears and grizzlies with cubs are particularly dangerous.

• Use extreme caution if you come across a dead animal. A bear may be feeding on it.

• Watch for signs of bear activities such as fresh diggings or scats.

• Keep dogs under strict control. They can easily disturb a bear and then lead it back to you.

• Bells and noisemakers or simply a steady chatter on the trail will alert bears that you are in the area and reduce the chance of surprising them.

• Anglers should be careful when walking alongside rivers or lakes since bears are often attracted to the same area. Do not clean fish or store bait and fish near camp.

• In most cases, bears will avoid humans. If a bear approaches, try to stay calm and move slowly away. It's almost impossible to outrun a bear. You can drop something as you retreat to distract the bear.

• Attempt to determine if it's a black or grizzly bear. The color is not a very reliable indicator. Grizzlies have a distinctive hump on their shoulders and are much larger than black bears. You may find refuge by climbing a tree, but it's not a guarantee since some bears will climb after you.

• Grizzlies will occasionally make bluff charges. If it's the real thing, curl up on the ground and try to protect your vital organs and clasp your hands over the back of your neck. Play dead.

Hunting

Alberta offers many hunting opportunities, governed by strict regulations to ensure well-being of the species. Hunting is not permitted in the national parks.

Bird hunters have their choice

White-tailed Ptarmigan

The white-tailed ptarmigan is a camouflage expert. In summer, its feathers are a mottled grey, white, brown, and black to match the background of its mountain habitat. As winter approaches, it molts, shedding the dark feathers in favor of white plumage to blend in with the snow.

Ptarmigan adults are about 25 centimetres in length. They nest on the ground and seldom fly. They are residents of the upper subalpine and alpine regions of the mountains.

Ptarmigan commonly startle hikers and cross-country skiers in the backcountry. The birds are difficult to see because they lie perfectly still when humans or predators are near. If you inadvertently approach their hiding spot, they will wait until the last moment before flapping their wings and clucking as they escape.

of waterfowl and upland game birds. The most common birds hunted in the province are ducks, geese, Hungarian partridge, ruffed grouse, and ring-necked pheasant.

Big game animals range from deer to woodland caribou and grizzlies.

Detailed hunting regulations are available from Alberta Fish and Wildlife, Main Floor, North Tower, Petroleum Plaza, 9945 - 108th Street, Edmonton AB T5K 2G6.

Horse Riding

Horsebackriding is ideal for experiencing the wilderness.Riding is available on the prairies and foothills as well as throughout the mountains. For opportunities to enjoy trail rides and the guest ranches, see Listings.

Motorcycling

The Alberta Forest Service has vast tracts of land available for off-highway motorcycle riding and all-terrain vehicles.

Mountain Park, 75 kilometres southeast of Hinton, has a loading ramp for all-terrain vehicles. The Ghost District on Highway 940 northwest of Cochrane has designated trails.

The McLean Creek area of Kananaskis Country, southwest of Calgary also has designated trails.

Mountaineering

The Rockies readily stir the adventurous spirit in many mountain visitors, but special care is needed for anyone who wants to venture onto the steep slopes.

Fortunately, there are plenty of skilled mountaineers who offer guided ascents and instruction. Contact:

Banff Alpine Guides, Box 1025,
    Banff AB T0L 0C0
Canadian School of
    Mountaineering, Box 723,
    Canmore AB T0L 0M0
Jasper Climbing Schools and
    Guide Service, Box 452, Jasper
    AB T0E 1E0
Lac Des Arcs Climbing School,
    1116 - 19th Avenue NW,
    Calgary AB T2M 0Z9
Yamnuska Inc., Box 1920 TA,
    Canmore AB T0L 0M0

Watersports

Alberta may be a landlocked province but there are refreshing lakes, sandy beaches, and good places for boating throughout the province.

Waves

Engineers and construction crews have also been busy helping mother nature to create water playgrounds. There are even swimming pools in Calgary and Edmonton with wave machines to make up for the absence of ocean-front property in the province and they provide year-round body surfing.

The "Blue Thunder" at West Edmonton Mall's waterpark is billed as the world's largest indoor-wave pool. There is a second wave pool in Edmonton at the Mill Woods Recreation Centre.

In Calgary, regional leisure centres such as Village Square and Southland are equipped with wave machines. The pools can accommodate up to 700 people. High-powered fans are adapted to produce waves of 1.5 metres or more.

Waterslides

There are also indoor and outdoor waterslides throughout the

An ice-climber scales the frozen surface of the Weeping Wall, along the Icefields Parkway. Mountaineers climb year-round in the Canadian Rockies. Ice-climbers use sharp hand-tools and spiked crampons on their boots to grip steep snow and ice.

Top: Sightseers take in the scenery on a leisurely float trip down the Bow River between Banff and Canmore. Raft tour operators offer a variety of trips on quiet water as well as thrilling whitewater.

Bottom: Outdoor waterslides are great for cooling off in summer. Indoor slides are open year-round with several found in both Calgary and Edmonton.

province. For summer fun, try the Wild Rapids Water Slide in Sylvan Lake (Lakseshore Drive), the Bonzai Water Slide Park in Calgary (Macleod Trail at Heritage Drive), Wild Water Aquatic Park in Edmonton (Highway 16 at Winterburn Road), and Riverside Amusement Park in Medicine Hat (Trans-Canada Highway).

The West Edmonton Mall has two renowned waterslide towers, "Twister" and "Screamer" for year-round thrills. The Douglas Fir Resort in Banff also has an indoor slide, as do the leisure centres in Calgary.

SuperGuide recommends:
Chestermere Lake (Highway 1A east of Calgary) This reservoir is popular with both waterskiers and windsurfers.

Elkwater Lake, Cypress Hills Provincial Park It is a welcome oasis southeast of Medicine Hat. There is a nice beach and swimming area with a jump for adventurous waterskiers.

Sylvan Lake (west of Red Deer) The water is warm and there are fine beaches, but it can be crowded in midsummer.

Sikome Lake, Fish Creek Provincial Park This man-made lake in south Calgary can be nearly unbearably crowded when a heat wave hits the city but it is refreshing if you can arrive early in the day.

Waterton Lakes, Waterton Lakes National Park They are too cool for swimming, but the windsurfing is fine. Emerald Bay (by the townsite) has a sunken boat for scuba divers to explore.

Lesser Slave Lake Alberta's third largest lake, 250 kilometres north of Edmonton has warm water in summer and some of the longest and best beaches in the province.

Ma-Me-O Beach Provincial Park, Pigeon Lake (west of Wetaskawin) The beach is small but ideal for sunbathing, swimming, and windsurfing.

Whitewater Rafting

The churning rivers that spill out of the mountains provide wild rides and incredible scenery for those who don't mind getting a little wet; well, maybe more than a little wet. In fact, most operators provide wet suits to keep you warm despite the crashing waves and the occasional water fights that break out on group tours.

A sailboarder prepares to take to the water on Pigeon Lake. Westerly winds make Alberta lakes and reservoirs prime spots for sailboarding. Wetsuits and drysuits are needed in most areas since the water is often too cold for comfort.

There are also quieter tours for those who just want to float down a smooth stretch of water and take in the views on the Bow River near Banff and the Athabasca River near Jasper.

Coyote

Coyotes are found throughout Alberta and are members of the wild dog family. An average male coyote weighs about 14 kilograms and measures 1.2 metres from its nose to the tip of its bushy tail. Females are slightly smaller. A coyote resembles both a German shepherd dog and a fox. Coyotes are greyish brown, greyer on top and browner on the sides, with light-coloured bellies. Rodents make up the bulk of their diet, although they will scavenge for food and will occasionally band together to hunt larger mammals. The typical home range for a coyote is 25 to 40 square kilometres. They are most often seen alone or in pairs.

Coyotes are wary of humans and will usually keep their distance. There have been coyote attacks in recent years, usually coyotes scavenging for food. One of the most serious incidents involved a young child. Caution is advised; coyotes are unpredictable.

Raft Trips

For short float trips, contact:

Rocky Mountain Raft Tours, Box 1771, Banff AB T0L 0C0
Bow River

Jasper Raft Tours, Box 398, Jasper AB T0E 1E0
Athabasca River

For wilder rides, contact:

Chinook River Sports, 7430 - 99th Street, Edmonton AB T6E 3R9
Red Deer and Highwood rivers

Hunter Valley Recreational Enterprises, Box 1620, Canmore AB T0L 0M0
Red Deer and Kananaskis rivers

Maligne River Adventures, Box 280, Jasper AB T0E 1E0
Maligne River

Mirage Adventure Tours, Box 233, Kananaskis Village AB T0L 2H0
Bow River

Mukwah Tours, 195, 601-10th Avenue SW, Calgary AB T2R 0B2
Red Deer River

Otter Rafting Adventures, 4919 - 49th Street, Red Deer AB T4N 1V2
Red Deer River

Riverbend Whitewater Rafting, Box 961, Red Deer AB T4N 5H3
Red Deer and North Saskatchewan rivers

The Adventure Group, 202 - 1414 Kensington Road N.W., Calgary AB T2N 3P9
Bow, Kananaskis, Highwood, Red Deer, and Ram rivers

WB Adventures, Box 3398 Stn. B., Calgary AB T2M 4M1
Red Deer River

Downhill Skiing

Albertans begin to get restless when the first snowfall arrives in early November. Some look south for ways to escape winter. Others cannot wait until the start of the ski season. By early December, the downhill and cross-country ski seasons begin at six major ski resorts in the Rockies and 30 smaller ski hills in the rest of the province. The best powder skiing often comes in February and early March.

The mountain resorts have the greatest variety of terrain, with runs to challenge expert skiers. **Nakiska**, in Kananaskis Country, was designed for the 1988 Winter Olympics. **Lake Louise** has hosted several World Cup events and **Sunshine Village** has also had its share of major races.

While speed is encouraged during races, the ski areas stress control for recreational skiers. Ski patrollers will not hesitate to order a reckless skier off the slopes.

Even though the mountain areas have some of the most challenging skiing in the world, novice and intermediate skiers have many choices as well. All the mountain resorts have a good balance of beginner, intermediate, and terrain.

Mount Norquay, in Banff, underwent a major expansion in 1991 to open up six new intermediate runs. It also has beginner slopes and the famed steep runs like the North American.

There is magnificent spring skiing (April-May) throughout the mountains. It is a time of year when skiers often choose a late

Resorts in the Canadian Rockies are among the finest downhill ski areas in the world. The season starts in November or December and lasts until late May. Nakiska, pictured above, was built for the 1988 Winter Olympics and has become a popular recreation area.

start to allow the snow to soften from the sunshine. A few brave souls will wear bathing suits to get a start on their tans. Good sunglasses and sunscreen are needed to avoid sunburn and snow blindness from the intense sunlight.

Lake Louise and Sunshine Village usually stretch the season longest. Sunshine often stays open until the last week of May.

There is little heli-skiing in Alberta but Canadian Mountain Holidays, the largest operator, and several others are based in Banff. They provide transportation to their lodges in British Columbia.

Cross-country Skiing

Nordic or cross-country skiers have as much choice as downhillers in the type of terrain to ski. There are hundreds of kilometres of groomed trails throughout the mountains and foothills with unlimited potential for experienced ski-tourers who want to strike off on their own.

SuperGuide recommends:
Canmore Nordic Centre, Kananaskis Country There are 56 kilometres of groomed runs at this recreation complex designed for the 1988 Winter Olympics. Many of the trails are strictly for well-conditioned racers but there are intermediate and beginner trails as well. There is a 2.5 kilometre loop with lights for night skiing.

Peter Lougheed Provincial Park, Kananaskis Country The 70 kilo-

metres of trails are among the best in the province with plenty of snow throughout the season. Trails can be crowded in mid-winter.

Ribbon Creek, Kananaskis Country Snow conditions tend to be quite variable, but the 54 kilometre trail network is easily accessible from the lodges in Kananaskis Village.

Lake Louise There is a wide range of terrain available and plenty of snow. The Lakeside trail is a level trail with lovely views of Chateau Lake Louise. Moraine Lake road is gently rolling and is often one of the first trails to open and one of the last to close.

Banff The Spray River trail is a popular well-groomed trail over easy terrain next to the Banff Springs Hotel.

Sunshine Village, Banff National Park The ski resort is known for its downhill runs, but it is also an excellent approach to magnificent Nordic trails above treeline.

Jasper The Cavell, Pyramid, and Athabasca Trails are all relatively short, easy trails adjacent to Jasper Park Lodge. There is variety on several trails at Maligne Lake.

Snowmobiling

The national and provincial parks are off-limits to snowmobiles, but there is terrain available on Alberta Forest Service territory and

other publicly owned land.

The Alberta Snowmobile Association can be contacted c/o Percy Page Centre, 11759 Groat Road, Edmonton AB T5M 3K6 (453-8668).

SuperGuide recommends:

McLean Creek There are more than 200 kilometres of groomed trails in the foothills 60 km southwest of Calgary.

Ghost District This forestry land 64 kilometres northwest of Calgary has close to 170 kilometres of groomed trails.

Eagle River There are about 130 kilometres of groomed trails near Whitecourt, 177 kilometres northwest of Edmonton.

Chambers Creek The provincial forest region 30 kilometres west of Rocky Mountain House has almost 90 kilometres of marked trails.

Atlas There are 70 kilometres of marked and unmarked trails, eight kilometres northwest of Blairmore in the Crowsnest Pass.

Winter safety
It's great to get out and enjoy the winter but special care is needed to cope with potential hazards.

Backcountry Travel
Travelling alone or allowing members of your group to become separated in the backcountry is dangerous.

Make and carry a basic survival kit: matches, a candle, pocket

Cross-country skiers get ready to hit the trails surrounding Skoki Lodge near Lake Louise. Nordic skiers can enjoy groomed trails in the mountains and foothills or venture into the backcountry and make their own tracks.

Avalanches pose a danger to backcountry travellers in winter. Staff in both national and provincial parks monitor conditions to determine where and when the risk is highest. Ski areas have control programs to minimize the danger on established runs.

knife, "space blanket," plastic garbage bags, and snacks. Even a short cross-country ski trip can turn into an overnight stay in the wilderness. In addition, carry extra clothing, water, high-quality sunglasses and sunscreen. And find out about avalanches and carry avalanche protection devices.

Avalanches

The Alberta Avalanche Safety Association provides information on the toll-free line, 1-800-772-2434.

Avalanches can be deadly and anyone heading into mountain terrain should be aware of the danger.

Avalanche expert Tony Daffern says the biggest mistake people make is not taking warnings seriously.

"The majority of accidents occur when the hazard is known to be high," he advises.

Specialists employed by the Canadian National Parks Service, ski resorts, and other agencies carefully monitor snow conditions throughout the winter and update avalanche forecasts frequently. Check with park officials or other local authorities before heading into mountainous terrain.

The downhill ski resorts have avalanche control programs where slopes are tested and occasionally slides are deliberately triggered to prevent a dangerous buildup of snow.

Groomed cross-country trails have been laid out to generally stay clear of common avalanche paths.

Some avalanche terrain is easy to spot since the slides leave a swath through forested areas.

Watch for other signs of avalanche activity, such as slopes where layers of snow have broken loose and form a jumbled mass at the bottom.

Take special care when travelling in the backcountry after a heavy snowfall and avoid steep terrain, especially if the slope is topped by a cornice, an overhanging lip of windblown snow. If you are travelling in a group and must cross a suspect slope, do it one at a time.

Skiers who venture into the backcountry should carry electronic avalanche beacons that aid in locating victims if they are caught in a slide. Lightweight snow shovels should also be carried by those who travel in potentially dangerous areas since time is crucial in rescuing someone trapped in a slide.

The chance of survival is slim for anyone buried for more than half an hour.

Anyone trapped in a slide should try a swimming motion to stay near the surface of the moving snow. If you are beneath the surface as the slide comes to a halt, try to make a bit of breathing room before the snowpack solidifies.

Hypothermia

Severe loss of body heat can be fatal but a few simple precautions will help guard against the cold in summer as well as winter. Good insulated clothing is important. Wool is one of the best materials since it provides warmth even when wet. A great deal of heat can be lost through the head so warm headgear is essential.

Carry extra layers of clothing when heading into the backcountry since conditions can quickly change in the mountains. Avoid alcohol since it speeds the loss of heat from the body's core. Food and other liquids will help the body produce its own heat. Warm drinks are especially good.

Watch for signs such as shivering and lethargy in members of your group.

Frostbite

High winds and cold temperatures can create very hazardous conditions. Exposed skin can freeze within minutes when the windchill is extreme.

Well-insulated wind resistant clothing is the best protection. Use balaclavas or other face covering in extreme cold.

Toes and fingers are particularly susceptible to frostbite and good boots and gloves or mitts are needed of winter.

On a journey, watch for early signs of frostbite in yourself and others. Skin will turn a pale white as it starts to freeze. Toes and fingers may go numb and will not warm up even with vigorous activity.

Sometimes there is relief for cold feet by loosening your boot laces and improving circulation. Cold hands can be warmed by swinging your arms to get more blood to your extremities.

Skin to skin warming helps and in extreme cases a companion's freezing feet can be protected by taking off the boots and putting the cold feet against your bare stomach.

Snowblindness and Sunburn

Spring skiers can bask in bright sunshine and work on an early tan, but high-quality sunglasses and sunscreen are needed to guard against bright sunshine that is intensified by high altitude and reflections off the snow. Even on cloudy days the hazard is great.

Dinosaurs

Albertosaurus was one of the most common dinosaurs in the region 75 million years ago. This predator had sharp teeth and powerful jaws, useful in attacking prey. The three-metre-tall dinosaur could move swiftly on powerful hind legs.

On a hot spring day in 1884, a field worker for the Geological Survey of Canada was gathering rock samples in the coal-rich badlands bordering the Red Deer River.

Joseph Burr Tyrrell was startled to see a huge skull embedded in the mud and rocks. The fossilized dinosaur became known as *Albertosaurus* and sparked the beginning of intense scientific interest that continues today.

Dinosaurs ruled the earth for 165 million years and although they have been extinct for 65 million years, they continue to cap-ture our imagination. Alberta, especially the badlands near Drumheller and Brooks, is recognized for its dinosaur fossils. Paleontologists have been studying the fossils for more than a century, and they have helped develop interpretive displays to give the rest of us a vivid impression of our planet in the distant past.

Origins

Scientists believe that the Earth was formed by a big bang or some other cataclysmic event 4.6 billion years ago. It took about one

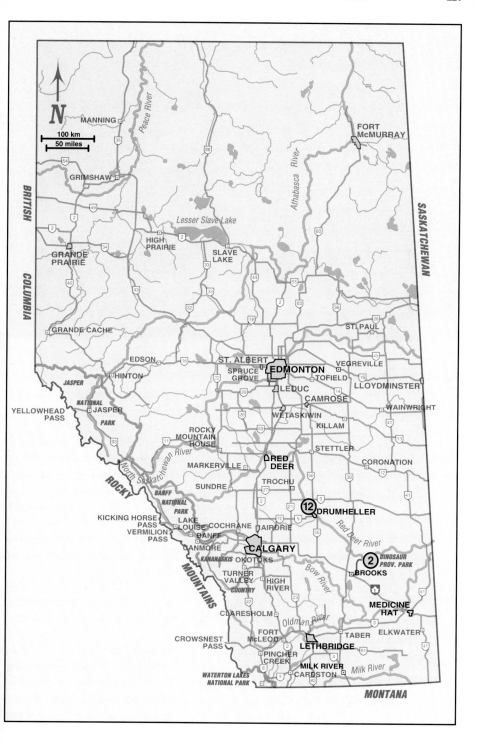

Edmontonia relied on spiked armor to ward off predators. With short legs and powerful grinding teeth, this dinosaur fed off low growth vegetation.

billion years for the simplest forms of life to arrive.

Since then, there has been a long process of evolution that has brought us to the life forms of today. Dinosaurs fit into a period known as the Mesozoic Era which began 230 million years ago and lasted until 65 million years ago. Humans have only been around for a fraction of that time – less than five million years.

Our knowledge about dinosaurs comes from fossils. When dinosaurs died, their remains were often scattered by scavengers. If they died in a wetland or riverbank area, their bodies were often encased by mud or sand. As they were buried, minerals seeped in and hardened or replaced the organic matter.

Paleontologists act like detectives piecing together clues found in fossilized bones, footprints, and other remnants to theorize about the apprearance and characteristics of the ancient reptiles.

Even dinosaur droppings and eggs became fossils. In 1987, a young girl discovered a dinosaur nesting site at Devil's Coulee in southern Alberta. Researchers were ecstatic when they probed the fossil bed and found softball-sized fossil eggs complete with embryos.

In 1841, British paleontologist Richard Owen came up with the term "dinosauria," which meant terrible lizard. Since then, more than 340 species of dinosaurs have been identified around the world. While the big ones such as the 15metre-long *Tyrannosaurus rex* have captured the attention of science-fiction writers and film- makers, many of the dinosaurs were quite small, less than a metre in height. At two metres in length, *Saurornitholestes* is the smallest species yet discovered in Alberta.

The term dinosaurs refers only to the prehistoric reptiles that lived on land. Bird-like fliers such as the *Pteranodon* are classified as pterosaurs. The prehistoric creatures who lived underwater are known as either ichthyosaurs or plesiosaurs.

The complicated names of dinosaurs stems from a combination of latin descriptions of distinguishing characteristics as well as the occasional use of the name of the discoverer or location of the find.

Scientists have identified about 35 species of dinosaurs in Alberta. That's only a small fraction of the total number, but sites in the province rank among the world's most important because the fossils are so plentiful and represent dinosaurs in the late stages of their development.

Alberta's environment was well-suited to the dinosaurs 75 million years ago and has proven to be quite good for dinosaur hunters in modern times.

Back in Mesozoic times, much of western North America was covered with shallow water. The Western Interior Seaway stretched from the Arctic Ocean to the Gulf of Mexico. As the Rocky Mountains gradually formed from changes in the earth's crust,

the western plains began to emerge as well. The retreating sea left rich sediments that turned into fertile river valleys and swamps. The warm climate enabled magnolias, giant redwoods, oak, willow, birch, and poplar to grow. The lush growth meant plenty of food for the dinosaurs. Millions of years later, some of that organic matter had turned into rich coal deposits.

The Ice Age that began two to three million years ago and continued off and on until 10,000 years ago dramatically reshaped the landscape of North America.

Tyrannosaurus rex was the largest carnivore (meateater). Adults grew up to 15 metres in length. Sharp teeth up to 18 centimetre long were well-suited to attacking prey.

Hoodoos provide exotic evidence of erosion. Sedimentary layers are constantly worn down by wind and rain, but rocks and boulders act as umbrellas in some areas. As the surrounding material is carried away, cement-like pillars are formed. Capstones can still be found atop some hoodoos.

One of the most powerful forces came from the surging meltwater as the glaciers retreated northward. In parts of southern Alberta, the water carved out new river valleys and cut deep into the earths surface revealing layers of sedminent that had built up over millions of years.

Early French fur traders who travelled across North America described the deep winding canyons of the Dakotas as "mauvaises terres à traverser." The translation, "bad lands to cross," has been shortened to "badlands" and is used to describe several deeply eroded land formations in the west.

Badlands continue to be highly susceptible to erosion. The mixture of soft materials such as sandstone and bentonitic clay is read-ily washed away with the rain. As the surface wears down, more and more fossils are exposed.

Dinosaur Hunters

There was intense scientific interest in dinosaurs in the late 1800s and rivals went to great lengths to discover new fossils and earn the honor of naming the species.

The competition was at its most fierce in the United States where wealthy paleontolgists Othniel Charles Marsh and Edward Drinker Cope continually tried to outdo one another.

The men had contempt for each other and sent out teams of workers in secrecy. The "bone war" as it came to be known led to a remarkable advancement in knowledge about dinosaurs. Only

nine species of dinosaurs had been identified in North America before the two men started their work.

They each accounted for a number of dramatic finds particularly in Wyoming and Colorado in the late 1870s. Over the years, they added an astounding 136 species to the list of dinosaurs found in North America.

American millionaire Andrew Carnegie fuelled the competition for dinosaurs spending $25 million at the turn of the century to unearth specimens for new museums in the United States.

There was only moderate interest in Canada at the time and fossil discoveries were usually side benefits of expeditions with other goals in mind. George M. Dawson was leading a survey team to map out the Canada-US boundary in 1874 when he made the first "official" discovery of dinosaur bones in Alberta along the Milk River valley.

Natives, of course, had come across countless fossils and regarded the large bones as belonging to ancient giant buffalo.

Joseph B. Tyrrell was working as Dawson's assistant in 1884, exploring for mineral wealth in southern Alberta for the Geological Survey of Canada. As he explored the Red Deer River valley by canoe, Tyrrell found not only the rich coal deposits in the Drumheller area, but also came upon an extensive fossil bed. He realized the importance of his find and collected several specimens and shipped them to Ottawa.

In 1888 and 1889 the Geologi-

Barnum Brown was among the most successul fossil hunters in the early 1900s. This *Corythosaurus* found north of the Red Deer River is now in the New York Museum of Natural History.

Fossils, reconstructed skeletons, and scale models bring the era of the dinosaurs to life in the Royal Tyrrell Museum of Palaeontology.

cal Survey sent Thomas C. Weston to continue research into the fossil beds along the Red Deer River. The first attempt ended in failure when his boat sank just a few kilometres downstream from his launch site. He returned with two better boats the following year and made a major discovery of fossils in the area now encompassed by Dinosaur Provincial Park, (See Scenic Drive 4.)

Research in the Drumheller area continued at a modest pace until 1909. Then, an Alberta rancher was visiting the American Museum of Natural History in New York and commented that there were plenty of fossils back home like those on display.

The Great Canadian Dinosaur Rush was on. Barnum Brown was sent up by the museum and shipped back boxcar loads of bones before Canadian officials began to see the need for collecting specimens to keep in Canada.

The Geological Survey of Canada hired American paleontologist Charles Sternberg and his sons to collect fossils for Canadian museums. The Sternberg and Brown teams returned year after year to find rich bounties of fossils. Occasionally, however, there were hard feelings when one group or the other felt its territory had been invaded. The flurry of activity quickly wore down and interest in dinosaurs declined over the next several decades.

In recent years with the renewed fascination with dinosaurs, the focus is on co-operation rather than competition. Specialists at the Royal Tyrrell Museum have worked closely on joint international projects as far away as China.

And dinosaur hunting has become very sophisticated in recent years. Paleontologists now have techniques to reduce the chance of destroying fragile specimens. That is why Alberta has enacted a strict law prohibiting amateurs from disturbing fossils. Anyone who makes a chance discovery should report the find to the nearest museum or other responsible authority.

Where to see Dinosaur Displays

Royal Tyrrell Museum of Palaeontology, Drumheller (Scenic Drive 12)
Unquestionably, the Tyrrell Museum is the place to begin for dinosaur hunters. Plan to spend at least half a day in the complex that covers 11,200 square metres.

The museum and labratory is tucked into the badlands six kilometres northwest of Drumheller. The museum, which opened in 1985, has "a celebration of life" as its theme. The entryway displays the variety of life in a mosaic of 190 illuminated photographs. A huge rotating globe gives visitors a sense of the cosmic influences that have shaped the earth over the past 4.6 billion years.

One imaginative display outlines the formation of the continents and the role of the ice ages in sculpting our landscapes.

Hands-on displays in the Science Hall provide lessons about the physical characteristics of our world and how they affect us.

The 3.6 billion-year story of life on our planet unfolds with an introduction to fossils and paleontology. A large window overlooks the preparation laboratory of the museum, where scientists study the fossils that are continually being unearthed.

The story of Charles Darwin's journeys and the development of his theories on evolution are outlined, along with the ways plants and animals have adapted to insure their survival.

A two-storey arboretum known as the Palaeoconservatory features over 100 species of plants that are descended from the vegetation that was prevalent from 15 million to 350 million years ago.

The showpiece of the museum is the expansive Dinosaur Hall with reconstructed skeletons and life-size replicas of the species that once ruled the earth.

In one corner, *Albertosaurus* looms three metres tall with jagged teeth and massive jaws. *Chasmosaurus*, with its sharp horns, hooked beak, and protective bony frill, is posed against a wall. *Edmontonia*, with its spiked and bony armor, stands in a forest clearing. The imposing *Tyrannosaurus rex* towers in the centre as if looking for its next meal.

The Royal Tyrrell Museum sits in the heart of the badlands near Drumheller. With the help of computer displays and an expansive mural, the Dinosaur Hall shows the ancient creatures and their habitat.

Modern technology is used to help tell an ancient story. Computer terminals are on hand for visitors find out the reasons for the specfic characteristics of the creatures.

Near the end of the tour, hypotheses are given about the extinction of the dinosaurs. And there are displays about the Ice Ages and the appearance of humans.

The Tyrrell Museum is open all year. Phone 823-7707 in Drumheller area or 294-1992 in Calgary.

Dinsoaur Provincial Park (Scenic Drive 4)

The badlands 48 kilometres northeast of Brooks are among the richest dinosaur fossil beds found anywhere. The 6000 square kilometre (15,000 acres) park is so important to all of us, it has been declared a World Heritage site.

In 1987, the **Tyrrell Museum** opened a **field station** in the park to serve as a base for continuing paleontological research as well as an interpretive centre for visitors. A *Chasmosaurus* skeleton is one of the most striking displays and there is a theatre with videos on the study of of dinosaurs. The field station is open year round. Phone 378-4342.

There are also interpretive hiking trails. The 3.2 kilometre **Quarry hiking trails** provide dramatic views of the badlands and one of the earliest dinosaur excavations in the province. Barnum

Brown found magnificent fossils in the area in 1913. One skeleton has been left embedded in the rocks as a display.

The 1.5 kilometre **Badlands Trail** leads into the eroded landscape that has provided so many clues about life on earth 75 million years ago.

The Calgary Zoo's Prehistoric Park (Scenic Drive 11)

A 2.6 square kilometre (6.5 acre) section of The Calgary Zoo has been been turned into display for more than 20 life-sized dinosaur replicas.

The well-known *Tyrannosaurus rex, Triceratops,* and *Stegosaurus* are all there. Park designers have also painstakingly interpreted the environment of the dinosaurs, recreating volcanoes, hoodoos, swamplands, mountains, and oceans.

The short interpretive trail through the ancient world of the dinosaurs complements the modern exhibits at the zoo since the issues of adaptation and extinction are crucial to present-day species.

The Prehistoric Park is open from mid-May to mid-November. Admission is included with the price of entry to the zoo. Phone 232-9300.

Provincial Museum of Alberta (Scenic Drive 12)

The Provincial Museum in Edmonton has a paleontology display as part of its overall display of Alberta's past.

There is a *Lambeosaurus* (duckbill) skeleton along with life-size replicas of *Corythosaurus* (duckbill), *Struthiomimus* (ostrich-like), and *Ankylosaurus* (armor-plated).

The museum is open year-round. Phone 427-1786.

Ten Prehistoric Favorites

Albertosaurus (Alberta lizard)
Adult length: 8-10 metres
It was an *Albertosaurus* skull that Joseph Tyrrell found in 1884 that intensified the interest in Alberta's fossil beds. *Albertosaurus* was the most prevalent of the large meat-eaters in the region 75 million years ago. This predator used its powerful jaws and long, sharp teeth to attack its prey. Arms were puny with two fingers on each hand.

Ankylosaurus (fused lizard)
Adult length: 10 metres
This plant-eater had plenty of protection. It was about the size of a tank with armor to match. Bony, spiked plates covered its back, tail, and flanks. A heavy knob on the end of its tail could be used as a club. With small teeth and weak jaws, it survived on soft low-growing vegetation.

Chasmosaurus (opened lizard)
Adult length: 5 metres
With a pronounced beak and strong scissor-like teeth, *Chasmosaurus* could feed off tough vegetation. Its most distinctive feature is a bony frill on its skull that

protected the vulnerable neck area from attack. It was a typical ceratopsian with one horn on its nose and two above its eyes.

Edmontosaurus
(Edmonton lizard)
Adult length: 15 metres
This three-tonne plant eater was the largest hadrosaur or duck-billed dinosaur in Alberta. It had about a thousand teeth to help in grinding up its food. With good hearing, smell, and eyesight, *Edmontosaurus* could sense danger and flee from predators by running on powerful hind legs.

Dinosaurs ruled the world for millions of years. *Albertosaurus* and other giant reptiles flourished along the coast of a shallow inland sea that covered much of North America. Reasons for their extinction remain a mystery.

Lambeosaurus

Albertosaurus

Pachycephalosaurus

Ankylosaurus

Chasmosaurus

Struthiomimus

Edmontosaurus

Triceratops

Hypacrosaurus

Tyrannosaurus rex

Hypacrosaurus
(High-ridge lizard)
Adult length: 9 metres
This duck-billed dinosaur is of special significance since the finding of fossilized eggs containing embryos in southern Alberta's Devil's Coulee. It is another of the plant-eating duck-billed dinosaurs. The name refers to a high ridge that ran along the back that may have served to regulate body heat.

Lambeosaurus (Lambe's lizard)
Adult length: 15 metres
Aside from its massive size, this duck-billed dinosaur could be distinguished by its prominent crest or headpiece. The crest was a combination of a blade-like flap in front and a sharp spike pointing backward. The tall *Lambeosaurus* could choose between vegetation growing high in trees or low on the forest floor.

Pachycephalosaurus
(Thick-headed lizard)
Adult length: 7 metres
This two-legged plant-eater is best known for its skullcap that was up to 25 centimetres thick. The smooth top of the skullcap was fringed with knobs and spikes. *Pachycephalosaurus* likely used its head as a battering ram in fights with other members of its own species, much the same as modern day goats and bighorn sheep.

Struthiomimus (Ostrich mimic)
Adult length: 4 metres
Ornithomomimids or bird-mimic dinosaurs did not fly but were fast sprinters, their main form of protection from predators. This toothless dinosaur was shaped like an ostrich, but did not have feathers. It likely ate low-growing plants, insects, and small lizards and other animals.

Triceratops (Three horned face)
Adult length: 9 metres
Triceratops is the best known and one of the largest ceratopsians (horned dinosaurs). It was also

Dinosaur replicas are presented in their appropriate environments at the Calgary Zoo's Prehistoric Park. Designers have created models of volcanos, badlands and even a lake to show the ancient creatures in life-like settings. The Petro-Canada office tower indicates the modern world beyond park boundaries.

Bony frill extending from back of skull protected neck of the *Chasmosaurus.* Strong scissor-like teeth could cut through tough vegetation.

one of the fiercest of the plant-eaters and powerful enough to take on most predators. Adults weighed more than five tonnes. Their heads were enormous, measuring about one-third of the total length.

Tyrannosaurus rex (Tyrant lizard)
Adult length: 15 metres
Tyrannosaurus has earned a reputation as the most fearsome of the dinosaurs. It was the largest meat-eater, with powerful jaws and up to 60 sharp teeth, some 18 centimetres long. *Tyrannosaurus* could run quickly on powerful hind legs, but may have preferred to scavenge for food.

And Then There Were None

One of the greatest quests in science is the search for the reason that dinosaurs became extinct, along with the vast majority of other species on earth, about 65 million years ago.

One hypothesis suggests that early species of mammals were beginning to flourish and thrive on a diet that included dinosaur eggs. Another suggestion has the plant-eating dinosaurs suffering from changes in their food source. Evolving vegetation may have become difficult to digest or even poisonous to the plant-eaters. Their demise would have killed off their predators as well.

Both those theories have been weakened by arguments that the departure of the dinosaurs was relatively abrupt, and the impact of mammals or changing food sources would have caused a more gradual change. Also a high percentage of marine life and other land-based animals perished with the dinosaurs.

One of the most credible suggestions is that a devastating event caused a sudden change in the earth's atmosphere. Some scientists believe that a giant asteroid collided with the earth. If a 10 kilometre diameter asteroid struck the planet, it would have created a deep crater up to 150 kilometres in diameter.

The collision would have thrown up a dense cloud of material that could have shrouded the earth and blocked out the sun for months. The atmosphere would become cool. As the particles settled, they may have created acid

Brian Cooley
Commercial Sculptor/
Dinosaur Models

When I graduated from the Alberta College of Art in 1979, my first job was at the Calgary Zoo, where I worked on creating the landforms for the Prehistoric Park.

I got into dinosaurs at the Tyrrell Museum in Drumheller – the fleshed-out, life-sized dinosaurs, such as *Albertosaurus* and the armored dinosaur. The work is challenging: creating particular translucent skin textures; experimenting with different materials and transporting completed dinosaurs like *Tyrannosaurus rex* (12 metres long, 5.5 metres tall) to far away places.

As soon as a project to create a dinosaur starts you have to obtain research information. Fortunately the Tyrell Museum is full of people who know about dinosaurs. With dinosaurs, or anything else, you start with measurements – in this case, of the fossil bones. I find out the exact size of everything and the proportions. Then I try to find out about the dinosaur's lifestyle. For example, where did this particular dinosaur live? What did it eat? How fast did it move? These are not easy questions to answer. I make sketches and they are reviewed by the paleontologists.

Then, working in metric, I will create a model at one-tenth the final size. Here I will try to work out the musculature, skin colour and texture, and so on. The model is also reviewed and changed and modified. Once approved, I go on to create the life-sized dinosaur.

Of my work so far, I think the dinosaurs are most satisfying. With something like a horse, you see the horse, you know what a horse looks like, and so you're not amazed to see that you have created a horse. But with dinosaurs, there are shocking moments. We'd be working away on it, working away on it, and we'd step back from the dinosaur and have an eerie feeling. It's like you just caught a glimpse of something from a long time ago, from some other world.

Bleriot ferry operates mid-April to early November taking vehicles across the Red Deer River. The cable ferry was built in 1913 and is the oldest of its kind in Alberta. There is no charge for the short ride.

rain. The disruption to plant and animal life may have been too severe for them to survive.

The asteroid theory is supported by evidence in the layers of the earth. A heavy concentration of the element iridium is found in many parts of the world, at a depth in the sediments that represents a time close to the era of mass extinction. Iridium is relatively rare on earth, but more common in asteroids.

Whether the dinosaurs died from a devastating event or for some other reason, they will continue to spark scientific debate and stir our imaginations.

Scenic Drive 12: Dinosaur Trail

This 48 kilometre drive along the banks of the Red Deer River is an ideal trip combined with a visit to the Royal Tyrrell Museum of Palaeontology, near Drumheller.

Start in Drumheller and drive northwest on Secondary Road 837, which is also known as South Dinosaur Trail. **Prehistoric Park**

(1), about one kilometre from the city, features life-size dinosaur models in a natural setting. There is an admission charge.

The highway passes several old mine sites carved into the layered riverbanks. The **Orkney Hill Viewpoint** (2) is a good stop to view the river valley and badlands.

Take the turnoff for the **Bleriot Ferry** (3) and hitch a free ride on one of the last remaining cable ferries in the province. The ferry, which can carry up to eight vehicles, runs from 7 am to 11 pm daily, from mid-April to early November. The Bleriot Ferry Campground on the west side of the river offers basic facilities only.

The North Loop of Dinosaur Trail follows Secondary Road 838 back to Drumheller. The **Horsethief Canyon** (4) viewpoint offers a remarkable view of a landscape etched by erosion.

Dinosaur Trail Campground (5) is a good spot for an overnight stay. Canoe rentals are available. Phone 823-9333. The nearby Dinosaur Trail Golf and Country Club is a nine hole public course. Phone 823-5622.

Watch for **The Little Church** (6) by the roadside. The popular description of the tiny building is that it can seat thousands, but only six at a time.

Of course, the main attraction is the **Royal Tyrrell Museum of Palaeontology** (7), six kilometres northwest of Drumheller.

McMullen Island (8), five kilometres northwest, is part of Midland Provincial Park and offers a good riverbank picnic spot.

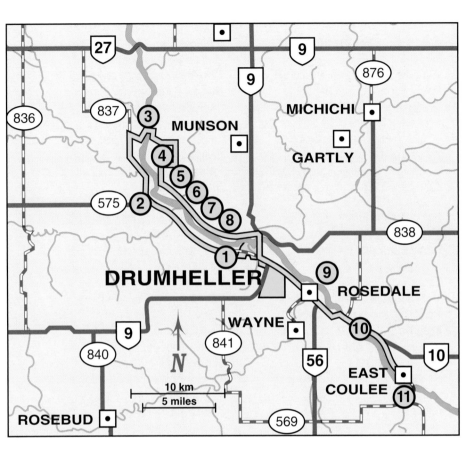

The Dinosaur Trail loop can be combined with a 25 kilometre drive southeast of Drumheller on Highway 10 to East Coulee. This route also follows the Red Deer River and winds through an area steeped with coal mining history.

Stop for a stroll across the restored suspension bridge at **Rosedale (9)**, 8.5 kilometres southeast of Drumheller. The footbridge was built for miners who had to cross the river to reach the Star Coal Mine.

Watch for **hoodoo formations (10)**, 18 kilometres from the city. Natives believed that the sandstone pillars formed by erosion were petrified giants. They are excellent subjects to photograph, but are fragile, and visitors are advised not to climb on them.

East Coulee housed 3500 people during the peak of coal mining in the 1930s. There are not many residents left in the area but some of the buildings remain. The old school house has been turned into a museum and cultural centre.

The nearby **Atlas Coal Mine (11)** has been designated a historic site primarily because of the tipple structure, used to sort ore, is still in place.

Some Alberta Place Names

Athabasca: where there are reeds [Cree]
Banff: Banffshire, Scotland
Bragg Creek: George Bragg, early settler
Bruderheim: home of the brothers, named after an early Moravian settlement
Canmore: after Canmore (large-headed), Malcolm III, King of Scotland (d. 1093)
Claresholm: Clare's home, after a woman who lived there
Dunvegan: Dunvegan castle of the McLeods, Scotland
Drumheller: Samuel Drumheller, coal pioneer
Eclan: based on tabernacle, Taber is adjacent to Eclan, nacle reversed
Etzikom: valley coulee [Blackfoot]
Exshaw: son-in-law of Sir Sandford Fleming, who was a director of the local cement company
Hobbema: Meyndert Hobbema, Dutch painter (1638-1709)
Indus: Indus River, Pakistan
Innisfail: Innisfail, Ireland
Jasper: Jasper Hawes, in charge of the North West Company trading post in the area, in 1817
Leduc: Rev. Hippolyte Leduc, Oblate missionary (1918)
Ma-me-mo Beach: place of many shore birds [Cree]
Markerville: C.P. Marker, former dairy commissioner of Alberta
Marlboro: after a marl deposit in the area, a lime deposit used to make cement

Medicine Hat: named for headdress of Blackfoot medicine man
Nakamun Park: song of praise [Cree]
Namao: sturgeon [Cree]
Okotoks: rock [Blackfoot]
Onefour: located in Township 1, Range 4, west of the 4th Meridian
Ozada: forks of the river [Stoney]
Patience: required to travel early roads in the area
Penhold: after pen nib sticking in map at this location during CPR naming meeting
Pincher Creek: after pincers lost in creek by early prospectors
Ponoka: elk [Blackfoot]
Ricinius: caster oil plant [Latin]
Scandia: Scandinavian settlement
Seebe: river [Cree]
Stettler: Carl Stettler, homesteader in the area from Bern, Switzerlan
Sundre: Sundre, Norway
Trochu: Armand Trochu, early French trader
Vegreville: Father Valentin Vegreville, early missionary
Vermilion: after colour from iron in springwater of the area
Wabamun Lake: mirror [Cree]
Wetaskiwin: Peace Hills

For more see: *2000 Place Names of Alberta*, by Eric and Patricia Holmgren. Modern Press, Saskatoon (1972)

Listings

"Don't Miss It" Calendar

Check locally for exact dates and locations. Note: (403) is the area code for telephone calls to all of Alberta.

JANUARY

Jasper Winter Festival
Skiing, dogsledding, ice-sculpting, and more.
Jasper Park Chamber of Commerce, 852-3858

FEBRUARY

Banff/Lake Louise Winter Festival
Good fun and winter outdoor sports. Many events including the Mountain Madness Relay Race.
Banff/Lake Louise Chamber of Commerce, 762-3777

Calgary Winter Festival
More than two hundred sporting, cultural, and community events for all.
Calgary Convention & Visitors Bureau, 262-2766 or 1-800-661-1778

MARCH

Lake Louise Annual Loppet
One of Alberta's oldest organized cross-country ski races. This family event has participation from young and old, novice to expert.
Banff/Lake Louise Chamber of Commerce, 762-3777

APRIL

Red Deer: Silver Buckle Rodeo
See top cowboys compete in pro rodeo.
David Thompson Country Tourist Council, 342-2032

MAY

Edmonton and Calgary: International Children's Festivals
Two festivals featuring entertainment for the young and young-in-spirit, with jugglers, clowns, mimes, puppeteers, and singers from all over the world.
Edmonton Convention & Tourism Authority, 422-5505 or 988-5455
Calgary Convention & Visitors Bureau, 262-2766 or 1-800-661-1778

JUNE

Banff Festival of the Arts
(June-August)
A celebration of the performing and visual arts in the heart of the Rocky Mountains, with opera, musical comedy, poetry readings, dance, theatre, music, workshops, and more, including free arts events in and around Banff.
Banff/Lake Louise Chamber of Commerce, 762-3777

Calgary International Jazz Festival & Edmonton Jazz City International Festival
Both festivals feature the latest in jazz music, with concerts and happenings throughout the cities.
Calgary Convention & Visitors Bureau, 262-2766 or 1-800-661-1778

Red Deer Highland Games
Enjoy Scottish culture and entertainment at Western Canada's largest Highland Games.
David Thompson Country Tourist Council, 342-2032

Edmonton: The Works: A

Visual Arts Celebration
Edmonton is turned into a living art gallery, as artists and artisans fill downtown streets, parks, and art galleries with creations.
Edmonton Convention & Tourism Authority, 422-5505 or 988-5455

Ponoka Annual Stampede
Held in the centre of Alberta's ranching country, this professional rodeo is considered second only to the Calgary Stampede.
David Thompson Country Tourist Council, 342-2032

Drumheller: Broncosaurus Days
Country rodeo and town funfest in the dinosaur lands.
Big Country Tourist Association, 823-5885

JULY

Vegreville: Ukrainian Pysanka Festival
A celebration of Ukrainian cultural heritage in Alberta, with folk dancing and singing, authentic costumes, and crafts demonstrations including *pysanka*, the art of Easter egg decoration.
Lakeland Tourist Association, 645-2913

Calgary Exhibition and Stampede
Calgary goes western for ten days, with top-ranked rodeo events including chuckwagon racing, agricultural and craft exhibits, carnival, native encampments, flapjack breakfasts, saloons, and square dancing in the streets.
Calgary Convention & Visitors Bureau, 262-2766 or 1-800-661-1778

Red Deer: Westerner Days
Country fair with midway, exhibits, casino, livestock shows, entertainment, and more.
David Thompson Country Tourist Council, 342-2032

Edmonton: Klondike Days
Edmontonians dress-up and re-live the gold rush days of the 1890s, with parades, gold-panning, World Champion-ship Sourdough Raft Race, Sunday Promenade, and pancake breakfasts through-out the city.
Edmonton Convention & Tourism Authority, 422-5505 or 988-5455

Medicine Hat: Exhibition and Stampede
Chuckwagon races, rodeo, and a variety of entertain-ment.
South-East Alberta Travel and Convention Bureau, 527-6422

Red Deer: International Air Show
The sunny skies of Alberta welcome the world's best aerial artists, with individual and team performances.
David Thompson Country Tourist Council, 342-2032

Lethbridge: Whoop-Up Days
Let out a yell and enjoy this annual rodeo, parade, and agricultural fair.
Chinook Country Tourism Association, 320-1222 or 1-800-661-1222

AUGUST

Edmonton: Heritage Festival
Dozens of outdoor pavilions feature nonstop international dancing, singing, arts and crafts, costumes, and more.
Edmonton Convention & Tourism Authority, 422-5505 or 988-5455

Edmonton: Folk Music Festival
Enjoy folk music from traditional bluegrass to modern jazz. Fun for the whole family.
Edmonton Convention & Tourism Authority, 422-5505 or 988-5455

Edmonton: Fringe Theatre Festival
One of North America's most exciting alternative perform-ance festivals, with more than one hundred new interna-tional productions of plays, music, mime, dance, and street entertainment.
Edmonton Convention & Tourism Authority, 422-5505 or 988-5455

SEPTEMBER

Calgary: Spruce Meadows Masters Tournament
Watch internationally known horses and riders compete in show jumping at one of North America's finest equine facilities.
Calgary Convention & Visitors Bureau, 262-2766 or 1-800-661-1778

SEPTEMBER-NOVEMBER, JANUARY-MAY

Calgary & Edmonton: Trade/ Consumer Shows
Theme shows for sportsmen, home improvements, automobiles, and more at Calgary's Roundup Centre, Stampede Park and Edmon-ton's AgriCom, Edmonton Northlands.
Calgary Exhibition & Stampede, 261-0101 and 1-800-661-1260
Calgary Convention & Visitors Bureau, 262-2766 or 1-800-661-1778
Edmonton Northlands, 471-7210

Edmonton Convention & Tourism Authority, 422-5505 or 988-5455

NOVEMBER

Banff: Festival of Mountain Films
Nonstop viewing of the best mountain films from around the world.
Banff/Lake Louise Chamber of Commerce, 762-3777

Edmonton: Canadian Finals Rodeo
This is it, the rodeo that decides the cowboy champi-ons of Canada.
Edmonton Convention & Tourism Authority, 422-5505 or 988-5455

DECEMBER

Edmonton and Calgary: First Night Festivals
On December 31, bring in the New Year with a night of family entertainment held in various locations around town.
Edmonton Convention & Tourism Authority, 422-5505 or 988-5455
Calgary Convention & Visitors Bureau, 262-2766 or 1-800-661-1778

Travel Information

For personal travel counselling, call Travel Alberta: 1-800-661-8888 (from Canada and the continental US), 1-800-222-6501 (from within Alberta), or write: Travel Alberta, PO Box 2500, Edmonton AB T5J 2Z4.

Alberta Information Offices

Alberta
Alberta Tourism
Main Floor
City Centre Building
10155 - 102nd Street
Edmonton AB T5J 4L6
427-4321

Alberta Tourism Information
Centre
Government Centre South
McDougall School
455 - 6th Street SW
Calgary AB T2P 4E8
1-800-222-6501

Ontario
Suite 1110, 90 Sparks Street
Ottawa ON K1P 5B4
(613) 237-2615

United States
Suite 3535
333 South Grand Avenue
Los Angeles CA 90071
(213) 625-1256

27th Floor
General Motors Building
767 - 5th Avenue
New York, NY 10153
(212) 759-2222

United Kingdom
1 Mount Street
Berkeley Square
London, England W1Y 5AA
011-441-491-3430

Germany (and German-speaking Europe)
Office of the Commissioner
General
Ms. Karin R. Teubert
c/o Touristik Dienst
Alte Dorfstrasse 21
6457 Maintal 2
Germany

Hong Kong
Room 1003-4
Admiralty Centre
Tower Two, Harcourt Road
Central Hong Kong
011-852-5-284-729

Japan
Alberta Office
17th Floor, New Aoyama
Building (West)
1-1, 1-Chome,
Minamiaoyama
Minato-Ku, Tokyo 107
011-81-3-475-1171

Currency and Banking

The money system in Canada is based on Canadian dollars and cents, with the dollar divided into one hundred cents. There are different colored paper bills for $2 and up; lower amounts, including the $1 coin called a "loonie," are coinage. U.S. money is accepted at a limited number of commercial establishments around the province. For the best exchange rate to Canadian dollars, visitors are encouraged to convert foreign funds at a bank, trust company, or currency exchange desk. Traveller's checks and major credit cards are also accepted by most businesses.

Weather

The Alberta climate is as varied as its terrain – if you don't like the weather, wait a few minutes and it will change! In general, Alberta is cool, sunny, and dry, with warmer, drier weather in south and southeastern Alberta, and cooler, wetter weather in the mountains.

Spring usually starts defrosting Alberta in May, with temperatures climbing above freezing and light rain showers into June. However, there will be snow and freezing evening temperatures in the mountain areas through the end of June.

July and August are the summer months in Alberta, with long, warm, sunny days. The sun rises in the wee hours of the morning and sets as late as 10 or 11 pm in some parts of the province. Temperatures typically range in the mid-twenties Celsius in central Alberta, rising to the thirties Celsius in southern Alberta. When the sun goes down, so do the temperatures, and it's not unusual to have the day cool off more than 10° C within an hour of sunset. August also brings occasional thunderstorms and, late August into early September, there may be a rare hailstorm or even light snow.

In early September, there's often a taste of winter, and a few evenings with below freezing temperatures. Then, the weather warms up again through early October, bringing Indian Summer. The days grow visibly shorter;

daytime temperatures average 6° C to 10° C; evening temperatures drop below freezing; and the trees blazon yellow gold around the province.

Winter in Alberta can be quite cold, though dry. Temperatures of -15° C to -20° C are not uncommon, and strong winds in open areas can blow the light dry snow into blizzard conditions. Some parts of Alberta, such as Calgary, do enjoy a regular respite from winter due to a warm, dry wind off the east slopes of the Rockies called a chinook (shi-nook'). When a chinook starts, temperatures may rise more than 15° C in one hour, melting all the snow, greening the land, and sometimes even tricking the trees into budding in the belief that spring is here! The sky is overcast and calm, and a bright sunny arch, called a chinook arch, can be seen in the sky to the west over the mountains. A chinook may last for days, then as suddenly as it began, it will stop and temperatures will drop back to their normal lows.

Temperature Chart

40° C   a summer heat wave
30° C   a hot day
20° C   room temperature
0° C   water freezes
-10° C   a pleasant winter day
-30° C   a cold winter day

Access

Most visitors to Alberta arrive via Calgary or Edmonton, or via Vancouver in British Columbia. Each of these cities has an international airport, served by major airlines. Charter air services are also available; contact the Alberta Aviation Council, 67 Airport Rd, Edmonton, Alberta, phone 451-5289.

Canada's main east-west highway, the Trans-Canada (Highway 1) runs through Banff, Calgary, and Medicine Hat across southern Alberta. Alberta's main north-south highway (Highway 2) crosses into Alberta at the US border of Piegan/Carway, and from there goes north through Fort Macleod, Calgary, Red Deer, and Edmonton. There is regular motorcoach service between all major centres. Passenger train service is limited. Car rental agencies have offices at airports and downtown in all major centres. There are also a number of companies offering a variety of Alberta tours.

Calgary to:

- Banff 129 km / 80 miles
- Drumheller 136 km / 84 miles
- Edmonton 292 km / 181 miles
- Fort Macleod 168 km / 104 miles
- Jasper (via Hwy 93) 412 km / 255miles
- Lethbridge 202 km /125 miles
- Medicine Hat 299 km / 185 miles
- Lake Louise 183 km / 114 miles

Edmonton to:

- Jasper 366 km / 227 miles
- Lloydminster 248 km / 154 miles

Driving in Alberta

Your driver's license, from any country, is valid while vacationing in Alberta, up to a maximum of three months in Canada. You should carry your motor vehicle registration forms, and if you are driving a rental vehicle, a copy of the rental contract is required. Proof of a valid auto accident insurance policy must also be carried: obtain a Canadian Non-Resident Inter-Provincial Motor Vehicle Liability Insurance Card from your insurance company before you go.

Highway distance is measured in kilometres; one km = 5/8 mi. To calculate approximate mileage, multiply kilometres by 0.6.

Speed is measured in kilometres per hour (km/h). Within a city, driving speed is usually posted 50 km/h, or approximately 30 mph; major highways may be posted at 100 km/h, or approximately 62 mph.

Gasoline is sold by the liter. One imperial (British) gallon equals 4.5 litres; one US gallon equals 3.8 litres. Unleaded gasoline is available at self-serve and full-serve service stations, and so is diesel fuel and propane.

Seat belts are mandatory in Alberta. Motorcyclists must wear helmets. Right turn on red is permitted after a full stop. U-turns are permitted at any non-signalized intersection, unless posted otherwise. Speed limit is 50 km/h or as posted. Watch for slower limits in designated playground zones and school zones.

Drivers must yield to pedestrians. Pedestrian crosswalks are marked, and some have overhead, flashing lights activated by pedestrians.

For 24 hour road condition reports, phone the Alberta Motor Association in Calgary at 246-5853, or Edmonton at 471-6056. For detailed road information, phone the Government of Alberta Transportation Department during business hours Monday to Friday, at 297-6311, Calgary, or 427-2731, Edmonton.

Metric/Imperial Conversion Table

1 centimetre (cm)	0.394 inches
1 metre (m)	3.28 feet
1 kilometre (km)	0.62 miles
1 hectare (ha)	2.47 acres
1 square kilometre (sq km)	
	0.386 square miles
1 kilogram (kg)	2.205 pounds
1 tonne	0.9842 UK tons
	1.102 US tons
1 litre (L)	0.22 Imp. gallons
	0.264 US gallons
1° Celsius (C)	1.8° Fahrenheit (F)

0° Celsius = 32° Fahrenheit

National Parks

A national park motor vehicle entry permit sticker is required and can be purchased at park gates (cash only) or at Alberta Motor Association offices. Permits are available for one day, four days, and full year.

A national parks angling licence is required for fishing. Contact a national park information centre.

Parks Canada, Western Region
  Mailing Address:
PO Box 2989, Station M
Calgary AB T2P 3H8
  Location:
Room 520, 220 - 4th Ave SE
Calgary
292-4401

Banff National Park
PO Box 900
Banff AB T0L 0C0
762-3324
762-4256 Information Centre

Elk Island National Park
Site 4, RR 1
Fort Saskatchewan AB T8L 2N7
992-6380

Jasper National Park
PO Box 10
Jasper AB T0E 1E0
852-6161
852-6176 Information Centre

Waterton Lakes National Park
Waterton Park, AB T0K 2M0
859-2224

National Historic Park

Rocky Mountain House National Historic Park
Box 2130
Rocky Mountain House AB T0M 1T0
845-2412

Alberta Provincial Parks

The province of Alberta maintains 61 provincial parks (of which 24 offer telephone charge-card camping site reservations for summer), 45 recreation areas, three wilderness areas, and one ecological reserve.

Alberta Recreation and Parks Visitor Services Branch
Standard Life Centre
10405 Jasper Avenue
Edmonton AB T5J 3N4
427-9429

Kananaskis Country
Suite 412
1011 Glenmore Trail SW
Calgary AB T2V 4R6
297-3362

Forests and Wildlife

Alberta Energy/Forestry, Lands & Wildlife maintains an abundance of primitive campgrounds and recreational areas in the densely forested areas of Alberta, as well as managing wildlife regulations, including issuing hunting and fishing licenses. All persons between 16 and 65 years of age must have an Alberta angling license to fish any Alberta waters.
For more information, contact Alberta Energy/Forestry, Lands & Wildlife at:

Edmonton Information Centre,
Main Floor, Bramalea Building
9920 - 108th Street
Edmonton AB T5K 2M4
427-3590

Calgary Information Centre
Main Floor, Bantrel Building
703 - 6th Avenue SW
Calgary AB T2P 0T9
297-6324

Trail Rides and Guest Ranches

Contact: Alberta Outfitters
Association
Box 511, Claresholm
AB T0L 0T0 (625-2931)

Fly-In Fishing

Andrews Lake Lodge and
Camps
Box 5846, Stn. L, Edmonton
AB T6C 4G3 (464-7537)

Christina Lake Lodge
General Delivery, Conklin
AB T0P 1H0 (559-2224)

Grist Haven Lodge
Box 1350, Grand Centre
AB T0A 1T0 (594-1254)

Gypsy Lake Lodge
Box 5508, Fort McMurray
AB T9H 3G5 (743-3176)

Island Lake Lodge
Box 5694, Fort McMurray
AB T9H 3G6 (743-0214)

Kimowin Lake Lodge
Box 461, Vermilion
AB T0B 4M0 (853-2290)

Margaret Lake Lodge
Box 113, Grande Prairie
AB T8V 3A1 (532-8247)

Namur Lake Lodge
Box 5941, Fort McMurray
AB T9H 4V9 (791-9299)

Tapawingo Lodge
Box 900, Manning
AB T0H 2M0 (836-3345)

Winefred Lake Lodge
Conklin AB T0P 1H0
(551-1913)

Bow River Float Fishing

Alberta Drift Inc.
222 Midridge Crescent
Calgary AB T2X 1C6
(256-9172)

Barry White's Bow River
Anglers
Box 8451, Stn F, Dept. A G
Calgary AB T2J 2V6
(252-1827)

Blue Ribbon Drift Charters
1152 Ninga Rd NW, Calgary
AB T2K 2P1 (275-5220)

Bow River Company
Box 15, Site 9, RR 1 DeWinton
AB T0L 0X0
(256-9020)

Bow Valley Guides
Box 3949, Stn B, Calgary
AB T2M 3M5 (276-5013)

Great Waters Alberta
Box 9071, Stn F, Calgary
AB T2J 5S7 (271-5460)

Northwest Guide Service
28 Deer Lake Close SE
Calgary AB T2J 5X7
(278-9302)

Silvertip Outfitters
Box 48181, Midlake
RPO,Calgary AB T2X 3C9
(256-5018)

Special D Outfitters
58 Rosewood Dr, Sherwood
Park AB T8A 0L9 (467-9761)

Water Boatman Ltd.
612 Queensland Drive SE
Calgary AB T2J 4G7
(271-0799)

West Winds
Fishing Charter Ltd.
220 Silvercreek Way NW
Calgary AB T3B 4H5
(286-4359)

Powwows

Alberta Tourism keeps up-to-date information on powwow schedules throughout the summer, and can be contacted at 1-800-222-6501 within Alberta or 1-800-661-8888 elsewhere in North America. Edmonton callers can phone 427-4321.

Rodeos

See pages 78 and 83.

Tax Refunds for Travellers

Although Alberta has a non-refundable provincial room tax of 5 percent, rebates are available for visitors on the 7 percent federal GST (Goods and Services Tax) paid on short-term accommodation (less than one month) and most goods taken home. GST rebate forms are available at Canada Customs, most Visitors Bureaus, Duty-Free Shops, and major shopping centres. Qualifying purchases must total at least $100, and original itemized receipts must be included. (They will be returned.) Rebate forms with receipts may be submitted in person at participating Canadian Duty Free Shops for cash rebates (daily limit of $500), or mailed to Revenue Canada, Customs and Excise. Forms must be submitted within one year of purchase date.

For more information, call 1-800-66VISIT (668-4748) within Canada, or 1-613-991-3346 outside Canada, or write:
Revenue Canada, Customs and Excise
Visitors' Rebate Program

Postal Services

Canadian stamps may be purchased and letters and parcels mailed at post offices and designated postal stations. Look for independent postal stations in mall kiosks, pharmacies, and small stores. Some all-night groceries offer 24 hour postal service. Be sure to use the correct postage – note that the same postage rate is used for both postcards and letters.

Customs and Immigration

Citizens or permanent residents of the US must show proof of citizenship, such as a birth certificate, naturalization certificate, or passport, upon request. Non-US citizens should check with the nearest Canadian consulate for passport and visa requirements. Persons under 18 unaccompanied by an adult should have a letter of authorization from a parent or guardian to travel in Canada.

Bringing Pets

A dog or cat from the United States must have a certificate signed by a licensed Canadian or US veterinarian certifying that the dog or cat has been vaccinated against rabies during the preceding three years. The certificate must also carry an adequate and legible description of the dog or cat and date of vaccination. The certificate will be initialled by the inspecting official at the customs port of entry. Note that the certificate is also needed for re-entry into the United States, so make sure that the vaccination does not expire while travelling in Canada. Puppies and kittens under three months of age and "Seeing Eye" dogs from the United States are exempt from these rules, and verbal information of good health from the importer is acceptable.

Holidays

The following legal holidays are observed in Alberta. Banks, post offices, liquor outlets, schools, and many stores are closed on these dates.

New Year's Day	January 1
Family Day	February 19
Good Friday	March/April
Easter	March/April
Victoria Day	May 24, if a Monday, or the closest prior Monday
Canada Day	July 1
Alberta Heritage Day	August (first Monday)
Labour Day	September (first Monday)
Thanksgiving Day	October (second Monday)
Remembrance Day	November 11
Christmas Day	December 25
Boxing Day	December 26

Liquor Laws

Liquor may be consumed with meals at licensed dining lounges and restaurants; liquor service alone is available in licensed beverage rooms. For both, liquor service is limited by law to certain hours of operation. Check locally for details.

Liquor supplies may be purchased at Alberta government liquor stores. Look in the white pages of the telephone directory under Alberta Liquor Control Board for store locations and hours of operation. Many stores now accept major credit cards. Most hotels also sell liquor for off-premise consumption; some also have cold beer outlets. There are also a limited number of privately operated wine boutiques.

You must be at least 18 years of age to consume liquor in Alberta.

It is unlawful to consume liquor in a place other than a residence, temporary residence, or licensed premises, and it is against the law to convey liquor in a place other than a residence, temporary residence, or licensed premises, and it is against the law to convey liquor in a vehicle, unless the liquor is sealed, in a luggage compartment, or out of reach of the driver.

EDMONTON

Access

By Plane

Most visitors to Edmonton arrive by air at the Edmonton International Airport, located 29 km south of the city centre. From the airport, it is about 40 minutes to downtown by taxi or Grey Goose Airporter Van (463-7520). Some airlines also offer service to the convenient Edmonton Municipal Airport, only a ten minute taxi ride to the city centre.

By Rail

Regular east-west transcontinental passenger rail service is available through Via Rail Canada Inc. (1-800-561-8630.) Points served include Toronto, Winnipeg, Saskatoon, Jasper, and Vancouver. The train station is located at 10004 - 104th Avenue. For train arrival and departure information call 422-6032.

By Bus

Regular long-distance bus service is available at the Greyhound Terminal, 10324 - 103rd Street (421-4211), as well as luxury motor coach Red Arrow Express (424-3339 and 1-800-232-1958) from downtown hotels to major Alberta cities.

Motor coach sightseeing tours of Edmonton are offered by a number of companies including Edmonton Transit's Route 123 (421-4636) and Royal Tours (424-8687).

By Car

The Yellowhead Highway (Highway 16) passes through Edmonton, linking the mountains of British Columbia to the west with the prairies of Saskatchewan and Manitoba to the east.

From the south, Edmonton can be reached on Highway 2; it is 514 km north of the United States border.

Edmonton is also the original southern access to the Alaska Highway, "The First Route to the Last Frontier." From Edmonton, it is around 3100 km to Fairbanks, Alaska. For more information on this route, contact the Midnight Twilight Tourist Association, 1 Sturgeon Rd, St. Albert AB T8N 0E8, 458-5600, or Alberta Tourism, 1-800-661-8888.

There are a number of rental car companies in Edmonton, with offices at both airports plus downtown locations. Check the telephone directory.

Visitor Information

For travel counselling, phone the Edmonton Convention and Tourism Authority at 422-5505 and 988-5455. Visitor Information Centres are operated year round at these locations:
• Gateway Park, Highway 2 South, 2404 Calgary Trail Northbound SW
• Edmonton Convention Centre, 9797 Jasper Avenue
• Edmonton International Airport, Lower Arrivals Level. Additional booths are set up during the summer.

Alberta Tourism provides tourist information at the City Centre Building, 10155 - 102nd Street (427-4321), and toll-free information through: 1-800-222-6501 (within Alberta) 1-800-661-8888 (outside Alberta, including US)

Talking Community Pages

For 24-hour recordings describing current Edmonton events, call the touch-tone operated Talking Community Pages at 493-9000, and touch the four digit code for the information required:
Visitor Information (Locations and Hours) 4340
Sightseeing Tours 4341
Downtown Attractions 4342
Old Strathcona Attractions 4343
North Edmonton Attractions 4344
South Edmonton Attractions 4345
East Edmonton Attractions 4346
West Edmonton Attractions 4347
Family Fun 4220
See the front of the Edmonton Yellow Pages telephone directory for complete code listing.

Telephone Information
Time 421-1111
Weather 468-4940
Road Reports (24 hrs) 471-6056
For even more telephone information, get yourself to a touch-tone telephone and call the Talking Community Pages at 493-9000, and touch 9930 for a demonstration. You can listen to recorded messages on everything from local events to camping tips, at no extra charge other than that of the call itself. A complete listing of touch codes is in the front of the Yellow Pages telephone directory.

Emergency

Dial 911 for immediate police, fire, or ambulance aid.

Deaf Person's Emergency
TTY/TDD: 425-1231;
M-33: 426-1987

Dental Emergency
West
Drs. Azarko and Zuch
483-7079
South
Tridont Dental Centre
434-9566
University of Alberta
Emergency Dental Clinic
492-6854

Veterinary Emergency
Veterinary Emergency Service (open nights, weekends, holidays) 433-9505

Medical Care
There are a number of walk-in medical clinics open seven days a week, 9 am - 11 pm. The following clinics offer 24 hour service:
Allin Clinic 482-7551
Links Clinic 454-0351
Check Yellow Pages telephone directory under "Physicians & Surgeons" for details.

Poison Centre
1-800-332-1414

Suicide/Distress Line
482-HELP (4357)

Legal Help
Lawyer Referral Service (Law Society of Alberta)
1-800-661-1095
Legal Aid Society 427-7575

Other Emergency Phone Numbers
See front pages of telephone directory.

Getting Around Edmonton

Layout
Edmonton is designed on a grid system. Streets run north-south, avenues run east-west, and both are numbered progressively in both directions starting from the southeast corner of Edmonton. The North Saskatchewan River cuts through the city diagonally, from southwest to northeast, and is crossed by ten bridges. A current Edmonton street map is useful.

Highways
Some highways are named for all or part of their distance. Here is a list of the major ones and their numbered equivalents:
Argyll Road / 63rd Avenue
Calgary Trail Northbound / 103rd Street
Calgary Trail Southbound / 104th Street
Jasper Avenue / 101st Avenue
Whitemud Drive / 43rd Avenue
Whyte Avenue / 82nd Avenue
Yellowhead Trail / 125th Avenue
See the back of the White Pages telephone directory for a complete listing of named buildings, apartments, and streets.

Rules of the Road
Bus and taxi lanes are often found on one-way streets, for their exclusive use only. You may get a ticket or be towed if you drive, park, or stop in such marked lanes.

During morning and evening rush hours, some major downtown access roads use one opposite lane of traffic to ease congestion to and from downtown. Also, parking on some roads is prohibited at this time. Towaway zones are strictly enforced.

Metered downtown parking as well as pay lot parking is available. Some short-term street parking is available.

A number of downtown businesses participate in the "Park in the Heart" program and distribute courtesy parking coupons to their customers for reduced rate parking in designated areas. See the downtown map in the Yellow Pages telephone directory for parking areas. For more information on downtown parking, call the Talking Community Pages at 493-9000 and touch 4281.

Traffic Circles
Edmonton is known for its traffic circles, although many are being phased out or updated with traffic lights. If you're not used to driving through traffic circles, here are some tips.

On approaching a traffic circle, look ahead and clearly spot where you plan to leave the circle. Then, enter the traffic circle in the right lane, if you're getting out at the first or second exit; enter in the left lane if you're getting out at the second or third exit. Within the circle, you must yield to vehicles on the left. To get out of the circle, signal your intentions, stay in the same lane, and cautiously exit.

Taxis
Although taxis may be hailed on the street, it is more usual to phone ahead. Check the

telephone directory, or use one of the taxi company direct courtesy phones located in the lobbies of major hotels and stores.

Public Transportation

Edmonton Transit operates buses and Light Rail Transit (LRT). Maps, schedules, and passes (day, monthly, and ticket books) are available from the Downtown Information Centre at 100A Street and Jasper Avenue, and from Edmonton Transit Customer Services, Churchill LRT Station (99th Street and 102A Avenue). Phone 421-4636 for route and schedule information.

Note that you may ride free on the downtown LRT 9 am to 3 pm, Monday to Friday; and Saturdays from 9 am to 6 pm. The downtown free zone extends from Churchill to Grandin (Government Centre) stations.

Shopping

Although West Edmonton Mall is probably the most famous (and often most crowded) shopping center in the city, Edmonton provides many interesting shopping experiences.

Edmontonians tend to shop downtown during the week, and at the wide variety of shopping malls throughout the city during evenings and the weekend. Twenty-four hour shopping is still rare in Edmonton, with only some neighbourhood convenience stores operating around the clock.

There are four major Canadian department stores in Edmonton: The Bay, Eaton's, Sears, and Woodward's. All have stores in major malls. The Bay, Eaton's, and Woodward's also have stores downtown.

Downtown

Downtown Edmonton, centered around 101st Street and 102nd Avenue, boasts the best selection of goods and services in northern Alberta, plus plenty of parking.

Pedway System

A "Pedway System" connects most major buildings through clearly marked paths ("follow the feet") that run above street level across bridges, at street level through buildings and outdoor walkways, and below street level through well-lighted and secure tunnels and the occasional parking garage.

Pedway maps are available through the Edmonton Convention and Tourism Authority, and can be also obtained at numerous downtown locations.

Pedway Shopping

One major pedway shopping stroll through downtown starts at Woodward's department store (100th Street and 102nd Avenue) and continues indoors through Edmonton Centre, Eaton Centre, Eaton's department store, Manulife Place, Hudson's Bay Centre, and The Bay department store.

If you need a break after experiencing Edmonton Centre's more than 140 stores and restaurants, Eaton Centre's 131, and Manulife's 75, you can play (or watch) nine holes of golf on the Royal Greens Golf Course inside Eaton Centre. Groups can book usage of the chess/checkerboard located in the nearby food court. This is no ordinary board – it's inlaid in the floor and comes complete with life size checkers and the world's largest registered chess set! Tournaments are often held here. The top floor of Eaton Centre features a luxury suite hotel, as well as Canada's largest Cineplex Odeon movie theatre.

Warehouse Shops

Step outside of Eaton's, and go to the corner of 102nd Avenue and 103rd Street, and enjoy the change of pace at the Boardwalk Market, a renovated warehouse featuring unique restaurants, snack stands, arts and crafts stalls, and live entertainment.

Elegant Shopping

If you're interested in fine furs, there are a number of stores clustered along Furrier Row, 103rd Street and Jasper Avenue.

Just west of downtown, along 100th Avenue and Jasper Avenues, from 110th Street to 125th Street, you'll find numerous art galleries, high fashion shops, and elegant boutiques. Major stops include June's House of Fashion (11302 - 100th Avenue), LeMarchand Mansion (11523 - 100th Avenue), and The High Street Shops (102nd Avenue and 125th Street.)

Ethnic Shopping

Ethnic shopping (and dining) can be found on the east side of downtown, from 97th

Street to 95th Street, between Jasper Avenue and 107th Avenue. There are shops, restaurants, bookstores, and more, featuring a number of Edmonton's ethnic communities including Chinese, Vietnamese, Jewish, Italian, and Ukrainian. Chinatown itself is heralded by the ornate China Gate over 102nd Avenue (Harbin Road) at 97th Street. And, while you're there, be sure to visit the adjacent City Farmers' Market.

Markets

Located in the heartland of Alberta, Edmonton boasts the most farmers' markets within one locality in Alberta. Farmers' markets feature individually operated stalls with seasonal goods, fruits, vegetables, home baking, eggs, fresh and frozen fish, meat and poultry, homemade sausage, plants, crafts, leather goods, and more.

Call the Edmonton Convention and Tourism Authority at 422-5505 and 988-5455 for dates, times, and locations, particularly for seasonal markets.

• Callingwood Mall, 6655 - 178th Street; Sundays, mid-May to September.

• Capilano Shopping Centre, 5004 - 98th Avenue; Saturdays, mid-July to September.

• City Farmers' Market, 10165 - 97th Street; Monday to Saturday, year-round.

• Fort Edmonton Park, southwest end of Quesnell Bridge; Sunday and Holiday Monday afternoons, mid-May to August.

• Millwoods Recreation Centre, 7207 - 28th Avenue;

Thursday evenings, July to September.

•Old Strathcona Bus Barn, 103rd Street and 83rd Avenue; Saturdays year-round; Tuesday afternoons, mid-May to September.

In addition to farmers' markets, there are flea markets offering a variety of new and used merchandise. The major one in Edmonton is the Ninety Ninth Street Shoppers Flea Market, 9908 - 65th Avenue. Call 435-2768.

Old Strathcona

Old Strathcona is an historic area, located south of downtown, and centered around Whyte Avenue and 104th Street. The University of Alberta campus is to the west at 114th Street. Strathcona was incorporated as a town in 1899, became a city in 1907, and amalgamated with Edmonton in 1912. The Old Strathcona Foundation was founded in 1974 to preserve and revitalize this area, which contains many buildings designated as Registered Historical Resources.

Shopping in Old Strathcona is a mix of the traditional and the trendy, with boutiques, restaurants, specialty shops, and a massive farmers' market. The Strathcona Public Building ("Old Post Office"), on the corner of Whyte Avenue and 105th Street, is now Strathcona Square, a festival market with shops and restaurants.

West Edmonton Mall

(See p. 160 and Scenic Drive 10.)

What to Wear

Edmontonians dress for the weather and the occasion – business or casual as appropriate.

Summer days are warm and dry, with plenty of sunshine. During the long days of June, there can be almost seventeen hours of daylight. Temperatures are cooler in the early morning and evening, so people usually wear sweaters, jackets, or layered clothing to be comfortable throughout the day.

Spring and autumn are pleasant, and the weather is excellent for hiking, cycling, golf, tennis, and more.

Rain showers occur, so bring an umbrella or raincoat.

Media

Both daily Edmonton newspapers, the *Edmonton Journal* and the tabloid *Edmonton Sun*, are published mornings. All are available in stores and coin-operated street boxes.

There are eighteen local AM and FM radio stations, three major local television channels, and a wide range of US networks and special interest channels available on cable television.

Places to Stay

Contact the Edmonton Convention and Tourism Authority at 422-5505 and 988-5455.

Restaurants

Edmonton features a wide range of ethnic cuisine, from Arabic to Ukrainian, as well as North American restaurants featuring Alberta beef.

CALGARY

Access

By Plane

Most visitors to Calgary arrive by air at the Calgary International Airport. From the airport, located in the north end of Calgary, it is about 25 minutes to downtown by taxi or Airporter Bus (291-3848).

By Rail

Regular passenger rail service through Calgary is no longer available. East-west travel is now served through Edmonton, north of Calgary. For information, call Via Rail Canada Inc., 1-800-561-8630. Rail sightseeing tours are sometimes available; check with Calgary Convention & Visitors Bureau at 262-2766 and 1-800-661-1778.

By Bus

Regular long-distance bus service is available at the Greyhound Terminal, 9th Avenue and 16 Street SW (265-9111), as well as luxury motor coach Red Arrow Express (531-0355 and 1-800-232-1958) from downtown hotels to major Alberta cities. Motor coach sightseeing tours out of Calgary are offered by a number of companies including Brewster Transportation & Tours, 221-8242.

By Car

Canada's main east-west highway, the Trans-Canada Highway 1, passes through Calgary, becoming 16th Avenue North within city limits.

Alberta's major north-south highway, Highway 2, bisects Calgary as a limited access highway bypass called Deerfoot Trail.

Visitor Information

For travel counselling, phone the Calgary Convention & Visitors Bureau at 262-2766 and 1-800-661-1778. Year round information booths are operated at these locations:
• 237 - 8th Avenue SE
• Canada Olympic Park, TransCanada Highway and Bowfort Road NW
• Calgary International Airport, Arrivals level
• 6220 - 16th Avenue NE.
Additional booths are set up during the summer.

Alberta Tourism provides tourist information in the McDougall Centre, 455 - 6th Street SW. Phone: 1-800-222-6501 (within Alberta) 1-800-661-8888 (outside Alberta, including US)

For a 24-hour recording describing current Calgary events, call the touch-tone operated *Talking Yellow Pages* at 521-5222, and touch 8950 to access the Fun Line.

Telephone Information

Time & Temperature 263-3333

Weather (Calgary and Banff) 275-3300

Road Reports (24 hrs) 246-5853

For more telephone information, use a touch-tone telephone to call the *Talking Yellow Pages* at 521-5222, and touch 2222 for a directory. You can listen to recorded messages on everything from local events to the crime of the week, at no extra charge other than that of the call itself. A complete listing of touch codes is in the front of the Yellow Pages telephone directory.

Emergency

Dial 911 for immediate police, fire, or ambulance aid.

Deaf Person's Emergency 233-2210

Dental Emergency
Northeast
Marlborough Dental Centre 235-6440
Northwest
Drs. Chernecki and Hucal 297-0220
Parkdale Dental Emergency Clinic 283-5596
Southeast
Fish Creek Health Care Centre 271-7770
Southwest
Braeside Dental Centre 251-1055
Chinook Dental Centre 258-3911

Veterinary Emergency
Calgary North Veterinary Hospital & Emergency Service (24 hrs) 277-0135
Calgary Animal Emergency Clinic (open nights, weekends, holidays) 269-7822

Medical Care
There are a number of walk-in medical clinics open seven days a week, 9 am - 11 pm. Check Yellow Pages telephone directory under "Physicians & Surgeons" for details.

Poison Centre 670-1414
Distress Centre/Drug Centre 266-1605

Legal Help
Lawyer Referral Service (Law Society of Alberta) 228-1722
Legal Aid Society 297-2260

Other Emergency Phone Numbers
See front pages of telephone directory.

What to Wear

During Stampede Week, Calgarians indulge their cowboy yearnings and dress western; however, most of the time people wear normal business or sports clothing as appropriate.

In summer, the weather may be hot, sunny, and dry during the day, but cools down rapidly in the evening. Buildings may or may not be air-conditioned, so Calgarians are used to wearing clothing that may be layered, and put on or off as the location demands. Always carry an extra sweater or jacket to be sure. For the occasional rainy day, bring a sporty rain parka or traditional trench coat. Umbrellas don't hold up in the high Alberta winds.

Media

Both daily Calgary newspapers, the *Calgary Herald* and the tabloid *Calgary Sun*, are published mornings, as well as a Calgary edition of the *Globe and Mail*. All are available in stores and coin-operated street boxes.

There are sixteen local AM and FM radio stations, three major local television channels, and a wide range of US networks and special interest channels available on cable television.

Shopping

Calgarians tend to shop downtown during the week, and at the wide variety of shopping malls throughout the city during evenings and the weekend. Twenty-four hour shopping is still rare in Calgary, with only some neighbourhood convenience stores operating around the clock.

There are four major Canadian department stores in Calgary: The Bay, Eaton's, Sears, and Woodward's. All have stores in major malls in town, and The Bay and Eaton's also have stores downtown.

Downtown

Downtown shopping in Calgary is a real treat, with a wide variety of stores, restaurants, and services. Easy access is provided by the free C-Train service along 7th Avenue S.

Outdoor Strolls

The Stephen Avenue Mall runs along 8th Avenue S on both sides of Centre Street. It's a favourite place for lunchtime strolls on sunny days, with street entertainment, numerous shops, and interesting people-watching.

Plus 15 Walkway

For pleasurable downtown walking in any weather, travel through the Plus 15 walkway system that connects many office, retail, and cultural buildings through enclosed elevated bridges at least 15 feet (4.5 m) above grade level. There are now 47 bridges over streets and between buildings and 12 km of indoor public walkways available downtown, with more under construction. Maps are available through the Calgary Convention & Visitors Bureau.

The Plus 15 system is clearly marked by blue and white maps and pictographs of a man with a white stetson cowboy hat. Overhead signs at all bridges list compass direction and next destination. **North** has pictures of fish, since the Bow River is to the North of downtown; **East** is represented by a fort, since Fort Calgary is to the East of downtown; **South** is represented by trains, since the Canadian Pacific Railway runs on the south edge of downtown; and **West** is symbolized by the mountains seen to the west from downtown.

The unique design of the signage, with the +15 indicated in solid circle patterns, is based on the Blackfoot Native usage of circles to represent stars on teepees, and their use of repetitive elements to indicate direction. You'll find lines of solid circles on +15 floors to guide you through open areas to the next bridge. The signage is all in blue and white, the colors of a clear sky, to show that the weather inside the Plus 15 is always pleasant, no matter what is happening outdoors.

Plus 15 Shopping

One good Plus 15 shopping stroll starts at Bow Valley Square (6th Avenue and 1st Street SW), through The Bay department store, Scotia Centre, to the multilevel shops of Toronto Dominion Square.

Be sure to take a rest here and enjoy the gorgeous Devonian Gardens at the top level of Toronto Dominion Square. There are more than 16,000 subtropical and local plants and trees, ponds, and waterfalls within this one hectare (2.5 acre) glassed-in garden oasis. Occasionally, there is entertainment during the lunch hour, and there are frequent art exhibits as well.

From Toronto Dominion Square, you can continue on the +15 walkway west through Calgary Eaton Centre, Eaton's department store, and Penny Lane (8th Avenue and 5th Street SW), or head south on the +15 to shop at Bankers Hall (9th Avenue and 3rd Street SW).

Kensington
On the north side of the Bow River across from downtown, you'll find the Kensington/ Louise Crossing shopping area. It runs north and west from the Louise Bridge at Memorial Drive and 10th Street NW. There are a number of specialty gift and craft shops, cafes, new and "gently worn" clothing shops, art galleries, and more in this established Calgary neighborhood.

17th Avenue
The 17th Avenue shopping district starts at the Stampede Grounds at Macleod Trail SE and increases in elegance as it reaches 4th Street SW through 14th Street SW, at the base of the Mount Royal district and its exceptional homes.

The shops clustering around 17th Avenue and 8th Street SW, including the multilevel indoor Mount Royal Village, feature internationally known names in fashion, art, decoration, jewellery, and gourmet delights. The area also boasts a wide variety of cafés and restaurants, from casual bagelries to elegant eateries.

You might also wish to detour off 17th Avenue for a while and explore the unusual shops, boutiques, trendy cafes and restaurants along 4th Street SW, from 15th Avenue SW south to Elbow Drive SW.

Inglewood Historic Area
Inglewood is located along 9th Avenue SE just east of Fort Calgary and near the Calgary Zoo. It is Calgary's oldest settled neighborhood, with more than two hundred pre-1914 buildings, a number of which have been desig-nated as Provincial Historic Resources. Shopping includes a number of second hand stores, unusual restaurants, book stores, and shops with character.

Markets
Calgary has two farmers' markets. The oldest is the Farmers' Own Farmers Market, 5600 - 11th Street SE. It is usually open Friday, Saturday, and Sunday during May to October, and Saturdays only the rest of the year. Phone 243-0065 to confirm dates and times. The second farmers' market is at the Crossroads Market, 2222 - 16th Avenue NE. There is also a flea market selling a variety of new and used merchandise. There are more than 400 booths within the massive 9300 square metre (100,000 sq ft) market area. Crossroads Market is open Saturday and Sunday year-round (291-5208).

The other major flea market in Calgary, also open Saturday and Sunday year-round, is the Firepark Market (707 Barlow Trail SE), located at Barlow Trail and Memorial Drive. It can be reached by car or by taking the Whitehorn C-Train to the Barlow/Max Bell station.

Getting Around Calgary

Layout

Calgary is divided into the four compass quadrants of north, south, east, and west, and all addresses are identified by quadrant. Streets run north-south, avenues run east-west and both are numbered progressively in both directions starting at Centre Street and Centre Avenue.

The street/avenue addressing scheme works fairly well close to downtown – as long as the quadrant (NE, SE, NW, SW) is given. However, subdivision addresses are usually combinations of the subdivision name plus some minor variation, such as Rundlehill Road or Rundlehill Place. Be sure to get the correct address and clear directions. A current Calgary street map is particularly useful if you're going outside of the immediate downtown area.

Rules of the Road

During morning and evening rush hours, some major downtown access roads use one opposite lane of traffic to ease congestion to/from downtown. Also, parking on some roads is prohibited at this time. Towaways zones are strictly enforced.

Metered downtown parking as well as pay lot parking is available. Some free street parking is available, subject to a two hour limit downtown.

Non-resident visitors to Calgary can obtain three-day parking passes good for free parking at meters and city-operated parking lots. Passes can be picked up (and renewed) at any Calgary Convention & Visitors Bureau Information Centre.

Taxis

Although taxis may be hailed on the street, Calgarians usually phone ahead. Check the telephone directory, or use one of the taxi company direct courtesy phones located in the lobbies of major hotels and stores.

Public Transportation

Calgary Transit operates buses and Light Rail Transit (LRT), called the C-Train. Maps, schedules, and passes (day, monthly, and ticket books) are available from the Information Centre at 206 - 7th Avenue SW, opposite The Bay department store. Phone 276-7801 for route and schedule information.

Note that you may ride free anytime on the downtown C-Train within the 7th Avenue Free Fare Zone, which extends along 7th Avenue from 10th Street SW to 3rd Street SE.

Places to Stay

In Calgary, there are four major locations to stay: Downtown/Central/Southwest (SW), Airport (NE), Motel Village/University (NW), and Macleod Trail (S). For more information, contact the Calgary Convention & Visitors Bureau at 262-2766 and 1-800-661-1778.

Restaurants

With its long-standing Chinese community, Calgary boasts some of the best Chinese food in North America. Dim Sum is a favourite on weekends, and is sometimes available during the week as well. A number of Chinese restaurants are clustered around 4th Avenue and Centre Street S downtown. For a treat, try some take-out sweets from one of the many oriental bakeries in the area.

Italian restaurants and shops can be found in Bridgeland, along First Avenue NE, from Edmonton Trail NE eastward.

Photography Credits

In the following list, photographs are indicated by page number. When there are two photographs on a page, the top or left photograph is indicated as "A" and the bottom or right photograph is indicated as "B".

Contemporary photographs:

Alberta Tourism: 11, 19, 22, 29, 30, 35, 47, 55, 57, 62, 69, 70A, 70B, 71A, 71B, 74, 83, 87, 129, 130, 146, 149, 151, 152, 154, 162, 164, 170, 185, 187, 189, 190, 192, 193, 194, 201, 202, 203, 213A, 213B, 226, 229, 236

Calgary Convention and Visitors Bureau: 165

City of Edmonton, Parks and Recreation: 75

Don Harmon: 24, 53, 105, 106, 107, 116, 119, 122, 140

Carole Harmon: 25A, 26A, 28, 37, 44, 86, 98, 102, 108, 109A, 109B, 110A, 112, 113B, 120, 124, 125, 136, 145, 198, 207, 212, 216

Stephen Hutchings: 25B, 25C, 26B, 27, 38, 51, 104, 110B, 115, 118, 123, 137, 138, 143, 206, 209, 217

Postcard Factory, courtesy of West Edmonton Mall: 158, 160, 161

Paul Beck: 15, 36, 43, 80, 85, 97, 155, 156, 157

Esther Schmidt: 31, 214

Dennis Schmidt: 95

Catherine Burgess: 61

R.D. Muir, courtesy of Wood Buffalo National Park: 34

Pacific Rim National Park: 41

Elk Island National Park: 49

Sire Records Company: 89

Yoho National Park: 117

R.W. Sandford: 127

Doug Leighton: Front cover, 2, 8, 14A, 18, 45, 93, 94, 111, 121, 180, 196, 215

Joan Wagner: 256

Graeme Pole: 208

Brad Watson, courtesy Calgary Flames: 178

Bruce Patterson: 14B, 16, 20, 32, 42, 58, 63, 64, 67, 90A, 90B, 91, 96, 133, 135, 169, 171, 173, 175, 176, 182, 183, 204, 211, 219, 222, 224, 225, 228, 231, 233, 234

Cansport, courtesy Spruce Meadows: 179

Calgary Exhibition and Stampede: 66, 78, 79, 81, 82, 84

Historical photographs

Glenbow Archives, Calgary: Front Cover (inset), 17, 52, 54, 56, 59, 60, 72, 76, 77, 88, 101, 113A, 114, 131, 148, 166, 167, 172, 227

Whyte Museum of the Canadian Rockies: 100, 126

Emergencies

Dial 911 for immediate
police, fire, or ambulance
aid.

Edmonton:
Poison Centre
  1-800-332-1414
Distress Centre/Drug Centre
  482-4357 (HELP)
See p. 245

Calgary:
Poison Centre
  670-1414
Distress Centre/Drug Centre
  266-1605
See p. 248

About the author

Bruce Patterson has lived in
Alberta since 1974 and
travelled extensively
throughout the province. He
worked for the *Calgary
Herald* for 15 years including
a four-year assignment as the
newspaper's reporter in
Banff.

Newspaper assignments
included coverage of the 1978
Commonwealth Games in
Edmonton and the Nordic
events of the 1988 Winter
Olympics held in Canmore.
He also wrote about outdoor
recreation and travel.

In 1982, Patterson was a
support team member of the
first Canadian expedition to
Mount Everest. His first book,
Canadians on Everest, is an
account of that successful
climb and subsequent
expeditions to the world's
highest mountain.

Since 1989, he has been a
freelance writer living in
Claresholm with his wife,
Joan Wagner.